The Footprints of the Ancients

The Footprints of the Ancients

Readings in World History from Hammurabi's Code to the Letters of Columbus

Edited by
Andrew Fogleman
California State University, Fullerton

FIAT LUX PRESS
LOS ANGELES

Published by
Fiat Lux Press
1623 Central Avenue Suite 145
Cheyenne, Wy 82001

ISBN-13: 978-0-692-15735-0
ISBN-10: 0692157350

Stella, Emily, and Blaise
sine qua non

"Questions ought to serve to excite tender readers to a zealous inquiry into truth and so sharpen their wits. The master key of knowledge is, indeed, a persistent and frequent questioning. Aristotle, the most clear-sighted of all the philosophers, was desirous above all things else to arouse this questioning spirit, for in his *Categories* he exhorts a student as follows: "It may well be difficult to reach a positive conclusion in these matters unless they be frequently discussed. It is by no means fruitless to be doubtful on particular points. "By doubting we come to examine, and by examining we reach the truth.""[1]

-Peter Abelard, *Sic et non*

---

[1] Peter Abelard, "Prologue," in James Harvey Robinson, *Readings in European History* (Boston: Ginn, 1904): 1: 451.

Preface

Ad fontes was a Renaissance dictum that expressed the desire to "(return) to the sources" of ancient classical or Christian writings. In doing so, Renaissance humanists of the 14th to the 16th centuries believed they gained a purer and more authentic experience of the past. They referred to these literary endeavors as keeping to "the footprints of the ancients."[1] I have attempted to channel this same spirit with the production of this world history reader. This book provides an impressionistic sample of the many rich written sources of world history up to the 16th Century C.E. Of course, these texts by no means exhaust the writings of the many regions and time periods covered, nor do these excerpts give a full account of the sources themselves. Source books such as this one are never fully completed but rather only abandoned to publication at some point. It is my hope that this introduction to some of the sources of world history will cause its readers to pursue these texts in their original entirety or use them as a launch pad for other sources of the period not covered in this collection.

In compiling the sources for this book, I have relied on the expertise of the various translators cited. To make these translations more readable for my students, I have "modernized" many of the texts. This means that I have replaced antiquated and lesser-known words with modern counterparts. At times I have also altered the sentence structure of original translations—generally by reducing the length and complexity of sentences—to make the meaning of these texts more readily accessible to my students. In doing so, I have always aimed at preserving the original sense of the translation. Please note ellipses where they occur, as they indicate omitted material and will give some

---

[1] See Document 10:1: Erasmus, *To Cornelius Gerard.*

sense of my editorial impact on the texts. Too often, students give up on primary sources because of the challenge of archaic language and unfamiliar syntax. It is my hope that the modernized versions of these texts, the analytical instruction of the introduction, and prompts throughout the book will encourage modern students to keep to "the footprints of the ancients."

Andrew Fogleman
Los Angeles, California

Contents

Preface viiii

Introduction... xii

Chapter 1: Law and Religion in Southwest Asia

   1.1 *The Code of Hammurabi* (ca. 1750 B.C.E) 1

   1.2 *The Bible* (ca. 600—ca. 400 B.C.E) 10

Chapter 2: Indian Society and Buddhism

   2.1 *Rigveda* (1900—1100 B.C.E). 22

   2.2 *The Buddha* (4th Century B.C.E). 26

   2.3 *Bhagavad Gita* (5th—2nd Century B.C.E).............................. 34

   2.4 *The Code of Manu* (200 B.C.E.—200 C.E.) 40

   2.5 *The Lotus Sutra* (1st Century B.C.E.—2nd Century C.E.)........ 47

Chapter 3: Ancient China

   3.1 *Dao De Jing* (ca. 4th Century B.C.E) 50

   3.2 *The Instructions of Yi* (1000 B.C.E.—200 B.C.E) 55

Chapter 4: The Greeks

   4.1 Hesiod, *Works and Days* (700 B.C.E.) 58

   4.2 Homer, *Iliad* (8th Century B.C.E.)...................................... 62

   4.3 Plato, *Apologia of Socrates* (ca. 399 B.C.E.). 71

   4.4 Pericles, *Funeral Oration* (431 B.C.E.)............................... 79

   4.5 Xenophon, *The Spartans* (ca. 380 B.C.E.) 84

   4.6 Aristotle, *On the Generation of Animals* (4th Century B.C.E.).......... 88

Chapter 5: Rome and the Christians

   5.1 Livy, *The History of Rome* (27-9 B.C.E.) 94

   5.2 The *New Testament* (ca. 30-ca. 70 C.E.). 100

   5.3 Pliny, *Letters to and from Emperor Trajan* (112 C.E.) 108

   5.4 Tertullian, *Apology* (197 C.E.). 112

5.5   *The Martyrdom of Saints Perpetua and Felicitas* (203 C.E.) 119

Chapter 6: The Spread of Christianity

6.1   Saint Benedict of Nursia, *The Rule* (ca. 530)............................ 129

6.2   Saint Augustine, *On Christian Doctrine* (397) 139

Chapter 7: The Expansion of Islam

7.1   *The Qur'an, Surah 2* (609-632) 145

7.2   *The Pact of Umar* (637) 168

Chapter 8: The Middle Ages

8.1   *Feudal Homage* (13th and 14th Century) 171

8.2   Fulcher of Chartres, *History of the Expedition* (1095)................. 174

8.3   King John of England, *Magna Carta* (1215) 180

8.4   Peter Abelard, *Sic et Non* (ca. 1125) 188

8.5   Saint Thomas Aquinas, *Summa Theologica* (1268) 195

8.6   *Student Drinking Songs* (13th Century)... 203

Chapter 9: The Americas

9.1   Bernal Díaz, *The Conquest of New Spain* (ca. 1570) 205

Chapter 10: Renaissance Humanism and the Reformation

10.1   Desiderius Erasmus, *To Cornelius Gerard* (1492) 220

10.2   Niccolò Machiavelli, *The Prince* (1513)..................................... 225

10.3   Martin Luther, *Ninety-Five Theses* (1517) 233

10.4   Martin Luther, *Of Preachers and Hearers* (1522) 237

10.5   Ignatius of Loyola, *The Spiritual Exercises* (ca. 1548) 244

Chapter 11: Exploration and the Global Economy

11.1   Christopher Columbus, *First Letter* (1493) 248

11.2   Pope Paul III, Sublimis Deus (1537) 258

11.3   Bartolomé de Las Casas, *The Devastation of the Indies* (1542) ...262

11.4   Juan Ginés De Sepúlveda, *On the Just Causes for War Against the Indians* (1545) 271

11.5   Bernal Díaz, *The Conquest of New Spain* (1570) 276

Introduction

The Renaissance dictum *ad fontes*, or "(return) to the sources!" expressed the desire to bypass medieval textbook-like summaries of ancient writings for reading the actual texts, ideally in their original languages. In reading ancient texts, Renaissance humanists of the 14th to the 16th centuries believed they experienced a purer version of the classical and Christian past. They "returned to the sources" by uncovering little-known manuscripts from ancient monasteries, edited these texts for a wider readership, debated their meanings, and sought to apply the things they learned to their public lives. They referred to these literary endeavors as keeping to "the footprints of the ancients."[1] The present book seeks to channel this humanistic spirit and apply it to the sources of world history. In doing so, it will be useful at the outset to reflect upon the types of source materials that link us to the past and set up some goals for analyzing them.

The past is different than history. The past is all the events leading up to this moment, reading this sentence. ...and now this sentence, too! The past is ever expanding into the present. In contrast, history is the stories we tell about past events. We base these stories on fragments of the past that come down to us. Textual fragments, such as a law, a love letter, or graffiti offer us some access to the world of their creators. Non-textual fragments, such as Galileo's telescope or a shrunken head, operate in the same way but without words. Historians use both types of textual remains, or *primary sources*, to ground the stories they tell in something concrete, something real. If we agree that our only access to the past comes by way of primary sources, then we need to be very careful about how we read and interpret them. The quality of things we

---

[1] See Document 10:1; Erasmus, *To Cornelius Gerard.*

claim to know about the past depends entirely on our ability to analyze these sources effectively.

But what exactly can a source tell us? For this book, I want to highlight two elements of a text: 1) what the source plainly indicates—a **description**—and 2) the larger significance of the source—an **inference**. A description simply restates the content of the source itself and summarizes its plain meaning. An inference, on the other hand, suggests the range of conclusions that might be reasonably drawn from the source about the community that produced the text or was affected by it. An inference thus moves beyond the mere description of the source itself and speculates about its larger historical significance. For example, if we discovered a collection of love letters from, say 15th-century France, we could use them to infer what other love letters from the same era and location might contain. We could use the details of the gender relations and social expectations in our initial trove of letters as evidence, hinting at the larger social or gender-based norms of the world of the authors. As such, inferences are informed guesses about the worlds beyond the text. Of course, the more love letters discovered from the same time and area, the safer it becomes to generalize about these matters. Historians support their inferences with additional primary and secondary sources. All of this, however, starts with understanding what a source says (a **description**) and speculating about its historical meaning for its period (an **inference**). These are the essential analytical skills of every historian, and the ones we will practice throughout the course of this book. Consider the following examples of a description and inference drawn from an excerpt of *The Law Code of Hammurabi*:

Text: Hammurabi's Code (ca. 1800 B.C.E.)
209. If a seignior struck a(nother) seignior's daughter and has caused her to have a miscarriage, he shall pay ten shekels of silver for her fetus.

210. If that woman has died, they shall put his daughter to death.

Description: Hammurabi's Code notes that a fine of ten shekels is imposed when a seignior injures another seignior's daughter, resulting in a miscarriage (*Hammurabi's Code*, p. 27). Additionally, the death of an accused man's daughter is the punishment for killing a seignior's daughter, who is pregnant.

Inference: Laws 209 and 210 show us that the assumed value of a seignior (or free-born) fetus in Babylon was ten shekels, and this is less than the value of a daughter. The text also reveals that daughters were seen as an extension of the property or resources of Babylonian men. A daughter's death, in this case, is meant to balance the loss of the injured (male) party even though she had nothing to do with the incident. So we can see that Babylonian lawmakers were in some way interested in fair and balanced outcomes to disputes and that women did not have the same legal standing as men did in the society.

In the example above, the laws governing the death of a seignior fetus and daughter hint at larger themes of justice, equity, compensation, and social and gender differences within Babylon during the period of Hammurabi's *Law Code*. Inferences ask how the particular examples in a source participate in larger social trends. In the selections throughout the book, I will include some possible themes for you to consider while reading the source to help you generate inferences. Let's consider a second example, this time from the *Bhagavad Gita*:

Themes: duty (dharma) and justice

Text: Bhagavad Gita (5th—2nd Century B.C.E.)
And seeing all his kinsmen standing (in both armies), the son of Kunti (Arjuna) was overcome by excessive pity, and spoke thus despondingly.... "What joy shall be ours, O Krishna, after killing Dhritarashtra's sons? We shall only incur sin, killing these felons. It is not proper for us to kill our own kinsmen, the sons of Dhritarashtra.

For how, O Krishna, could we be happy after killing our own relatives?"

[Krishna responded,] "...engage in battle, O descendant of Bharata (Arjuna), for he who thinks he kills and he who thinks he is killed, both know nothing. The one does not kill, and the other is not killed. A man is not born, nor does he ever die, nor, having existed, does he ever cease to exist.... The soul, O descendant of Bharata, within everyone's body is indestructible. Therefore you ought not to grieve for any being. Have regard for your own duty; you should not fail, for there is nothing better for a Kshatriya than a righteous battle."

Description: In this portion of the *Bhagavad Gita*, Krishna encourages Arjuna to fulfill his duty and fight in a battle against his relatives despite Arjuna's reservations. He tries to soften the consequences of these actions by explaining that the death of the body does not affect the real core of a person, which abides in one's eternal soul. Rather than destroying a person forever, Krishna describes physical death as only moving from one body to the next.

Inference: This excerpt reveals attitudes about duty (*dharma*) and justice in Indian society. We see that fulfilling one's caste-related duties in India is more important than the apparent injustices such actions might create, such as killing relatives in Arjuna's extreme example.

Now it's your turn. Write a description and inference for the following selection.

Themes: gender and natural order

Text: Ban Zhao, *Lessons for Women* (ca. 80 C.E.)

"As *Yin* and *Yang* are not of the same nature, so man and woman differ in behavior. The virtue of *Yang* is firmness; *Yin* is manifested in yielding. Man is honored for strength; a woman is beautiful on account of her gentleness. Hence there arose the common saying, 'A man born like a wolf may, it is feared, become a weak monstrosity; a woman though born like a mouse may, it is feared, become a tiger.'"

Description:_____

_____

_____

Inference:_____

_____

_____

You are now *doing* history, which is considerably more fun than simply learning it. Neat and tidy historical summaries didn't satisfy humanists of the past. They wanted to engage, debate, and learn from original sources directly. They understood that doing history is an art, which involves meticulous observation (**description**) as well as wonder (**inference**) about the past and it's meaning for the present. It is my hope that for those who would "keep to the footprints of the ancients" this book will help them do the same.

Chapter 1:
Law and Religion in Southwest Asia

DOCUMENT 1-1

The Code of Hammurabi

CA. 1750 B.C.E

Hammurabi (c. 1810—1750 BCE) reigned as the sixth king of the First Babylonian Dynasty from 1792 to 1750 BCE. He dramatically expanded his father's empire, uniting all of Mesopotamia through a series of military campaigns. Though not the first historical example of law, Hammurabi's Code is remarkable for its length and complexity. It contains 282 laws and deals with infractions as important as murder and as mundane as the wages of an ox driver. As such, it is an invaluable resource for historians of Babylonian society. The Code survives on a series of tablets but is most commonly associated with a large basalt stele in the shape of a giant index finger. The stele features the text of the Code in Akkadian, the common language of Babylon, as well as a carving of Hammurabi receiving the Code from the God Shamash (or possibly Marduk).

Themes: justice, equity, compensation, punishment, gender

The Code of Hammurabi King of Babylon, ed. Robert Francis Harper (Chicago: The University of Chicago Press, 1904), 3, 9, 11, 17, 19, 45, 49, 51, 53, 55, 73, 75, 77, 79, 81, 97. Modernized by Andrew Fogleman.

The Prologue

When the lofty Anu, king of the Anunnaki, And Enlil,[1] lord of heaven and Earth, he who determines the destiny of the land, committed the rule of all mankind to Marduk, the chief son of Ea; When they made him great among the Igigi;[2] When they pronounced the lofty name of Babylon; When they made it famous among the quarters of the world and in its midst established an everlasting kingdom whose foundations were firm as heaven and earth—At that time, Anu and Enlil called me, Hammurabi, the exalted prince, the worshiper of the gods, to cause justice to prevail in the land, To destroy the wicked and the evil, to prevent the strong from oppressing the weak, to go forth like the Sun over the Black Head race, to enlighten the land and to further the welfare of the people. Hammurabi, the governor named by Enlil, am I, who brought about plenty and abundance… the favorite of Nana, am I. When Marduk sent me to rule the people and to bring help to the country, I established law and justice in the land and promoted the welfare of the people.

1. If a man bring an accusation against a man, and charge him with a (capital) crime, but cannot prove it, he, the accuser, shall be put to death.

16. If a man harbor in his house a male or female slave who has fled from the palace or from a commoner,[3] and do not bring him (the slave) forth at the call of the commandant, the owner of that house shall be put to death.

25. If a fire breaks out in a man's house and a man who goes to extinguish it desires the furniture of the owner of the house, and takes the furniture of the owner of the house, that man shall be thrown into that fire.

---

[1] Or "Bel."
[2] **The Igigi**: Servants of Enlil (or Bel).
[3] Or "freeman."

127. If a man points the finger[4] at a priestess or the wife of another and cannot justify it, they shall drag that man before the judges and brand his forehead.

128. If a man takes a wife and does not arrange with her the (proper) contracts, that woman is not a wife.

129. If the wife of a man is discovered lying with another man, they shall bind them and throw them into the water. If the husband of the woman wants to save his wife, or if the king wants to save his male servant, (he may).

130. If a man abducts the (betrothed) wife of another who has not known a male and is living in her father's house, and he is discovered lying with her, that man shall be put to death and that woman shall go free.

131. If a man accuses his wife and she has not been discovered lying with another man, she shall take an oath in the name of god and she shall return to her house.

132. If the finger has been pointed at the wife of a man because of another man, and she has not been discovered lying with another man, for her husband's sake she shall throw herself into the river.[5]

133. If a man is captured and there are provisions in his house. His wife shall protect herself (with them) and she shall not enter into another house.

---

[4] **Points the finger:** a form of accusation.

[5] This act refers to a water ordeal practiced in many premodern societies. The accused was thrown (or in this case threw herself) into a deified river. If the accused survived, he or she was considered innocent of the charge. See Kathryn E. Slanski, "The Law of Hammurabi and Its Audience" *Yale Journal of Law & the Humanities* 24, no. 1 (2013): 3, 4.

134. If a man is captured and there are no provisions in his house and his wife enters into another house, that woman has no blame.

135. If a man is captured and there are no provisions in his house, and his wife openly enter into another house and bears children; if later her husband returns to his city, that woman shall return to her husband (and) the children shall stay with their father.

136. If a man desert his city and flee and afterwards his wife enters into another house; if that man returns and seeks to take his wife, the wife of the fugitive shall not return to her husband because he hated his city and fled.

137. If a man wants to put away a concubine who has borne him children or a wife who has presented him with children, he shall return to that woman her dowry and shall give to her the income of field, garden and goods and she shall bring up her children; from the time that her children are grown up, from whatever is given to her children they shall give to her a portion corresponding to that of a son and the man of her choice may marry her.

138. If a man wants to divorce his wife who has not borne him children, he shall give her money to the amount of her marriage settlement and he shall make good to her the dowry, which she bought from her father's house and then he may divorce her.

139. If there was no marriage settlement, he shall give to her one mina[6] of silver for a divorce.

140. If he is a commoner, he shall give her one-third mina of silver.

142. If a woman hates her husband, and says (to him), "You cannot have me," they shall inquire into her behavior for any defects; and if she has been a careful wife and is without reproach (even though) her

---

[6] Or "mana" of silver.

husband has been going about and greatly belittling her, that woman has no blame. She shall receive her dowry and shall go to her father's house.

143. If she has not been a careful wife, has gossiped about, has neglected her house, and has belittled her husband, they shall throw that woman into the water.

144. If a man takes a wife and that wife gives a maidservant to her husband (for the purposes of children) and she bear (him) children; if that man (still) wants to take a concubine, they shall not allow it.

145. If a man takes a wife and she does not bear him children and he wants to take a concubine, that man may take a concubine and bring her into his house. That concubine shall not rank (equally) with his wife.

146. If a man takes a wife and she gives a maid servant to her husband (for the purpose of children), and that maid servant bears children and afterwards assumes (an equal) rank with her mistress; because she has borne children, her mistress may not sell her for money, but she may reduce her to bondage and count her among the maidservants.

147. If she has not borne children, her mistress may sell her for money.

148. If a man takes a wife and she becomes afflicted with disease, and if he wants to take another, he may. His wife, who is afflicted with disease, shall not be put away. She shall remain in the house which he has built and he shall care for her as long as she lives.

149. If that woman does not want to remain in her husband's house, he shall make good to her the dowry which she brought from her father's house and she may go.

150. If a man gives to his wife, field, garden, house or goods in a sealed deed, after (the death of) her husband, her children cannot make claim

against her. The mother after her (death) may will (the property) to her child who she loves, but not to a brother. ...

153. If a woman brings about the death of her husband for the sake of another man, they shall impale her.

154. If a man has sex with his daughter, they shall expel that man from the city.

155. If a man has betrothed a bride to his son and his son has had sex with her, and if he (the father) afterward also has sex with her, they shall bind that man (the father) and throw him into the water.

156. If a man has betrothed a bride to his son and his son has not had sex with her but he himself has sex with her, he shall pay her one-half mana of silver and he shall make good to her whatever she brought from the house of her father and the man of her choice may take her.

157. If a man has sex with his mother after (the death of) his father, they shall burn both of them.

195. If a man strikes his father, they shall cut off his hand.[7]

196. If a man destroys the eye of another man, they shall destroy his eye.

197. If one breaks a man's bone, they shall break his bone.

198. If one destroy the eye of a commoner or break the bone of a commoner, he shall pay one mina of silver.

199. If one destroys the eye of a man's slave or break a bone of a man's slave he shall pay one-half his price.

---

[7] Or "fingers."

200. If a man knocks out a tooth of a man of his own rank, they shall knock out his tooth.

201. If one knocks out a tooth of a commoner, he shall pay one-third mina of silver.

202. If a man strikes the person of a man (i.e., commit an assault) who is his superior, he shall receive sixty strokes with an ox-tail whip in public.

203. If a man strikes another man of his own rank, he shall pay one mina of silver

204. If a commoner strikes a commoner, he shall pay ten shekels[8] of silver.

205. If a man's slave strikes a man's son, they shall cut off his ear.

206. If a man strikes another man in a quarrel and wound him, and he swears, "I struck him without intent." He shall be responsible for the (cost of the) physician.

207. If (he) die as the result of the blow, he shall swear (as above), and if he be a man,[9] he shall pay one-half mina of silver.

208. If (he) be a commoner, he shall pay one-third mina of silver.

209. If a man strikes a man's daughter and brings about a miscarriage, he shall pay ten shekels of silver for her fetus.

210. If that woman dies, they shall put his daughter to death.

211. If, by the blow, he brings about a miscarriage to the daughter of a commoner, he shall pay five shekels of silver.

---

[8] Fifty Shekels makes one mina.
[9] i.e., a noble man.

212. If that woman dies, he shall pay one-half mina of silver (for the fetus).

213. If he strikes the female slave of a man and bring about a miscarriage, he shall pay two shekels of silver (for the fetus).

214. If that female slave dies, he shall pay one-third mina of silver.

215. If a physician operates on a man for a severe wound with a bronze lancet and saves the man's life; or if he opens an abscess (in the eye) of a man with a bronze lancet and saves the man's eye, he shall receive ten shekels of silver (as his fee).

216. If he is a commoner, he shall receive five shekels.

217. If it is a man's slave, the owner of the slave shall give two shekels of silver to the physician.

218. If a physician operates on a man for a severe wound with a bronze lancet and cause the man's death; or opens an abscess (in the eye) of a man with a bronze lancet and destroy the man's eye, they shall cut off his hand.[10]

219. If a physician operates on a slave of a commoner for a severe wound with a bronze lancet and causes his death, he shall restore a slave of equal value.

220. If he opens an abscess (in his eye) with a bronze lancet, and destroy his eye, he shall pay silver to the extent of one-half of his price.

229. If a builder build a house for a man and does not make its construction firm, and the house which he has build collapses and causes the death of the owner of the house, that builder shall be put to death.

---

[10] Or "fingers."

230. If it causes the death of the son of the owner of the house, they shall put to death a son of that builder....

282. If a male slave says to his master, "You are not my master," and his master proves that he is his slave. They shall cut off the slave's ear.

Description:_____

_____

_____

Inference:_____

_____

_____

Questions:

1. Is there evidence in this text that Hammurabi thought this was a just law code?

2. What role does social class play in punishments and fines? Find specific examples to support your answer.

3. How are women treated in this law code?

4. Did any of the statutes or penalties in the Code surprise you? If so which ones and why?

DOCUMENT 1-2

The Bible

CA. 600—CA. 400 B.C.E.

"[F]or I the Lord your God am a jealous God..."

Genesis and Exodus are the first two books of the Jewish Torah and Christian Old Testament. While the Talmud attributes these books Moses's authorship, modern scholars suggest they were written over time by various authors. The book of Genesis recounts the story of creation and the promises God made to the Hebrew patriarchs (Abraham, Isaac, and Jacob). The Book of Exodus tells of God's miraculous deliverance of the Hebrews from Egypt and the establishment of a covenant relationship with God based their faithfulness to his holy law. These books present a monotheistic view of the world, where God is transcendent and not part of nature.

Themes: ethical choice, covenant relationship, monotheism

The Book of Genesis

In the beginning when God created the heavens and the earth, ²the earth was a formless void and darkness covered the face of the deep, while a wind from God swept over the face of the waters. ³Then God said, 'Let there be light'; and there was light. ⁴And God saw that the light was good; and God separated the light from the darkness. ⁵God called the light Day, and the darkness he called Night. And there was evening and there was morning, the first day.

⁶And God said, 'Let there be a dome in the midst of the waters, and let it separate the waters from the waters.' ⁷So God made the dome and separated the waters that were under the dome from the waters that were above the dome. And it was so. ⁸God called the dome Sky. And there was evening and there was morning, the second day.

⁹And God said, 'Let the waters under the sky be gathered together into one place, and let the dry land appear.' And it was so. ¹⁰God called the dry land Earth, and the waters that were gathered together he called Seas. And God saw that it was good. ¹¹Then God said, 'Let the earth put forth vegetation: plants yielding seed, and fruit trees of every kind on earth that bear fruit with the seed in it.' And it was so. ¹²The earth brought forth vegetation: plants yielding seed of every kind, and trees of every kind bearing fruit with the seed in it. And God saw that it was good. ¹³And there was evening and there was morning, the third day.

¹⁴And God said, 'Let there be lights in the dome of the sky to separate the day from the night; and let them be for signs and for seasons and for days and years, ¹⁵and let them be lights in the dome of the sky to give light upon the earth.' And it was so. ¹⁶God made the two great lights—the greater light to rule the day and the lesser light to rule the night—and the stars. ¹⁷God set them in the dome of the sky to give light upon the earth, ¹⁸to rule over the day and over the night, and to separate the light from the darkness. And God saw that it was good. ¹⁹And there was evening and there was morning, the fourth day.

²⁰And God said, 'Let the waters bring forth swarms of living creatures, and let birds fly above the earth across the dome of the sky.' ²¹So God created the great sea monsters and every living creature that moves, of every kind, with which the waters swarm, and every winged bird of every kind. And God saw that it was good. ²²God blessed them, saying, 'Be fruitful and multiply and fill the waters in the seas, and let birds multiply on the earth.' ²³And there was evening and there was morning, the fifth day.

²⁴And God said, 'Let the earth bring forth living creatures of every kind: cattle and creeping things and wild animals of the earth of every kind.' And it was so. ²⁵God made the wild animals of the earth of every kind, and the cattle of every kind, and everything that creeps upon the ground of every kind. And God saw that it was good.

²⁶Then God said, 'Let us make humankind in our image, according to our likeness; and let them have dominion over the fish of the sea, and over the birds of the air, and over the cattle, and over all the wild animals of the earth, and over every creeping thing that creeps upon the earth.'

²⁷ So God created humankind in his image,
  in the image of God he created them;
  male and female he created them.

²⁸God blessed them, and God said to them, 'Be fruitful and multiply, and fill the earth and subdue it; and have dominion over the fish of the sea and over the birds of the air and over every living thing that moves upon the earth.' ²⁹God said, 'See, I have given you every plant yielding seed that is upon the face of all the earth, and every tree with seed in its fruit; you shall have them for food. ³⁰And to every beast of the earth, and to every bird of the air, and to everything that creeps on the earth, everything that has the breath of life, I have given every green plant for food.' And it was so. ³¹God saw everything that he had made, and indeed, it was very good. And there was evening and there was morning, the sixth day.

[Chapter 2]

⁷ then the LORD God formed man from the dust of the ground, and breathed into his nostrils the breath of life; and the man became a living being. ⁸ And the LORD God planted a garden in Eden, in the east; and there he put the man whom he had formed. ⁹ Out of the ground the LORD God made to grow every tree that is pleasant to the sight and

good for food, the tree of life also in the midst of the garden, and the tree of the knowledge of good and evil....

[15] The LORD God took the man and put him in the garden of Eden to till it and keep it. [16] And the LORD God commanded the man, "You may freely eat of every tree of the garden; [17] but of the tree of the knowledge of good and evil you shall not eat, for in the day that you eat of it you shall die."

[18] Then the LORD God said, "It is not good that the man should be alone; I will make him a helper as his partner." [19] So out of the ground the LORD God formed every animal of the field and every bird of the air, and brought them to the man to see what he would call them; and whatever the man called every living creature, that was its name. [20] The man gave names to all cattle, and to the birds of the air, and to every animal of the field; but for the man there was not found a helper as his partner. [21] So the LORD God caused a deep sleep to fall upon the man, and he slept; then he took one of his ribs and closed up its place with flesh. [22] And the rib that the LORD God had taken from the man he made into a woman and brought her to the man. [23] Then the man said,

"This at last is bone of my bones
    and flesh of my flesh;
this one shall be called Woman,
    for out of Man this one was taken."

[24] Therefore a man leaves his father and his mother and clings to his wife, and they become one flesh. [25] And the man and his wife were both naked, and were not ashamed.

[Chapter 3]

[1] Now the serpent was more crafty than any other wild animal that the LORD God had made. He said to the woman, "Did God say, 'You shall not eat from any tree in the garden'?" [2] The woman said to the serpent,

"We may eat of the fruit of the trees in the garden; ³ but God said, 'You shall not eat of the fruit of the tree that is in the middle of the garden, nor shall you touch it, or you shall die.'" ⁴ But the serpent said to the woman, "You will not die; ⁵ for God knows that when you eat of it your eyes will be opened, and you will be like God, knowing good and evil." ⁶ So when the woman saw that the tree was good for food, and that it was a delight to the eyes, and that the tree was to be desired to make one wise, she took of its fruit and ate; and she also gave some to her husband, who was with her, and he ate. ⁷ Then the eyes of both were opened, and they knew that they were naked; and they sewed fig leaves together and made loincloths for themselves.

⁸ They heard the sound of the LORD God walking in the garden at the time of the evening breeze, and the man and his wife hid themselves from the presence of the LORD God among the trees of the garden. ⁹ But the LORD God called to the man, and said to him, "Where are you?" ¹⁰ He said, "I heard the sound of you in the garden, and I was afraid, because I was naked; and I hid myself." ¹¹ He said, "Who told you that you were naked? Have you eaten from the tree of which I commanded you not to eat?" ¹² The man said, "The woman whom you gave to be with me, she gave me fruit from the tree, and I ate." ¹³ Then the LORD God said to the woman, "What is this that you have done?" The woman said, "The serpent tricked me, and I ate." ¹⁴ The LORD God said to the serpent,

"Because you have done this,
    cursed are you among all animals
    and among all wild creatures;
upon your belly you shall go,
    and dust you shall eat
    all the days of your life.
¹⁵ I will put enmity between you and the woman,
    and between your offspring and hers;

he will strike your head,
  and you will strike his heel."

[16] To the woman he said,

"I will greatly increase your pangs in childbearing;
  in pain you shall bring forth children,
yet your desire shall be for your husband,
  and he shall rule over you."

[17] And to the man he said,

"Because you have listened to the voice of your wife,
  and have eaten of the tree
about which I commanded you,
  'You shall not eat of it,'
cursed is the ground because of you;
  in toil you shall eat of it all the days of your life;
[18] thorns and thistles it shall bring forth for you;
  and you shall eat the plants of the field.
[19] By the sweat of your face
  you shall eat bread
until you return to the ground,
  for out of it you were taken;
you are dust,
  and to dust you shall return."

[20] The man named his wife Eve, because she was the mother of all living. [21] And the LORD God made garments of skins for the man and for his wife, and clothed them.

[22] Then the LORD God said, "See, the man has become like one of us, knowing good and evil; and now, he might reach out his hand and take also from the tree of life, and eat, and live forever"— [23] therefore the LORD God sent him forth from the garden of Eden, to till the ground

from which he was taken. ²⁴He drove out the man; and at the east of the garden of Eden he placed the cherubim, and a sword flaming and turning to guard the way to the tree of life.

[Chapter 6]

¹When people began to multiply on the face of the ground, and daughters were born to them, ²the sons of God saw that they were fair; and they took wives for themselves of all that they chose. ³Then the Lord said, 'My spirit shall not abide in mortals for ever, for they are flesh; their days shall be one hundred and twenty years....'

⁵The Lord saw that the wickedness of humankind was great in the earth, and that every inclination of the thoughts of their hearts was only evil continually. ⁶And the Lord was sorry that he had made humankind on the earth, and it grieved him to his heart. ⁷So the Lord said, 'I will blot out from the earth the human beings I have created— people together with animals and creeping things and birds of the air, for I am sorry that I have made them.' ⁸But Noah found favour in the sight of the Lord.

⁹These are the descendants of Noah. Noah was a righteous man, blameless in his generation; Noah walked with God. ¹⁰And Noah had three sons, Shem, Ham, and Japheth.

¹¹Now the earth was corrupt in God's sight, and the earth was filled with violence. ¹²And God saw that the earth was corrupt; for all flesh had corrupted its ways upon the earth. ¹³And God said to Noah, 'I have determined to make an end of all flesh, for the earth is filled with violence because of them; now I am going to destroy them along with the earth. ¹⁴Make yourself an ark of cypress wood; make rooms in the ark, and cover it inside and out with pitch.... ¹⁷For my part, I am going to bring a flood of waters on the earth, to destroy from under heaven all flesh in which is the breath of life; everything that is on the earth shall die. ¹⁸But I will establish my covenant with you; and you shall

come into the ark, you, your sons, your wife, and your sons' wives with you. [19]And of every living thing, of all flesh, you shall bring two of every kind into the ark, to keep them alive with you; they shall be male and female. [20]Of the birds according to their kinds, and of the animals according to their kinds, of every creeping thing of the ground according to its kind, two of every kind shall come in to you, to keep them alive. [21]Also take with you every kind of food that is eaten, and store it up; and it shall serve as food for you and for them.' [22]Noah did this; he did all that God commanded him.

[Chapter 7]

[11]In the six-hundredth year of Noah's life, in the second month, on the seventeenth day of the month, on that day all the fountains of the great deep burst forth, and the windows of the heavens were opened. [12]The rain fell on the earth for forty days and forty nights. [13]On the very same day Noah with his sons, Shem and Ham and Japheth, and Noah's wife and the three wives of his sons, entered the ark, [14]they and every wild animal of every kind, and all domestic animals of every kind, and every creeping thing that creeps on the earth, and every bird of every kind— every bird, every winged creature. [15]They went into the ark with Noah, two and two of all flesh in which there was the breath of life. [16]And those that entered, male and female of all flesh, went in as God had commanded him; and the Lord shut him in.

[17]The flood continued for forty days on the earth; and the waters increased, and bore up the ark, and it rose high above the earth. [18]The waters swelled and increased greatly on the earth; and the ark floated on the face of the waters. [19]The waters swelled so mightily on the earth that all the high mountains under the whole heaven were covered; [20]the waters swelled above the mountains, covering them fifteen cubits deep. [21]And all flesh died that moved on the earth, birds, domestic animals, wild animals, all swarming creatures that swarm on the earth, and all human beings; [22]everything on dry land in whose nostrils was the

breath of life died. [23]He blotted out every living thing that was on the face of the ground, human beings and animals and creeping things and birds of the air; they were blotted out from the earth. Only Noah was left, and those that were with him in the ark. [24]And the waters swelled on the earth for one hundred and fifty days.

[Chapter 8]

[6]At the end of forty days Noah opened the window of the ark that he had made [7]and sent out the raven; and it went to and fro until the waters were dried up from the earth. [8]Then he sent out the dove from him, to see if the waters had subsided from the face of the ground; [9]but the dove found no place to set its foot, and it returned to him to the ark, for the waters were still on the face of the whole earth. So he put out his hand and took it and brought it into the ark with him. [10]He waited another seven days, and again he sent out the dove from the ark; [11]and the dove came back to him in the evening, and there in its beak was a freshly plucked olive leaf; so Noah knew that the waters had subsided from the earth. [12]Then he waited another seven days, and sent out the dove; and it did not return to him any more.

[13]In the six hundred and first year, in the first month, on the first day of the month, the waters were dried up from the earth; and Noah removed the covering of the ark, and looked, and saw that the face of the ground was drying. [14]In the second month, on the twenty-seventh day of the month, the earth was dry. [15]Then God said to Noah, [16]"Go out of the ark, you and your wife, and your sons and your sons' wives with you...

[20]Then Noah built an altar to the Lord, and took of every clean animal and of every clean bird, and offered burnt-offerings on the altar. [21]And when the Lord smelt the pleasing odour, the Lord said in his heart, 'I will never again curse the ground because of humankind, for the inclination of the human heart is evil from youth; nor will I ever again destroy every living creature as I have done.

The Book of Exodus

[Chapter 20]

[1]Then God spoke all these words:

[2]I am the Lord your God, who brought you out of the land of Egypt, out of the house of slavery; [3]you shall have no other gods before me.

[4]You shall not make for yourself an idol, whether in the form of anything that is in heaven above, or that is on the earth beneath, or that is in the water under the earth.

[5]You shall not bow down to them or worship them; for I the Lord your God am a jealous God, punishing children for the iniquity of parents, to the third and the fourth generation of those who reject me, [6]but showing steadfast love to the thousandth generation of those who love me and keep my commandments.

[7]You shall not make wrongful use of the name of the Lord your God, for the Lord will not acquit anyone who misuses his name.

[8]Remember the sabbath day, and keep it holy. [9]For six days you shall labour and do all your work. [10]But the seventh day is a sabbath to the Lord your God; you shall not do any work—you, your son or your daughter, your male or female slave, your livestock, or the alien resident in your towns. [11]For in six days the Lord made heaven and earth, the sea, and all that is in them, but rested the seventh day; therefore the Lord blessed the sabbath day and consecrated it.

[12]Honour your father and your mother, so that your days may be long in the land that the Lord your God is giving you.

[13]You shall not murder.

¹⁴You shall not commit adultery.

¹⁵You shall not steal.

¹⁶You shall not bear false witness against your neighbour.

¹⁷You shall not covet your neighbour's house; you shall not covet your neighbour's wife, or male or female slave, or ox, or donkey, or anything that belongs to your neighbour.

¹⁸When all the people witnessed the thunder and lightning, the sound of the trumpet, and the mountain smoking, they were afraid and trembled and stood at a distance, ¹⁹and said to Moses, 'You speak to us, and we will listen; but do not let God speak to us, or we will die.' ²⁰Moses said to the people, 'Do not be afraid; for God has come only to test you and to put the fear of him upon you so that you do not sin.' ²¹Then the people stood at a distance, while Moses drew near to the thick darkness where God was.

²²The Lord said to Moses: Thus you shall say to the Israelites: 'You have seen for yourselves that I spoke with you from heaven. ²³You shall not make gods of silver alongside me, nor shall you make for yourselves gods of gold.

²⁴You need make for me only an altar of earth and sacrifice on it your burnt-offerings and your offerings of well-being, your sheep and your oxen; in every place where I cause my name to be remembered I will come to you and bless you.

Description:_____

_____

_____

Inference:_____

_____

_____

Questions:

1. What, if anything, stands out to you about this creation account?

2. What prompts God to destroy humankind? Why does he spare Noah?

3. What is the Hebrew God like? What characterizes his covenant relationship with humanity?

Chapter 2:
Indian Society and
Buddhism

DOCUMENT 2-1

Rigveda

1900—1100 B.C.E.

The Rigveda is a collection of ancient Indian hymns organized in ten books. It is the oldest of the four canonical texts of Hinduism known as the Vedas. The hymns are composed in honor of various deities and reveal ancient Indian conceptions of creation and cosmology. In the hymn below, Purusha's sacrifice gives rise to the world and human social hierarchy.

Themes: pantheism, caste system, social hierarchy

Hymn to Purusha

1. A thousand heads has Purusha, a thousand eyes, a thousand feet. On every side pervading (the) earth he fills a space ten fingers wide.

2. This Purusha is all that has been and all that is to be;
    The Lord of Immortality, which grows greater still by food.

"Hymn to Purusha," in *The Hymns of the Rigveda*, trans. Ralph T. H. Griffith, (Benares: E. J. Lazarus, 1897), 2: 517-520. Modernized by Andrew Fogleman.

3. So mighty is his greatness; indeed, greater than this is Purusha. All creatures are one-fourth of him, and three-fourths is eternal life in heaven.

4. With three-fourths Purusha went up: one-fourth of him again was here. From there he strode out to every side, over what does not eats and what eats.

5. From him Viraj[1] was born; again Purusha from Viraj was born. As soon as he was born he spread eastward and westward over the earth.

6. When the gods prepared the sacrifice with Purusha as their offering, its oil was spring, the holy gift was autumn; summer was the wood.

7. They balmed[2] Purusha as a victim on the grass, born in earliest time. With him the Deities and all Sadhyas[3] and Rishis[4] sacrificed.

8. From that great general sacrifice the dripping fat was gathered up. He formed the creatures of the air, and animals both wild and tame.

9. From that great general sacrifice Rishis and Sama-hymns were born: Also spells and charms were produced; the Yajus[5] had its birth from it.

10. From it were horses born, from it all cattle with two rows of teeth: From it were generated cows, from it the goats and sheep were born.

---

[1] **Viraj**: a primeval being associated with creation.
[2] **Balmed**: To apply aromatic resin or oil.
[3] **Sadhyas**: lesser gods.
[4] **Rishis**: sages or saints.
[5] **Yajus**: sacrificial prayers or mantras.

11. When they divided Purusha how many portions did they make? What do they call his mouth, his arms? What do they call his thighs and feet?

12. The Brahman (priest caste)[6] was his mouth, of both his arms was the Rajanya (warrior caste)[7] made. His thighs became the Vaisya (merchant and artisan caste),[8] from his feet the Sudra (laborer or lower caste)[9] was produced.

13. The Moon was gendered from his mind, and from his eye the Sun had birth; Indra and Agni from his mouth were born, and Vayu from his breath.

14. Forth from his navel came mid-air; the sky was fashioned from his head, the earth from his feet, and from him came the regions. Thus they formed the worlds.

15. Seven fencing-sticks had he, thrice seven layers of fuel were prepared, When the gods, offering Purusha as a sacrifice, bound, as their victim

16. Gods, sacrificing, sacrificed the victim these were the earliest holy ordinances. The Mighty Ones attained the height of heaven, there where the Sadhyas, gods of old, are dwelling.

Description:_____

_____

_____

Inference:_____

_____

_____

---

[6] **Braman**: priest caste.
[7] **Rajanya**: warrior caste.
[8] **Vaisya**: merchant and artisan caste.
[9] **Sudra**: laborer or lower caste.

Questions:

1. Based on the hymn, how would you describe Purusha's relationship to the gods and the world?

2. Where do the various divisions among humanity come from, and why might this be significant to Indian society?

3. The hymn states that "Purusha is all that has been and all that is to be." How does this compare to other conceptions of divinity we have seen?

DOCUMENT 2-2

The Buddha

4ᵀᴴ CENTURY B.C.E.

"This mind has demolition reached, and seen the last of all desire!" - Buddha

These selections are taken from the Jataka tales of the Pali Scriptures, an important early source for the biography and sermons of the Buddha in the Theravada Buddhist tradition. They were preserved orally and committed to writing in 29 BCE. In the excerpt below, Siddhartha's father attempts to block his son's enlightenment in a selfish effort to ensure Siddhartha's succession to his throne. Siddhartha, however, experiences life beyond the palace walls and chooses to abandon his royal lineage, his wife and child, and caste expectations in search of enlightenment.

Themes: caste duty, asceticism, desire, enlightenment

The Young Gotamid Prince

Then said the king [to a group of elders], "What would my son see to make him retire from the world?" "The four signs," they answered. "What four?" "A decrepit old man, a diseased man, a dead man, and a monk." "From this time forth," said the king, "let no such persons be allowed to come near my son. It will never do for my son to become a Buddha. What I would wish to see is my son exercising sovereign rule

"The Buddha," in *Buddhism in Translation*, trans. Henry Clarke Warren (Cambridge, Harvard University Press, 1909), 53-59, 63, 64, 70, 71, 76-78, 80, 81, 83. Modernized by Andrew Fogleman.

and authority over the four great continents and the two thousand attendant isles, and walking throughout the heavens surrounded by a retinue thirty-six leagues in circumference." And when he had spoken, he placed guards for a distance of a quarter of a league in each of the four directions, in order that none of these four kinds of men might come within sight of his son....

And so the Future Buddha began to grow, surrounded by an immense retinue, and in great splendor....

The Great Retirement

Now on a certain day the Future Buddha wished to go to the park, and told his charioteer to make ready the chariot. Accordingly, the man brought out a sumptuous and elegant chariot, and adorning it richly, he harnessed to it four state-horses and of the Sindhava breed, as white as the petals of the white lotus, and announced to the Future Buddha that everything was ready. And the Future Buddha mounted the chariot, which was like a palace of the gods, and proceeded towards the park.

"The time for the enlightenment of prince Siddhartha is close," Thought the gods; "we must show him a sign." and they changed one of their number into a decrepit old man, broken-toothed, gray-haired, crooked and bent of body, leaning on a staff, and trembling, and showed him to the Future Buddha, but so that only he and the charioteer saw him.

Then the Future Buddha said to the charioteer, in the manner related in the Mahapadana—"Friend, who is this man? Even his hair is not like that of other men." And when he heard the answer, he said, "Shame on birth, since to everyone that is born, old age must come." And agitated in heart, Siddhartha returned and entered his palace.

"Why has my son returned so quickly?" asked that king. "Sire, he has seen an old man," was the reply; "and because he has seen an old man, he is about to retire from the world."

"Do you want to kill me, that you say such things? Quickly get ready some plays to be performed before my son. If we can but get him to enjoy pleasure, he will cease to think of retiring from the world." Then the king extended the guard to half a league in each direction.

Again on a certain day, as the Future Buddha was going to the park, he saw a diseased man, whom the gods had fashioned; and having again made inquiry, he returned, agitated in heart, and entered his palace.

And the king made the same inquiry and gave the same orders as before; and again extending the guard, placed them for a league around.

And again on a certain day, as the Future Buddha was going to the park, he saw a dead man whom the gods had fashioned; and having gain made inquiry, he returned, agitated in heart, and entered his palace.

And the king made the same inquiry and gave the same orders as before; and again extending the guard, placed them for a league around.

And again on a certain day, as the Future Buddha was going to the park, he saw a monk carefully and decently clad, whom the gods had fashioned; and he asked his charioteer, "Who is this man?"

Now although there was no Buddha in the world, and the charioteer had no knowledge of either monks or their good qualities, yet by the power of the gods he was inspired to say, "Sire, this is one who has retired from the world;" and he thereupon proceeded to sound the praises of the retirement from the world. The thought of retiring from the world pleased the Future Buddha, and he continued on until he came to the park....

At this juncture, Suddhodana, the king, having heard that the Siddhartha's wife had brought forth a son, sent a messenger, saying, "Announce the glad news to my son." On hearing the message, the Future Buddha said, "An impediment (*rahula*)[1] has been born; a fetter has been born."

At the same moment Kisa Gotami, a virgin of the warrior caste, ascended to the roof of her palace, and beheld that beauty and majesty of the Future Buddha, as he walked through the city; and in her pleasure and satisfaction at the sight, she burst forth into this song of joy:

> Full happy now that mother is,
> Full happy now that father is,
> Full happy now that wife is,
> Who owns this lord so glorious!"

On hearing this, the Future Buddha thought, "In beholding a handsome figure the heart of a mother attains Nirvana, the heart of a father attains Nirvana, the heart of a wife attains Nirvana. This is what she says. But wherein does Nirvana consist?" and to him, whose mind was already averse to passion, the answer came: "when the fire of lust is extinct, that is Nirvana; when the fires of hatred and infatuation are extinct, that is Nirvana; when pride, false belief, and all other passions and torments are extinct, that is Nirvana. She has taught me a good lesson. Certainly, Nirvana is what I am looking for. I feel moved to leave the household immediately and to retire from the world in search of Nirvana...."

[Siddhartha returns to the palace and takes a final look at his son before fleeing. As he leaves the city, Mara attempts to convince him to stay. In Buddhist literature, Mara is sometimes presented as a powerful deity or the personification of worldly desire.]

---

[1] Rahula, or impediment, is the name given to the Siddhartha's son.

At this moment came Mara, with the intention of persuading the Future Buddha to turn back; and standing in the air, he said,

"Sire, go not forth! For on the seventh day from now the wheel of empire will appear to you, and you shall rule over the four great continents and their two thousand attendant isles. Sire turn back!"

"Who are you?"
"I am Vasavatti."[2]

"Mara, I knew that the wheel of empire was on the point of appearing to me; but I do not wish for sovereignty. I am about to cause the ten thousand worlds to thunder with my becoming a Buddha."

"I shall catch you," thought Mara, "the very first time you have a lustful, malicious, or unkind thought." And like an ever-present shadow, he followed after, ever on the watch for some slip….

The Great Struggle

And the Future Buddha, thinking, "I will carry austerity to the uttermost," tried various plans, such as living on one sesame seed or on one grain of rice a day, and even ceased taking nourishment altogether, and moreover rebuffed the gods when they came and attempted to infuse nourishment through the pores of his skin. By this lack of nourishment his body became emaciated to the last degree, and lost its golden color, and became black, and his thirty-two physical characteristics as a great being became obscured. Now, one day, as he was deep in a trance of suppressed breathing, he was attacked by violent pains, and fell senseless to the ground, at one end of his walking-place…. But the Future Buddha recovered his consciousness, and stood up….

---

[2] **Vasavatti**: Another name for Mara.

Now the six years that the Great Being thus spent in austerities were like time spent in trying to tie the air into knots. And coming to the conclusion, "These austerities are not the way to enlightenment," he went begging through villages and market-towns for ordinary material food, and lived upon it. And his thirty-two physical characterizes as a great being again appeared, and the color of his body became like unto gold....

Then the Great Being [seeing a Bo-tree], said to himself, "this is the immovable spot on which all the Buddhas have planted themselves! This is the place for destroying passion's net!" [He] took hold of a handful of grass by one end, and shook it out there. And straightway the blades of grass formed themselves into a seat fourteen cubits long, of such symmetry of shape as not even the most skillful painter or carver could design.

Then the Future Buddha turned his back to the trunk of the Bo-tree and faced the east. And he made this mighty resolution, "Let my skin, and sinews, and bones become dry! And let all the flesh and blood in my body dry up! But never from this seat will I stir, until I have attained the supreme and absolute wisdom!" He sat himself down cross-legged in an unconquerable position, from which not even a hundred thunder-bolds at once could have moved him.

At this point the god Mara, exclaimed, "Prince Siddhartha is desirous of passing beyond my control, but I will never allow it!" Mara went and announced the news to his army, and sounding a war cry, drew out for battle. Now Mara's army extended in front of him for twelve leagues, and to the right and to the left for twelve leagues, and in the rear as far as to the confines of the world, and it was nine leagues high. And when it shouted, it made an earthquake like roaring and rumbling over a space of a thousand leagues. And the god Mara mounting an elephant, which was a hundred and fifty leagues high, and had the name "Girded with Mountains," caused a thousand arms to appear on his body, and with these he grasped a variety of weapons. Also in the remainder of that army, no two persons carried the same weapon; and diverse also in their appearances and countenances, the host swept on like a flood to overwhelm the Great Being....

Then he [Mara] caused a shower of rocks, in which immense mountain-peaks flew, smoking and flaming through the sky. But on reaching the Future Buddha they became celestial bouquets of flowers.... Then the hosts of the gods, when they saw the army of Mara flee, cried out, "Mara is defeated! Prince Siddhartha has conquered!..."

When thus he had attained omniscience, and was the center of such unparalleled glory and homage, many prodigies appeared about him, and he breathed forth that solemn utterance which has never been omitted by any of the Buddhas:

> "Through birth and rebirth's endless round,
> Seeking in vain, I hastened on,
> To find who framed this edifice
> What misery! —birth incessantly!
>
> O builder! I've discovered you!
> This fabric you will never rebuild!
> Your rafters are all broken now
> And the pointed roof lies demolished
> This mind has demolition reached,
> And seen the last of all desire!"

Description:_____

_____

_____

Inference:_____

_____

_____

Questions

1. Why do you think the four signs (a decrepit old man, a diseased man, a dead man, and a monk) caused Siddhartha to withdraw from the world?

2. What lesson does Siddhartha learn from his six years of austerities?

3. Consider the "solemn utterance" Buddha makes at the end of this excerpt. In it, what is the problem with life and what is the solution?

4. In what ways is the Buddha's life a critique of the Indian Vedic tradition, and in what ways does it perpetuate some of its religious ideas?

DOCUMENT 2-3

Bhagavad Gita

5ᵀᴴ—2ᴺᴰ CENTURY B.C.E.

"Performing the duty prescribed by nature, one does not incur sin." - Krishna

The Bhagavad Gita is drawn from a section of the Mahabharata, one of the major Sanskrit epics of ancient India. The Mahabharata follows the dynastic struggles of Kaurava and Pandava princes through a series of smaller stories, widely considered complete works in their own right. In the following excerpt, the Pandava Prince, Arjuna, finds himself conflicted over fulfilling his duty (dharma) when its outcome seems wrong. As a member of the warrior class (Kshatriya), Arjuna is duty-bound to fight in a war that would mean the death of his relatives (the Kauravas) and people that he respects. Arjuna stands before the assembled armies, conflicted over whether to fulfill his duty and hurt those he loves or reject his caste obligations altogether. At this moment, the divine being Krishna reveals himself as Arjuna's chariot driver and counsels him to fulfill his duty by joining the battle.

Themes: dharma (duty), violence, justice

... Then seeing (the people of) Dhritarashtra's [1] party regularly marshaled, [Arjuna] the son of Pandu, whose standard is the ape, raised his bow, after the discharge of arrows had commenced ... spoke these

"The Bhagavadgita," in *The Sacred Books of the East*, trans. Kashinath Trimbak Telang (Oxford: The Clarendon Press, 1882), 8: 39-46, 126-128, 130. Modernized by Andrew Fogleman.

[1] **Dhritarashtra**: The King who governs the territories in this dispute. Dhritarashtra's sons are the Kauravas, who are lined up in battle against their cousins, the Pandavas. Arjuna is a member of the Pandavas.

words to [his chariot driver] Krishna: "O un-degraded one, drive my chariot between the two armies, while I observe those, who stand here desirous to engage in battle, and with whom, in the labors of this struggle, I must do battle. I will observe those who are assembled here and who are about to engage in battle, whishing to do service in battle to the evil-minded son of Dhritarashtra."

Thus addressed by Gudakesa (i.e., Arjuna), O descendant of Bharata, Krishna placed that excellent chariot between the two armies, in front of Bhishma (the brother of Arjuna's grandfather) and Drona (Arjuna's beloved teacher) and all the kings of the earth, and said, O son of Pritha! Look at these assembled Kauravas."

There the son of Pritha (Ajuna) saw fathers and grandfathers, preceptors, maternal uncles, brothers, sons, grandsons, companions, fathers-in-law, as well as friends in both armies. And seeing all those kinsmen standing (there), the son of Kunti (Arjuna) was overcome by excessive pity, and spoke thus despondingly:

"Seeing these kinsmen, O Krishna! Standing here desirous to engage in battle, my limbs droop down; my mouth is quite dried up; a tremor comes on my body; and my hairs stand on end; the Gandiva (bow) slips from my hand...."

"What joy shall be ours, O Krishna, after killing Dhritarashtra's sons? We shall only incur sin, killing these felons. It is not proper for us to kill our own kinsmen, the sons of Dhritarashtra. For how, O Krishna,[2] could we be happy after killing our own relatives? Although having their consciences corrupted by avarice, they do not see the evils flowing from the extinction of a family, and the sin in treachery to friends, still O Krishna, should not we, who do see the evils flowing from the extinction of a family learn to refrain from that sin? On the extinction of a family, the eternal rites of families are destroyed. Those

---

[2] Or Madhava.

rites being destroyed, impiety predominates over the whole family. In consequence of the predominance of impiety, O Krishna, the women of the family become corrupt; and the women becoming corrupt, O descendant of Vrishni, intermingling of casts results; that intermingling necessarily leads the family and the destroyers of the family to hell; for when the ceremonies of (offering) the balls of food and water (to them) fail, their ancestors fall down (to hell). By these transgressions of the destroyers of families, which occasion intermingling of castes, the eternal rites of castes and rites, of families are subverted...." Having spoken thus, Arjuna cast aside his bow together with the arrows, on the battlefield, and sat down in (his) chariot, with a mind agitated by grief.

The Deity (Krishna) said: "You grieve for those who deserve no grief. Are your words then words of wisdom? Learned men grieve neither for the living nor the dead. Never did I not exist, nor you, nor these rulers of men; nor will any one of us ever hereafter cease to exist. As in this body, infancy and youth and old age come to the soul,[3] so does the acquisition of another body; the senses, O son of Kunti, which produce cold and heat, pleasure and pain, are not permanent, [but] they are ever coming and going. A sensible man is not deceived by them. Bear them, O descendant of Bharata, for, O chief of men, that sensible man whom they (i.e., the senses) afflict not, he merits immortality. There is no existence for that which is unreal; there is no non-existence for that which is real. And the correct conclusion about both is perceived by those who perceive the truth. That which pervades all of this is indestructible; no one can bring about the destruction of that inexhaustible (principle). The soul is eternal, indestructible, and indefinable, but these bodies are said to be perishable; therefore engage in battle, O descendant of Bharata, for he who thinks he kills and he who thinks he is killed, both know nothing. The one does not kill, and the other is not killed. A man is not born, nor does he ever die, nor, having existed, does he cease to exist. Unborn, everlasting,

---

[3] **Soul**: embodied (self).

unchangeable, and primeval, he is not killed when the body is killed. O son of Pritha, once a man understands that other men are indestructible, everlasting, unborn, and inexhaustible, whom could he kill? Whom could he cause to be killed? As a man, takes off old clothes, and puts on new clothes, so the soul that casts off an old body, goes to a new one. Weapons do not cut a man (into pieces); fired does not burn him, waters do not soak him; the wind does not dry him up. It is not dividable; it is not combustible; it is not to be moistened; it is not to be dried up. It is everlasting, all pervading, stable, firm, and eternal. It is said to be unperceived, to be unthinkable, to be unchangeable. There, knowing it to be such, you ought not to grieve, but even if you think that it is constantly born, and constantly dies, still, O you of mighty arms, you ought not to grieve thus. For to one that is born, death is certain; and to one that dies, birth is certain....

...This soul O descendant of Bharata, within every one's body is ever indestructible. Therefore you ought not to grieve for any being. Having regard to your own duty also, you ought not to falter, for there is nothing better for a Kshatriya than a righteous battle. Happy those Kshatriyas, O son of Pritha, who can find such a battle (to fight)—come of itself—an open door to heaven! But if you will not fight this righteous battle, then you will have abandoned your own duty and your fame, and you will incur sin....

The duties of Brahmanas, Kshatriyas, and Vaisyas, and of Sudras, too, O terror of your foes, are distinguished according to the qualities born of nature. Tranquility, restraint of the senses, penance, purity, forgiveness, straightforwardness, also knowledge, experience, and belief (in a future world), this is the natural duty of Brahmanas. Valor, glory, courage, dexterity, not slinking away from battle, gifts, exercise of lordly power, this is the natural duty of Kshatriyas. Agriculture, tending cattle, trade, (this) is the natural duty of Vaisyas. And the natural duty of Sudras, consists in service.

(Every) man intent on his own respective duties obtains perfection. Listen, now, how one intent on one's own duty obtains perfection. Worshiping, by (the performance of) his own duty, him from whom all things proceeded, and by whom all this is permeated, a man obtains perfection. One's duty, though defective, is better than another's duty well performed. Performing the duty prescribed by nature, one does not incur sin. O son of Kunti, one should not abandon a natural duty though tainted with evil; for all actions are enveloped by evil, as fire by smoke.

One who is self-retrained, whose understanding is unattached everywhere, from whom affection have departed, obtains the supreme perfection of freedom from action by renunciation. Learn from me, only in brief, O son of Kunti, how one who has obtained perfection attains the Brahman, which is the highest culmination of knowledge. A man possessed of a pure understanding, controlling his self by courage, discarding sound and other objects of sense, casting off affection and aversion; who frequents clean places, who eats little, whose speech, body and mind are restrained, who is always intent on meditation and mental abstraction, and has recourse to unconcern, who abandoning egoism, stubbornness, arrogance, desire, anger and (all) belongings, has no (thought that this or that is) mine, and who is tranquil, becomes fit for assimilation with the Brahman...."

Arjuna responded: "Destroyed is my delusion; by your favor, O un-degraded one! I (now) recollect myself. I stand freed from doubts. I will do your bidding."

Description:_____
_____
_____

Inference:_____
_____
_____

Questions:

1. According to Arjuna, what are the consequences of fighting against relatives and the "extinction of a family?"

2. Explain Krishna's analogy of the body and old clothes. What does he mean by it? Why does it matter to Krishna's advice in favor of fighting?

3. Arjuna is conflicted over doing his duty as a warrior (Kshatriya) and killing those he loves. How does the caste system factor into Krishna's solution to this difficulty?

4. What does Arjuna decide to do?

DOCUMENT 2-4

The Code of Manu

200 B.C.E.—200 C.E.

The Code of Manu is one of many ancient Hindu legal texts (Dharma-shastras), but came into prominence when translated into English in the 18th century and used as a basis for the British colonial Hindu Law. The law purports to be a discussion given by Manu, the ancient progenitor of humans, on societal duty (dharma). Its statutes highlight obligations and prerogatives of the various hierarchical divisions of Indian society. The excerpts below are organized thematically for the sake of comparison.

Themes: caste hierarchy, gender, social order, mixed races

I. 1. The great sages approached Manu,[1] who was seated with a collected mind, and, having duly worshipped him, spoke as follows:

I. 2. "Deign, divine one, to declare to us precisely and in due order the sacred laws of each of the [four chief] castes (varnas) and of the intermediate ones....

I. 31. But for the sake of the prosperity of the worlds, he caused the Bramana, the Kshatriya, the Vaisya, and the Sudra to proceed from his mouth, his arms, his thighs, and his feet....

"The Code of Manu," in *The Sacred Books of the East*, trans. and ed. F. Max Müller (Oxford: Clarendon Press, 1886), 25: 1, 13, 14, 24, 152, 195-197, 218, 219, 221, 301, 302, 310, 326, 400-402, 404, 406, 420, 422-423. Modernized by Andrew Fogleman.

[1] **Manu**: This deity holds various descriptions in Hindu mythology. Manu is often presented as an archetypal or first man, the son of Brahma.

I. 87. But in order to protect this universe, He, the most resplendent one, assigned separate [duties and] occupations to those who sprang from his mouth, arms, thighs, and feet.

I. 88. To Bramanas he assigned teaching and studying [the Vedas], sacrificing for their own benefit and for others, giving and accepting of alms.

I.89. The Kshatriya he commanded to protect the people, to bestow gifts, to offer sacrifices, to study [the Vedas], and to abstain from attaching himself to sensual pleasures.

I. 90. The Vaisya to tend cattle, to bestow gifts, to offer sacrifices, to study [the Vedas], to trade to lend money, and to cultivate land.

I. 91. One occupation only the lord prescribed to the Sudra, to serve meekly even these other three castes.

On duties

X. 80. Among the several occupations the most commendable are, teaching the Vedas for a Brahmana, protecting the people for a Kshatriya, and trade for a Vaisya.

X. 81. But a Brahmana, unable to subsist by his peculiar occupations just mentioned, may live according to the law applicable to Kshatriyas; for the latter is next to him in rank.

X. 95. A Kshatriya who has fallen into distress, may subsist by all these means; but he must never arrogantly adopt the mode of life prescribed for his betters.

X. 96. A man of low caste who through covetousness lives by the occupations of a higher one, the king shall deprive of his property and banish.

X. 97. It is better to discharge one's own [appointed] duty incompletely than to perform completely that of another; for he who lives according to the law of another [caste] is instantly excluded from his own.

X. 98. A Vaisya who is unable to subsist by his own duties, may even maintain himself by a Sudra's mode of life, avoiding however acts forbidden to him, and he should give it up, when he is able to do so.

On mixed races

X. 4. Brahmana, the Kshatriya, and the Vaisya castes (varna) are the twice-born ones,[2] but the fourth, the Sudra, has one birth only; there is no fifth [caste].

X. 5. In all castes (varna) those children only which are begotten in the direct order from wedded wives, equal in caste and married as virgins, are to be considered as belonging to the same caste as their fathers.

X. 14. Those sons of the twice-born, begotten with wives of the next lower castes, who have been enumerated in due order, they call by the name Anantaras (belonging to the next lower caste), on account of the blemish inherent in their mothers.

On duties and hierarchies

VII. 15. Through fear of him (the king) all created beings, both the immovable and the movable, allow themselves to be enjoyed and swerve not from their duties....

VII. 18. Punishment alone governs all crated beings, punishment alone protects them, punishment watches over them while they sleep; the wise declare punishment to be identical with the law.

----

[2] **Twice-born ones**: those of the Brahmin, Kshatriya, and Vaishya varnas who underwent a second, spiritual birth as a rite of passage.

VII.19. If punishment is property inflicted after due consideration, it makes all people happy; but inflicted without consideration, it destroys everything....

VII. 35. The king has been created to be the protector of the castes (*varna*) and orders, who, all according to their rank discharge their several duties.

On fines and penalties:

VIII. 267. A Kshatriya, having slandered a Brahmana, shall be fined one hundred panas; a Vaisya one hundred and fifty or two hundred; a Sudra shall suffer corporal punishment.

VIII. 268. A Brahmana shall be fined fifty panas for defaming a Kshatriya; in [the case of] a Vaisya the fine shall be twenty-five panas; in [the case of] a Sudra twelve.

VIII. 269. For offences of twice-born men against those of equal caste (varna), the fine shall be also twelve panas; for speeches which ought not to be uttered, that and every fine shall be double.

VIII. 270. A once-born man (a Sudra), who insults a twice-born man with gross invective, shall have his tongue cut out; for he is of low origin.

VIII. 271. If he mentions the names and castes of the (twice-born) in an insolent manner, an iron nail, ten fingers long, shall be thrust red-hot into his mouth.

VII. 272. If he arrogantly teaches Brahmanas their duty, the king shall cause hot oil to be poured into his mouth and into his ears.

VII. 273. He who through arrogance makes false statements regarding the learning of a caste-fellow, his country, his caste, or the rites by which his body was sanctified, shall be compelled to pay a fine of two hundred panas.

VII. 274. He who even in accordance with the true facts contemptuously calls another man one-eyed, lame, or the like [names], shall be fined at least one pana.

Women

V. 147. By a girl, by a young woman, or even by an aged one, nothing must be done independently, even in her own house.

V. 148. In childhood a female must be subject to her father, in youth to her husband, when her lord is dead to her sons; a woman must never be independent.

V. 149. She must not seek to separate herself from her father, husband, or sons; by leaving them she would make both [her own and her husband's] families contemptible.

V. 150. She must always be cheerful, clever in [the management of her] household affairs, careful in cleaning her utensils, and economical in expenditure.

V. 151. Him to whom her father may give her, or her brother with the father's permission, she shall obey as long as he lives, and when he is dead, she must not insult his memory.

V. 152. For the sake of procuring good fortune to brides, the recitation of benedictory texts (svastyayana), and the sacrifice to the Lord of creatures (Pragapati) are used at weddings; the betrothal by the father or guardian is the cause of the husband's dominion over his wife.

V. 153. The husband who wedded her with sacred texts, always gives happiness to his wife, both in season and out of season, in this world and in the next.

V. 154. Though destitute of virtue, or seeking pleasure elsewhere, or devoid of good qualities, (yet) a husband must be constantly worshipped as a god by a faithful wife.

V. 155. No sacrifice, no vow, no fast must be performed by women apart from their husbands; if a wife obeys her husband, she will for that reason alone be exalted in heaven....

V. 164. By violating her duty towards her husband, a wife is disgraced in this world, after death she enters the womb of a jackal, and is tormented by diseases the punishment of her sin....

V. 166. In reward of such conduct, a female who controls her thoughts, speech, and actions, gains in this life highest renown, and in the next world a place near her husband.

Duties of Vasya

IX. 326. After a Vaisya has received the sacraments and has taken a wife, he shall be always attentive to the business whereby he may subsist and to (tending cattle).

IX. 327. For when the Lord of creatures (Pragapati) created cattle, he gave them over to the Vaisya; to the Brahmana, and to the king he entrusted all created beings.

IX. 328. A Vaisya must never conceive this wish, "I will not keep cattle"; and if a Vaisya is willing to keep them, they must never be kept by men of other castes.

Duties of Sudra

IX. 334. But to serve Brahmanas who are learned in the Vedas, householders, and famous for virtue is the highest duty of a Sudra, which leads to blessedness.

IX. 335. A Sudra who is pure, the servant of his betters, gentle in his speech, and free from pride, and always seeks a refuge with Brahmanas, attains [in his next life] a higher caste.

VIII. 413. But a Sudra, whether bought or unbought, may be compelled to do servile work; for he was created by the Self-existent (Svayambhu) to be the slave of a Brahmana.

VIII. 414. A Sudra, though emancipated by his master, is not released from servitude; since that is innate in him, who can set him free from it?

Description:_____

_____

_____

Inference:_____

_____

_____

Questions:

1. Consider the following statute: "It is better to discharge one's own [appointed] duty incompletely than to perform completely that of another." What effect might a statute like this have had on ancient Indian society?

2. How is cast status translated in birth?

3. What role does punishment play in this system?

4. Did any of these statutes or punishments surprise you? If so, which and why?

5. How does the text compare with the Code of Hammurabi?

DOCUMENT 2-5

The Lotus Sutra

1ˢᵀ CENTURY B.C.E.—2ᴺᴰ CENTURY C.E.

The Lotus Sutra is one of the most widely known and influential sacred scriptures of East Asian Mahayana Buddhism. In it, Shakyamuni Buddha (Gautama Buddha) rouses from meditation and expounds the path of Buddhahood to thousands of listeners. He explains that all beings have the potential to become Buddhas because there are many paths to Buddhahood.

Themes: donors and enlightenment

And all in the world who are hearing or have heard the law from the mouth of the Buddhas, given alms, followed the moral precepts, and patiently accomplished the whole of their religious duties;

75. Who have acquitted themselves in point of zeal and meditation, with wisdom reflected on those laws, and performed several meritorious actions, have all of them reached enlightenment.

76. And such beings as were living patient, subdued, and disciplined, under the rule of the Buddhas of those times, have all of them reached enlightenment.

"The Lotus of the True Law," trans. H. Kern, in *Sacred Books of the East*, ed. Max Müller (Oxford, Clarendon Press, 1884), 21: 49, 50. Modernized by Andrew Fogleman.

77. Others also, who paid worship to the relics of the departed Buddhas, erected many thousands of Stupas[1] made of gems, gold, silver, or crystal,

78. Or built Stupas of emerald, cat's eye, pearls, excellent lapis lazuli, or sapphire; they have all of them reached enlightenment.

79. And those who erected Stupas from marble, sandal-wood, or eagle-wood; constructed Stupas from deodar[2] or a combination of different sorts of timber;

80. And who in gladness of heart built for the Buddhas Stupas of bricks or clay; or caused mounds of earth to be raised in forests and wildernesses in dedication to the Buddhas;

81. The little boys even, who in playing erected here and there heaps of sand with the intention of dedicating them as Stupas to the Buddhas, they have all of them reached enlightenment.

82. Likewise have all who caused jewel images to be made and dedicated, adorned with the thirty-two characteristic signs, reached enlightenment.

83. Others who had images of Buddhas made of the seven precious substances, of copper or brass, have all of them reached enlightenment.

84. Those who ordered beautiful statues of Buddhas to be made of lead, iron, clay, or plaster have reached enlightenment.

85. Those who made images [of the Buddhas] on painted walls, with complete limbs and the hundred holy signs, whether they drew them themselves or had them drawn by others, have reached enlightenment.

---

[1] **Stupa**: a dome-shaped Buddhist shrine.
[2] **Deodar**: A large cedar tree.

49

Description:_____
_____
_____

Inference:_____
_____
_____

Questions:

1. What type of people can reach enlightenment, according to this text?

2. Which actions lead to enlightenment?

3. Why would a text like this matter to wealthy Buddhist merchants?

Chapter 3:
Ancient China

Document 3-1

Laozi

Dao De Jing

CA. 4TH CENTURY B.C.E.

The Dao De Jing, translated as the "The Classic of the Way and its Power (or Virtue)" is an ancient Chinese philosophical text dealing with various topics ranging from the nature of the universe, to proper moral action, to political advice. It is a foundational text for both philosophical and religious Daoism. Its authorship is traditionally attributed to Laozi, though he may be a mythical figure. The excerpts below contain the pithy, cryptic aphorisms that have made this text a classic and also fueled debate over its meaning.

Themes: action vs. non-action, knowledge and learning, the Way (Dao)

1:1. The Way (*Dao*) that can be spoken of is not the enduring and unchanging Way. The name that can be named is not the enduring and unchanging name....

"The Tao Teh King," trans. James Legge, in *Sacred Books of the East*, ed. Max Müller (Oxford: Oxford University Press, 1891), 39: 47, 49, 52, 53, 65, 87, 89-91. Modernized by Andrew Fogleman.

3:1. Not to value and employ men of superior ability is the way to keep the people from rivalry among themselves; not to prize articles which are difficult to procure is the way to keep them from becoming thieves; not to show them what is likely to excite their desires is the way to keep their minds from disorder.

3:2. Therefore the sage, in the exercise of his government, empties their minds, fills their bellies, weakens their wills, and strengthens their bones.

3:3. He constantly [tries to] keep them without knowledge and without desire, and where there are those who have knowledge, to keep them from presuming to act [on it]. When there is this abstinence from action, good order is universal....

7:1. Heaven is long-enduring and earth continues long. The reason why heaven and earth are able to endure and continue thus long is because they do not live of, or for, themselves. This is how they are able to continue and endure.

7:2. Therefore the sage puts himself last, and yet he is found in the foremost place; he treats body as if it were foreign to him, and yet that body is preserved. Is it because he has no personal and private ends, that therefore such ends are realized? ....

9. 1. It is better to leave a vessel unfilled, than to attempt to carry it when it is full. If you keep feeling a point that has been sharpened, the point cannot long preserve its sharpness.

9:2. When gold and jade fill the hall, their possessor cannot keep them safe. When wealth and honors lead to arrogance, this brings evil on itself. When the work is done, and one's name is becoming distinguished, to withdraw into obscurity is the way of Heaven....

22. 1. The partial becomes complete; the crooked, straight; the empty, full; the worn out, new. He whose desires are few gets them; he whose desires are many goes astray.

22:2. Therefore the sage holds in his embrace the one thing of humility, and manifests it to all the world. He is free from self-display, and therefore he shines; from self-assertion, and therefore he is distinguished; from self-boasting, and therefore his merit is acknowledged; from self-complacency, and therefore he acquires superiority. It is because he is thus free from striving that no one in the world is able to strive with him.

22:3. That saying of the ancients that "the partial becomes complete" was not vainly spoken; all real completion is comprehended under it....

43:1. The softest thing in the world dashes against and overcomes the hardest; that which has no [substantial] existence enters where there is no crevice. I know hereby what advantage belongs to doing nothing.

43:2. There are few in the world who attain to teaching without words, and the advantage arising from non-action.

47:1. Without going outside his door, one understands all that takes place under the sky; without looking out from his window, one sees the Way (*Dao*) of Heaven. The farther that one goes out, the less he knows.

47:2. Therefore the sages got their knowledge without travelling; gave the [right] names to things without seeing them; and accomplished their ends without any purpose of doing so.

48:1. He who devotes himself to learning seeks from day to day to increase [his knowledge]; he who devotes himself to the Way seeks from day to day to diminish his doing.

48:2. He diminishes it and again diminishes it, till he arrives at doing nothing. Having arrived at this point of non-action, there is nothing that he does not do.

48:3. He who gets all-under-heaven as his own does so by giving himself no trouble. If one troubles himself, he is not equal to getting as his own all-under-heaven.

49:1. The sage has no invariable mind of his own; he makes the mind of the people his mind.

49:2. To those who are good, I am good; and to those who are not good, I am also good; and thus all get to be good. To those who are sincere, I am sincere; and to those who are not sincere, I am also sincere; and thus all get to be sincere.

49:3. The sage has in the world an appearance of indecision, and keeps his mind in a state of indifference to all. The people all keep their eyes and ears directed to him, and he deals with them all as his children.

Description:_____

_____

_____

Inference:_____

_____

_____

Questions:

1. How would you explain the role of language and knowledge in the following lines? "The Way (*Dao*) that can be spoken of is not the enduring and unchanging Way. The name that can be named is not the enduring and unchanging name."

2. How would you explain the role of action and non-action in the following lines? "He is free from self-display, and therefore he shines; from self-assertion, and therefore he is distinguished; from self-boasting, and therefore his merit is acknowledged; from self-complacency, and therefore he acquires superiority. It is because he is thus free from striving that no one in the world is able to strive with him."

3. Are the suggestion made in this excerpt practical? If not, are there benefits to this philosophy at all?

DOCUMENT 3-2

The Instructions of Yi

1000 B.C.E.—200 B.C.E.

The Book of Documents is one of the five classical works of ancient Chinese literature and served as a foundational text on Chinese political philosophy for over two millennia. The work is divided between the historical accounts of four dynasties: the semi-mythical Yu, the Xia, Shang, and Zhou. The excerpt below is taken from the section on the Shang dynasty. In it, the chief minister, Yî Yin, instructs a new king, Thâi Kiâ, on the nature of proper kingship following the death of his grandfather, Cheng Tang. Yi encourages Thâi to look to the actions of former kings as a model for his rule.

Themes: tradition, counsel, the power of the king

In the twelfth month of the first year, on [the day] Yi-khau, Yi Yin[1] Sacrificed to the former king [Cheng Tang] and presented the heir-king reverently before the shrine of his grandfather. All the princes from the domain of the nobles and the royal domain were present; all the officers also, each continuing to discharge his particular duties, were there to receive the orders of the chief minister. Yi Yin then clearly described the complete virtue of the meritorious ancestor for the instruction of the young king.

He said, "Oh! Of old the former kings of Xia cultivated earnestly their virtue, and then there were no calamities from Heaven. The spirits of

---

"The Instruction of YÎ," in *The Sacred Books of China*, trans. James Legge (Oxford: Clarendon Press, 1879), 3:92-95. Modernized by Andrew Fogleman.

[1] **Yi Yin**: Cheng Tang's royal minister.

the hills and rivers likewise were all in tranquility; and the birds and beasts, the fishes and tortoises, all enjoyed their existence according to their nature. But their descendant did not follow their example, and great Heaven sent down calamities, employing the agency of our ruler who was in possession of its favoring appointment. The attack [on Xia] may be traced to the orgies in Mingtiao,[2] but our rise began in Po. Our king of Shang brilliantly displayed his sagely prowess; for oppression he substituted his generous gentleness; and the millions of people gave him their hearts. Now your majesty is entering on the inheritance of his virtue; all depends on how you commence your reign. To set up love, it is for you to love your relations; to set up respect, it is for you to respect your elders. The commencement is in the family and the state; the consummation is in all within the four seas."

"Oh! The former king began with careful attention to the bonds that hold men together. He listened to correction, and did not seek to resist it; he conformed to the wisdom of the ancients; occupying the highest position, he displayed intelligence; occupying an inferior position, he displayed his loyalty; he allowed the good qualities of men whom he employed, and did not seek that they should have every talent; in the government of himself, he seemed to think that he could never sufficiently attain. It was thus he arrived at the possession of the myriad regions. How painstaking was he in these things!

"He extensively sought out wise men, who should [also] be helpful to you, his descendant and heir. He laid down the punishments for officers, and warned those who were in authority, saying, 'If you dare to have constant dancing in your palaces, and drunken singing in your chambers, that is called the fashion of sorcerers; if you dare to set your hearts on wealth and women, and abandon your selves to wandering about or to the chase, that is called the fashion of extravagance; if you dare to despise sage words, to resist the loyal and upright, to put far

---

[2] **Mingtiao**: present-day North Anyi, Xiyun and the site of the defeat of Jie, the last Xia king.

from you the aged and virtuous, and to seek the company of clever youths, that is called the fashion of disorder. Now if a high noble or officer be addicted to one of these three fashions with their ten evil ways, his family will surely come to ruin; if the prince of a country be so addicted, his state will surely come to ruin. The minister who does not try to correct such vices in the sovereign shall be punished with branding. These rules were minutely inculcated in the sons of officers and nobles in their lessons."

"Oh! Do you who now succeed to the throne revere these warnings in your person? Think of them! Sacred counsels of vast importance, admirable words forcibly set forth! The ways of God are not invariable: on the good-doer he sends down all blessings, and on the evil-doer he sends down all miseries. Do you but be virtuous, be it in small things or in large, and the myriad regions will have cause for rejoicing. If you be not virtuous, be it in large things or in small, it will bring the ruin of your ancestral temple."

Description:_____
_____
_____

Inference:_____
_____
_____

Questions:

1. How does this text reflect a Confucian philosophy of order?

2. What is the heir-king's relationship to the kings who have come before him?

3. According to this text, what role does Heaven play in politic?

Chapter 4:
The Greeks

DOCUMENT 4-1

Hesiod

Works and Days

700 B.C.E.

The Works and Days is an epic poem written by the Greek poet Hesiod (ca. 750—ca. 650). In it, Hesiod encourages his brother, Perses, to find satisfaction in honest labor by working the land left to him by his father. In the course of expounding on the arts of agricultural to his brother, Hesiod also recounts the origin of life's many difficulties. These he traces back to Prometheus, who in an effort to ease the lives of men, stole fire from the gods. When Zeus learned of it, he retaliated with a destructive gift.

Themes: nature of the gods, origins of women, nature of women

For the gods keep hidden away from men the means of life. Otherwise you would easily do work enough in a day to supply yourself for a full year, even if you remained idle. You could put away your rudder over the fireplace, and the fields worked by ox and a sturdy mule would be fallow. But Zeus in the anger of his heart hid it (i.e., the means of life),

Hesiod, "Works and Days," in *Homeric Hymns, Epic Cycle, Homerica*, trans. Hugh G. Evelyn White (London: William Heinemann, 1914): 2: 42-105. Modernized by Andrew Fogleman.

because crafty Prometheus deceived him; therefore Zeus planned miserable sorrows for men. He hid fire; but Prometheus, the noble son of Iapetus, stole it away from Zeus, the counselor, for men [and hid it] in a hollow fennel-stalk, so that Zeus, the thunderer, did not see it. But afterwards, Zeus who gathers the clouds said to him in anger:

"Son of Iapetus, surpassing all in cunning, are you glad that you have outwitted me and stolen fire? That theft will be a great plague to you and to men in the future. I will give men as the price for that fire an evil thing. A thing they will enjoy as they embrace their own destruction."

Thus said the father of men and gods, and laughed aloud. And he asked famous Hephaestus to quickly mix earth with water and to put in it the voice and strength of human kind, and fashion a sweet, lovely maiden-shape and face, like to the immortal goddesses; and [he asked] Athena to teach her needlework and the weaving of the varied web; and golden Aphrodite to shed grace upon her head and cruel longing and cares that weary the limbs. And he charged Hermes the guide, the Slayer of Argus, to put in her a shameless mind and a deceitful nature.

That is what he ordered. And they obeyed the lord Zeus the son of Cronos. Immediately the famous Lame God[1] molded clay in the likeness of a modest maid, as the son of Cronos desired. And the bright-eyed goddess Athena girded and clothed her, and the divine Graces and queenly Persuasion put necklaces of gold upon her, and the rich-haired Hours crowned her head with spring flowers. And Pallas Athena clothed her form with all manners of finery. Also the Guide, the Slayer of Argus,[2] contrived within her lies and crafty words and a deceitful nature at the will of loud thundering Zeus, and the Herald of the gods[3] put speech in her. And he called this woman Pandora,[4]

---

[1] **The Famous Lame God**: this is Hephaestus, a smithing god who made weapons for the gods.
[2] **The Guide, the Slayer of Argus**: the god Hermes.
[3] **The Herald of the gods**: the god Hermes.

because all they who dwelt on Olympus each gave [her] a gift, a plague to men who eat bread.

But when he had finished the sheer, hopeless snare, the Father sent glorious Argus-Slayer, the swift messenger of the gods, to take it to Epimetheus [5] as a gift. And Epimetheus did not think on what Prometheus had said to him, instructing him never take a gift from Olympian Zeus, but send it back for fear it might prove to be something harmful to men. But he took the gift, and afterwards, when the evil thing was already his, he understood.

For before this the tribes of men lived on earth remote and free from ills and hard toil and heavy sickness, which bring the Fates upon men; for in misery men grow old quickly. But the woman took off a great lid from a jar [she carried in] her hands and scattered all these, and her thought caused sorrow and mischief to men.

Only Hope remained there in an unbreakable home under the rim of the great jar, and did not fly out at the door; for before that, the lid of the jar stopped her, by the will of Aegis-holding Zeus who gathers the clouds. But the rest, countless plagues, wander among men; for earth is full of evils and the sea is full, too. Of themselves diseases come upon men continually by day and by night, bringing mischief to mortals silently; for wise Zeus took away speech from them. indeed, there is no way to escape the will of Zeus.

Description:_____

_____

_____

Inference:_____

_____

_____

[4] **Pandora**: the "all-endowed."
[5] **Epimetheus**: the brother of Prometheus.

Questions:

1. How would you describe the nature of the gods in this origin myth? What is man's relationship to the gods in this tale?

2. According to Hesiod, why are women created? And how does their creation affect men and the world?

3. Do you think a story like this would have affected the perception of women in Greek society?

Homer

Iliad

8ᵀᴴ CENTURY B.C.E.

"We have slain the noble Hector, whom, throughout their city, the Trojans ever worshipped like a god."-Achilles

The Iliad is an epic Greek poem attributed to Homer. It is one of the oldest extant works of Western literature. The poem's setting is the final weeks of the ten-year long siege of Troy by a coalition of Greek states. It focuses on a dispute within the Greek ranks between King Agamemnon and the warrior Achilles over the division of spoils. The selection below reveals attitudes toward the role of the gods, fate, and individual honor in Greek society.

Themes: honor, loyalty, violence, the nature of the gods

Achilles, the swift-footed, with stern look, thus answered:

"You, [Agamemnon] clothed in insolence and bent on dishonest gain! How shall any of the Greeks willingly obey you on the march, or bravely battling the enemy?

I did not come to this war because of any wrong done to me by the valiant sons of Troy.

The Iliad of Homer, trans. William Cullen Bryant (Boston: Houghton Mifflin Company, 1870), 1: 8, 9, 233, 234, 236, 237, 2: 94-97, 128-130, 267, 271, 272, 275, 276. Modernized by Andrew Fogleman.

I had no feud with them; they never took my cattle or horses, nor spoiled my harvest fields in Phthia's realm, deep-soiled and populous.

For many shadowy mountains and waters of the wide-resounding sea lies between us.

We followed you here to bring you glory in vengeance upon Troy for your grudge and Menelaus', you shameless one!

And yet you have neither care nor thanks for our sacrifices.

Now you threaten to take from me the prize[1] of my long toil in battle, which the Greeks decreed mine.

I have never taken an equal share with you of spoils when our Grecian host sacked some populous Trojan town.

My hands perform the harder tasks in all the tumults of the fight;

But when the spoils are shared, the largest portion is always yours,

While I, content with little gain, seek my ships, weary with combat.

I shall now go home to Phthia;[2] it is better to return with my beaked ships;

But here, where I am held in little honor, I think you will fail to gather spoils and wealth in large measure."

Agamemnon, king of men, answered Achilles: "Desert then, if you want; I do not ask you to stay for me; there are plenty of others who will give me honor, and, best of all, the all-providing Jove is still with me. I detest you the most of all the men ordained by him to govern; your delight is in contention, war, and bloody battles...."

---

[1] **Prize**: The slave, Breisis.

[2] **Phthia**: In Greek mythology, a city in ancient Thessaly and home of Achilles.

[In anger, Achilles returns to his tent and refuses to fight for Agamemnon. After losing efforts against the Trojans, messengers from Agamemnon seek to appease Achilles by offering to return the slave, Briseis, the cause of the feud and many other gifts if he will join the Greeks in war.]

[Agamemnon's messenger speaks], "…These gifts will [Agamemnon] bestow, but cool your anger. And if the son of Atreus[3] and his gifts still move you to rage, at least have pity on the afflicted Greeks, trapped in their camp. They would honor you as a god; and you will gain great glory as their champion. Kill Hector, who even now is near, and in a murderous frenzy boasts that none of chieftains whom the fleet of Greece brought equals his might." …

"I will not join in council or action with him (Agamemnon):

He has deceived and wronged me once, and now he cannot persuade me with words.

Let once suffice. I leave him to himself, to perish. All-providing Jupiter hath made him mad. I hate his gifts; I hold in utter scorn the giver." … "As many gifts as there are sands and dust of earth,—not even then shall Atreus' son persuade me, till I reap a just revenge for his foul deeds against me." …

[The battle rages on, and the Greeks continue to suffer. Patroclus, the fellow warrior and friend of Achilles, asks to wear Achilles's armor into battle in order to terrify the Trojans.]

Meanwhile, Patroclus stood beside his friend, the shepherd of the people, Peleus's son (Achilles), and shed hot tears, as when a fountain sheds dark waters streaming over a precipice.

---

[3] **Son of Atreus**: Agamemnon.

The great Achilles, swift of foot, saw and pitied him, and spoke these winged words:

"Patroclus, why do you cry like a girl...?

Patroclus, with a deep-drawn sigh, answered: "Do not be angry, Achilles, son of Peleus, bravest by far of all the Achaian army! For the Greeks are suffering. Their mightiest chiefs are within the ships, wounded or stricken down.... "give me the armor from your shoulders. I will wear your mail, and then the Trojans, at the sight, may think I am Achilles, and may pause from fighting, and the warlike sons of Greece, tired as they are will breath once more and find relief from the conflict. Then our refreshed troops will easily drive the weary Trojans back to their city and away from our tents and fleet."

[Achilles agrees.] "Put on my well-known armor; lead my Myrmidons[4] into the field, men that rejoice in war, since like a lowering cloud the men of Troy surround the fleet, and the Achaians[5] stand in narrow space close pressed beside the sea, and all the city of Ilium flings itself against them, confident of victory, now that the glitter of my helmet no more flashes before their eyes.

Yet very soon their flying host would fill the trenches here with corpses, had but Agamemnon dealt gently with me; and now their troops close around our army.

Tydides Diomed no longer wields the spear to rescue the Greeks;[6]

No more the shout of Agamemnon's hated throat is heard;

---

[4] **Myrmidons**: Achilles's army.

[5] **Achaians**: general name used by Homer for the Greeks.

[6] **Tydides Diomed**: One of the greatest Greek warriors in the *Iliad*. At this point in the story, Diomed is shot through the foot by an arrow from Paris and would not return to the battle.

But the man-queller, Hector, lifting up his voice, exhorts the Trojans, who, in throngs, raising the war-cry, fill the plain, and drive the Greeks before them.

Gallantly lead on the charge, Patroclus!

Rescue our good ships; Let not the enemy give them to the flames, and cut us off from our desired return.

Follow my counsel; bear my words in mind; Win for me great honor and renown among the Greeks, and they shall bring the beautiful maiden back with princely gifts…"

…Patroclus rushed onward, bent to wreak his fury on the Trojans. Fierce as Mars, three times he charged their troops with fearful shouts, and three times he laid nine warriors in the dust.

But as with god-like energy he made the fourth assault, then it was clearly seen that your life, Patroclus, was near its end, for then Phoebus[7] encountered you in that fierce strife.

Patroclus did not see him advancing in the clamor [of battle] for he moved unseen in darkness. Coming close behind, he smote the hero's back with an open palm between his ample shoulders, and his eyes reeled with the blow, while Phoebus struck the tall helm, that, clanking from his head, and rolled away under the horses' feet;

Its crest was stained with blood and dust, though dust had never defiled its horse-hair plum until that moment;

For once that helmet had guarded an illustrious head, that glorious brows of Peleus' son, and now Jove destined it for Hector, to be worn in battle, and his death was also near.

---

[7] **Phoebus**: the God Apollo

The spear Patroclus wielded, edged with brass, long, tough, and huge was broken in his hands, and his broad shield, dropping with its band, lay on the ground, while Phoebus, son of Jove, undid the latches of his armor. With mind bewildered and powerless limbs, Patroclus stood as thunderstruck.

Then a Dardanian named Euphorbus, son of Panthous, who excelled his comrades in the wielding of the spear, the chariot race, and horsemanship, approached and struck Patroclus in the back between the shoulder-blades with his powerful spear.

He had already dashed down twenty warriors from their chariots, while guiding his own, a learner in the art of war.

He (Euphorbus) was the first to throw the spear at you, Patroclus, but he did not kill you.

For, tearing its ash-colored shaft from his back, he fled, and blended with the multitude, nor dared await your coming, though you were unarmed, while weakened by that wound and by the blow given by the god (phoebus), Patroclus turned and sought shelter in the Grecian ranks;

But when Hector saw the gallant Greek wounded and retreating, he left his place among the troops, and, rushing forward pierced Patroclus with his spear below the belt, driving the weapon deep. The hero collapsed with armor clashing, and all the Greeks beheld his fall with grief…"

[*Achilles learns of Patroklus's death and, mad with rage, enters the battle. Hector flees and and Achilles pursues him around the walls of the city as the Gods decide the warriors' fates*]

"…The all-Father raised the golden balance high, and placing in the scales two lots which bring death's long dark sleep, —on lot for Peleus' son, and one for knightly Hector, —and held the balance by the middle.

Hector's fate sank down to Hades and Apollo left the field.

The blue-eyed goddess Pallas[8] then approached the son of Peleus with theses winged words: "Famous Achilles, dear to Jupiter! Now, at last we may return from this terrible war to the Achaian army and the fleet with glory as I hoped, with Hector slain.

He cannot escape now, even if the archer-god Apollo threw himself with passionate entreaty at the feet of Jove, the Aegis-bearer.

Stay and breathe a moment, while I go to him (Hector) and lure him to face you here....

[Pallas disguises herself as Deiphonbus, Hector's brother, and convinces Hector to stand and fight Achilles]

...So Hector, brandishing that sharp-edged sword, sprang forward, while Achilles opposite leaped toward him, all on fire with savage hate, holding his bright shield, nobly wrought, before him.

On his (Achilles) shining helmet waved the fourfold crest and golden tufts lavishly decorated by the hand of Vulcan.

As in the still hours of night, Hesper,[9] the fairest light of heaven, goes forth among the multitude of stars, so the keen blade of his spear shone brightly in the right hand of Peleus' son, as he confidently (went forth) to slay the noble Hector. [Achilles's] eye ran over Hector's glorious form, exploring where to plant a fatal wound.

The glittering armor of brass won from the slain Patroclus guarded well each part (of Hector's body), except where the collarbones divide the

---

[8] **Pallas**: Athena.
[9] **Hesper**: The evening star, Venus.

shoulder from the neck, and there appeared the throat, the spot where life is most in peril.

Through that part the noble son of Peleus drove his spear, and it went straight through Hector's tender neck…

[In triumph, Achilles declares] "Now then, youths of Greece, march on and chant a song of triumph, while, returning to the fleet, for we bring great glory with us; we have slain the noble Hector, whom, throughout their city, the Trojans ever worshipped like a god."

He spoke, and planning in his mind to treat the noble Hector shamefully, he bored holes behind the tendons of his feet between the heel and ankle;

Drawing through them leather cords, he tied them to his chariot, but left the head to drag in dirt.

And then he climbed the chariot, took the shining armor, and lashed to speed the horses, who raced with eagerness.

Dust arose, as Hector was dragged along, around the dead; His dark locks swept the ground.

That head, of late so noble in men's eyes, now lies deep amid the dirt, for that day Jove suffered the foes of Hector to insult his corpse in his own land.

His mother saw, and tore her hair, and flung her lustrous veil away and uttered piercing shrieks.

No less his father, who so loved him, piteously bewailed him; and in all the streets of Troy the people wept aloud, with such lament as if the towering Ilium[10] were in flames even to its highest roofs.

Description:_____

_____

_____

Inference:_____

_____

_____

Questions:

1. What role does individual honor play in this poem? Find specific examples.

2. How do the gods participate in this conflict? What does this tell us about the nature of the gods in relation to human affairs?

3. Why do you think this type of literature was so entertaining to the Greeks?

4. What sort of visual details are highlighted in this story? What might this say about the communities that enjoyed this poem?

---

[10] **Ilium**: Another name for Troy.

DOCUMENT 4-3

Plato

Apologia of Socrates

CA. 399 B.C.E.

"[A]n unexamined life is not worth living."-Socrates

An apologia (or apology) is a formal defense of one's actions or position. The following is an account of Socrates's apologia, or legal defense, against charges he faced in a trial at Athens in 399 BCE. In this text, written by Socrates's student, Plato (429—347 BCE), Socrates defends himself against accusations of impiety and corrupting the city's youth. He explains how a pronouncement from the Oracle of Delphi led him to seek wisdom and the resulting anger it produced among the city's elites. A jury of Athenian citizens eventually found Socrates guilty of these charges and sentenced him to death by way of drinking poison hemlock.

Themes: pursuit of truth, wisdom, individualism vs. communal harmony

... "I will bring the God of Delphi[1] to be witness of my wisdom, if it is indeed wisdom, and of its nature. You remember Chærephon. From youth upwards he was my comrade.... And you know too Chærephon's character: how passionate he was in pursuing everything he did. Once he went to Delphi and ventured to put this question to

---

Plato, "Apologia," in *The Trial and Death of Socrates*, trans. F. J. Church (London: Macmillan and Co., 1880), 36-39, 41, 48-53, 55, 56, 62, 63, 68. Modernized by Andrew Fogleman.

[1] **The God of Delphi**: Apollo.

the oracle,[2] ... he asked if there was any man wiser than I (i.e.,
Socrates) was and the priestess answered that there was no man [wiser].
He himself is dead, but his brother will confirm the truth of what I say.

Now see why I tell you this. I am going to explain to you the origin of
the prejudice against me. When I heard of the oracle I began to reflect,
what can the God mean by this strange saying? Certainly I know well
that I am not wise either more or less [than anyone else]. Then what
can he mean by saying that I am the wisest of men? It cannot be that
he is speaking falsely, for he is a god and cannot lie. And for a long
time I was at a loss to understand his meaning: then, very reluctantly, I
turned to seek for it (i.e., the truth of the oracle's statement) in this
manner. I went to a man who seemed wise, thinking that there, if
anywhere, I should prove that answer wrong, and be able to say to the
oracle, "You said that I am the wisest of men; but this man is wiser
than I am." So I examined him. I need not tell you his name. He was a
public man, but this was the result, Athenians. When I questioned him,
I came to see that, though many persons, and chiefly he himself,
thought that he was wise, yet he was not wise. And then I tried to show
him that he was not wise, though he thought that he was; and by that I
gained his hatred, and the hatred of many of the bystanders. So when I
went away, I thought to myself, "I am wiser than this man; neither of
us probably knows anything that is really good, but he thinks that he
has knowledge, when he has it not, while I, seeing that I have no
knowledge, do not think that I have." In this point at least, I seem to
be a little wiser than he is, as I do not think that I know what I do not
know. Next I went to another man, who seemed to be still wiser, with
just the same result. And there again I gained his hatred and the hatred
of many other men.

Then I went on to one man after another, seeing that I was gaining
their hatred, and in grief and fear at it, still I thought that I must set the

---

[2] **Oracle**: Apollo was thought to speak through a priestess known as the Oracle of
Delphi, or the *pythia*.

God's command above everything. So I had to go to every man who seemed to have any knowledge, and search for the meaning of the oracle; and, Athenians, I must tell you the truth; verily, by the Dog of Egypt, this was the result. It seemed to me, in the search which the God commanded me, that the men in greatest repute were the greatest in lacking wisdom, while others who were not considered great were much the better men.…

[In an attempt to further test the Oracle's saying, Socrates then seeks wisdom among the famous poets and artists of Athens only to discover that they too lack wisdom.]

This search, Athenians, has gained me much hatred of the very fierce and bitter kind, which has caused many false accusations against me. [Additionally] some call me wise. For bystanders always think that I am wise myself in any matter wherein I convict another man of ignorance. But in truth, my friends, perhaps it is God who is wise; and by this oracle he may have meant that man's wisdom is worth little or nothing. He did not mean, I think, that Socrates is wise. He only took me as an example, and made use of my name, as though he would say to men; "He among you is wisest, who, like Socrates, is convinced that he has little wisdom."

And therefore I still go about searching and testing every man whom I think wise, whether he is a citizen or a stranger, according to the word of God; and whenever I find that he is not wise, I point that out to him in the service of God.

And I am so busy in this pursuit that I have never had leisure to take any part worth mentioning in public matters,[3] or to look after my private affairs.

As a result, I am in very great poverty by my service to the God.

---

[3] **Public matters**: Politics.

And besides this, the young men who follow me about, who are the sons of wealthy persons and with much leisure, by nature delight in hearing men questioned. And they often imitate me among themselves and then they try their hand at questioning other people. And, I imagine, they find a many men who think that they know a great deal, when in truth they know little or nothing. And then the persons who are questioned become angry with me instead of with themselves and say that Socrates is an abominable fellow who corrupts the young. And when they are asked, Why? What does he do? What does he teach? They have nothing to say. But not to seem at a loss, they repeat the stock charges against all philosophers and say that he investigates things in the air and under the earth, and that he teaches people to disbelieve in the gods, and "to make the worst reason appear the better reason." For I guess that they would not like to confess the truth that they are … mere ignorant pretenders to knowledge. And so they have filled your ears with their fierce slanders for a long time, for they are zealous and fierce, and numerous.…

… Perhaps some one will say: "Are you not ashamed, Socrates, of following pursuits, which are likely now to cause your death?" I should make him a just reply, and say: "My friend, you do not speak well, if you think that a man of any worth at all should give any weight to the chances of life and death, and that he ought in this actions to regard anything but the question whether he is acting rightly or wrongly, and as a good or a bad man would act. According to you all, the demigods who died at Troy would be worthless men, and especially the son of Thetis (Achilles). He thought nothing of danger when the alternative was disgrace. For when his mother, a goddess spoke to him, as he was burning to slay Hector, I suppose in this fashion, "My son, if you avenge the death of your comrade, Patroclus, and kill Hector, you will also die, for "fate waits for you after Hector's death." He heard what she said, but scorned danger and death. He feared much more to live as a coward, and not to avenge his friends. "Let me punish the evil-doer and straightway die," he said, "that I may not remain here by the beaked ships, a scorn of men, encumbering the earth."[4] Do you suppose that he thought of danger and death? For in truth, Athenians, wherever a man's post is, whether he has chosen it for himself or has been placed at it by his commander, there to my mind, it is his duty to remain and face the danger, without thinking either of death or of anything else except disgrace. … At Delium, I remained [at my post] where they (i.e., the commanders) placed me like other men, and faced the danger of death; and it would a be monstrous action on my part if now, when the God commands me, as I am persuaded he does, to spend my life in philosophy and in examining myself and others, I were to desert my post from fear of death or of any other thing…

"Athenians, I hold you in the highest regard and love; but I will obey the God rather than you; and as long as I have breath and power I will not cease from philosophy, and from exhorting you and setting forth the truth to any of you whom I meet, saying as I do, "My excellent friend, you are a citizen of Athens, a city very great and very famous for wisdom and power of mind. Are you not ashamed of caring so much about making of money, and for reputation and honor? Will you not spend a thought or care on wisdom and truth and the perfecting of your soul?" …

"I have something more to say to you… Be sure that if you kill me, a man such as I say I am, you will harm yourselves more than you will harm me. Meletus and Anytus[5] can do me no harm; that is impossible for I do not think that the God will allow a good man to be harmed by a bad one. They may indeed kill me, or drive me into exile, or deprive me of my civil rights; and perhaps Meletus and others think these things [I do are] great evils. But I do not think so. I think that to do as he is doing, and to try to kill a man unjustly is a much greater evil. And now Athenians, I am not going to argue for my own sake at all as you might think, but for yours, that you may not sin against the God and

---

[4] Homer, *Iliad*. Xvii.
[5] **Meletus and Anytus**: the chief prosecutors of the case against Socrates.

reject his gift to you, by condemning me. If you put me to death, you will hardly find another man to fill my place. That God has sent me to attack the city (i.e., Athens), if I my use a ludicrous simile, just as if Athens were a great and noble horse, which was rather sluggish from its size and needed a horsefly[6] to rouse it; and I think that I am the horsefly that the God has set upon the city; for I never cease stinging you as it were at every point, and rousing, and exhorting, and reproaching each of you all day long. You will hardly find anyone else, my friends to fill my place; and if you take my advice, you will spare my life. You are angry, as sleepy persons are at being awakened, and of course, if you listen to Anytus, you could easily kill me with a single blow, and then sleep on undisturbed for the rest of your lives, unless the God cared for you and sent another man to arouse you....

... But throughout my life, both in private, and in any public matter in which I have been engaged, you will always find me the same; never bending to any man at all to do wrong, not even to those whom my slanderers assert to be my pupils. But I was never a teacher of any man. If any one, old or young, desired to hear me speak while I was about my mission, I never denied him. Nor do I speak for payment and refuse to speak if I am not paid; I offer myself to rich and poor alike to ask questions; and if any man will answer me, and then listen to my reply, he may. And I cannot justly be charged with causing any of these men to turn out a good or a bad citizen; for I never either taught or professed to teach any of them any knowledge. And if any man asserts that he ever learned or heard anything from me in private, which every one else did not hear as well, be sure he does not speak the truth.

Why is it then that people delight so much in my company? You have heard why, Athenians. I told you that whole truth when I said that they delight in hearing me examine persons who think that they are wise, when they are not. It is amusing enough to listen to that....

---

[6] Or gadfly.

... Perhaps someone will say, "Cannot you retire from Athens, Socrates, and remain silent?" It is the most difficult thing in the world to explain to you why I cannot do that. If I say that I cannot hold my peace, because that would be to disobey the God, you will likely think that I am not in earnest, and will not believe me. And if I tell you that no better thing can happen to a man than to speak every day about virtue, and the other matters on which you have heard me conversing, and examining myself and others, and that an unexamined life is not worth living, then you will believe me still less. But that is the truth, my friends, though it is not easy to convince you of it..."

[After some deliberation, Plato is condemned to death by a majority of the council.]

"Yet I have a request to make to them (i.e., the minority of judges that supported Socrates). When my sons grow up, visit them with punishment, my friends, and vex them just as I vexed you, if they seem to you to care for riches, or for any other thing, before virtue; and if they think that they are something when they are nothing at all, reproach them, as I reproached you, for not caring for what they should; and for thinking that they are something when they are not. And if you will do this, I myself and my sons will have received justice at your hands.

But now the time is come for us to go away, for me to die, and for you to live. Whether life or death is better is known only to the God.

Description:_____

_____

_____

Inference:_____

_____

_____

Questions:

1. What sends Socrates on his mission of questioning the wise men of Athens?

2. What parallel does Socrates draw between himself and Achilles?

3. Socrates asks that his life should be spared based on a service he provides to Athens. What is that service?

4. How do you read Socrates's tone? Does he come across as earnest or sarcastic? Find examples to support your view.

5. Athens is celebrated for its culture of philosophical inquiry. How do you square that tradition with Socrates's conviction and execution?

DOCUMENT 4-4

Pericles

Funeral Oration

431 B.C.E.

"For heroes have the whole earth as their tomb" -Pericles

The oration given below is attributed to the Greek statesman, Pericles (c. 495—429 BCE), at the conclusion of the first year of the Peloponnesian War (431—404 BCE). The speech was part of a traditional public funeral for Athenian warriors killed in battle. In the selections below, Pericles honors the memory of the fallen young men by celebrating the peculiar character of Athenian citizens and distinguishes them from their rivals, the Spartans.

Themes: political participation, citizenship, patriotism

"Our constitution does not copy the laws of neighboring states; we are a pattern to others rather than imitators. Our administration favors the many instead of the few; this is why it is called a democracy. If we look to the laws, they extend equal justice to all in their private differences; if to social standings, advancement in public life is based on reputation for ability. Class considerations are not considered over merit; nor does poverty block the way (to advancement), if a man is able to serve the state, he is not hindered by low status. Class considerations

---

"Funeral Oration of Pericles," in *The History of the Peloponnesian War*, trans. Richard Crawley (New York: E. P. Dutton & Co. INC, 1914), 121-128. Modernized by Andrew Fogleman.

The freedom, which we enjoy in our government, extends also to our ordinary life. There, far from a jealous surveillance over each other, we do not feel called upon to be concerned with our neighbor for doing what he likes, or even to indulge in those annoying looks, which though offensive, inflict no actual harm. But all this liberty in our private relations does not make us lawless as citizens. Our chief safeguard is the fear [of lawlessness], which teaches us to obey the magistrates and the laws, especially those that protect the injured, whether they are actually [mentioned] in the statue book, or belong to that code which although unwritten, still cannot be broken without acknowledged disgrace....

Turning to our military policy, there we are also different from our antagonists.[1] We throw open our city to the world, and never exclude foreigners by alien acts from any opportunity of learning or observing us, although the eyes of an enemy may occasionally benefit by this liberty; we trust less in system and policy than to the native spirit of our citizens. While in education, where our rivals seek after manliness by a painful discipline from their very cradles, at Athens we live exactly as we please, and yet are just as ready to encounter every legitimate danger. ...And yet with habits of ease, not labor, and courage of nature, not art, we are still willing to encounter danger. We have the double advantage of escaping the training for hardships in anticipation of facing them [and facing those hardships as] fearlessly as those who are never free from [training for] them.

Nor are these the only points in which our city is worthy of admiration. We cultivate refinement without extravagance and knowledge without effeminacy; wealth we employ more for use than for show, and place the real disgrace of poverty not in admitting to it but in declining to struggle against it. Our public men have besides politics, their private affairs to attend to, and our ordinary citizens though occupied with the pursuits of labor, are still fair judges of public matters, for, unlike any

---

[1] **Antagonists**: Pericles refers to the Lacedaemonians (or Spartans).

other nation, we regard him who take no part in these duties not as unambitious but as useless, we Athenians are able to judge all events well even if we cannot create them, and instead of looking on discussion as a barrier in the way of action, we think it an indispensable first step to any wise action at all. Again, in our endeavors we present the unique image of daring and deliberation too, each carried to its highest point, and both united in the same persons; although usually action is the fruit of ignorance, and hesitation, that of reflection. But the label of courage will surely be given most justly to those, who best know the difference between hardship and pleasure and yet are never tempted to shrink from danger.…

In short, I say that as a city we are the school of Hellas.[2] …For Athens alone is found greater than her reputation when tested, and no enemy beaten by her is indignant for being bested by such a city, and none of her subjects question her right to rule. Rather the admiration of ages now and to come will be ours, since we have left many witnesses of our power, and have proved it by many examples; and far from needing the likes of Homer to sing our praises, or other of his craft; [since] verses charm only for the moment and the impression which they leave melts away at the touch of fact. [However] we have forced every sea and land to be the highway of our daring, and everywhere, whether for evil or for good, have left imperishable monuments behind us. Such is the Athens for which these men, in their resolve not to lose her, nobly fought and died; and may every one of their surviving family members be ready to suffer in her cause, too.

…For in truth dedication to one's country's battles is a cloak that covers a man's other imperfections; since such good actions blot out the bad, and his merit as a citizen more than outweighs his faults as an individual. But none of these men allowed wealth, with its prospect of futures enjoyments, to unnerve his spirit, or poverty with its hope of a

---

[2] **The school of Hellas**: The citizens of Athens consider themselves as an example or the teacher of other Greek city-states.

day of freedom and riches to tempt him to shrink from danger. No, believing that vengeance upon their enemies was more to be desired than any personal blessing, and reckoning this to be the most glorious of hazards, they joyfully determined to accept the risk, exact their vengeance and to let their [other] wishes wait. And while committed to the hope the uncertainty of final success, in the business before them they acted boldly and trusted in themselves. Thus choosing to die resisting, rather than to live submitting, they retreated only from dishonor, but met anger face to face.

...For heroes have the whole earth as their tomb; and in lands far from their own, where the column with its epitaph declares it, there is enshrined in every breast an unwritten record with no tablet to preserve it, except that of the heart.

Yet you who are still of an age to beget children must bear up in the hope of having others in the place [of these men]. Not only will they help you to forget those whom you have lost, but they will also reinforce and a secure the state....

On the other hand, if I must say anything on the subject of female excellence to those of you who will now be widows, it is comprised in this brief exhortation: great will be your glory if you do not fall short of your natural character; and greatest is she who is the least talked of among the men, whether for good or for bad.

My task is now finished. I have performed it to the best of my ability, and in word, at least, the requirements of the law are now satisfied. If deeds be in question, those who are buried here have received part of their honors already, and for the rest, their children will be brought up until manhood at the public's expense; the state thus offers a valuable prize, as the garland of victory in this race of valor, for the reward both of those who have fallen and their survivors. And where the rewards for merit are greatest, there are found the best citizens. And now that you have brought to a close your lamentations for your relatives, you may depart."

Description:_____

_____

_____

Inference:_____

_____

_____

Questions:

1. According to Pericles, how are the Athenians different than the Spartans?

2. Consider the following claim: "[F]or, unlike any other nation, we regard him who take no part in these duties (i.e., politics) not as unambitious but as useless." What type of community would such expectations create?

3. What place does Pericles see for women in heroic Athens?

DOCUMENT 4-5

Xenophon

The Spartans

CA. 380 B.C.E.

Xenophon (430—354 BCE) was a philosopher, historian, and mercenary soldier. Although born an Athenian citizen, he fought in the armies of the Persian Cyrus the Younger with other Greek mercenary soldiers, including many Spartans. He was exiled from Athens for his association with Spartan military leaders (and perhaps Socrates) and retired from his military career in the Spartan-controlled territory of Scillus. In the following excerpts of his Polity of the Lacedaemonians (Spartans), Xenophon recounts their laws, institutions, and social practices.

Themes: gender, sex, procreation, family

I recall the astonishment with which I first noted the unique position of Sparta among the states of the Hellas,[1] its relatively sparse population and at the same time that extraordinary power and prestige of its community. I was puzzled to account for that fact. It was only when I came to consider the peculiar institutions of the Spartans that my wonderment ceased. Or rather, it was transferred to the legislator who gave them those laws, obedience to which has been the secret of their prosperity. I admire this legislator, Lycurgus,[2] and hold him to

---

Xenophon, "The Polity of the Lacedaemonians," in *The Works of Xenophon*, trans. H. G. Dakyns (London: Macmillan and Co., 1890), 2:295-297. Modernized by Andrew Fogleman.

[1] **Hellas**: Greece.
[2] **Lycurgus**: the legendary lawgiver credited with revolutionizing Spartan society.

have been one of the wisest of mankind. Certainly he was no servile imitator of other states. It was by a stroke of invention rather, and on a pattern much in opposition to the commonly-accepted one, that he brought his fatherland to this pinnacle of prosperity.

Take for example—and it is well to begin at the beginning—the whole topic of the producing and raising of children. Throughout the rest of the world the young girl, who will one day become a mother (and I speak of those who may be thought to be well brought up), is nurtured on the plainest food attainable, with the scantiest addition of meat or other condiments; while as for wine they train them either to total avoidance or to take it highly diluted with water. And in imitation, as it were, of the handicraft type, since the majority of artificers are sedentary, we the rest of the Hellenes, are content that our girls should sit quietly and work [spinning] wools. That is all we demand of them. But why should we think that women nurtured in this manner should produce a splendid offspring?

Lycurgus pursued a different path. Clothes were things he held, the production of which should well enough be left to female slaves. And, believing that the highest function of a free woman was the bearing of children, in the first place he insisted on the [physical] training of the body as necessary no less for the female than the male; and in pursuit of the same idea instituted competitive contests in running and feats of strength for women as for men. He believed that where both parents were strong, their children would be stronger still.

And likewise after marriage, in view of the fact that excessive sex is elsewhere permitted during the earlier period of matrimony, he adopted a principle directly opposite. He laid it down as an ordinance that a man should be ashamed to be seen visiting the room of his wife [for intercourse], whether going in or coming out. When they did meet under such restraint, the mutual longing of these lovers could not but be increased, and the child which might spring from such intercourse would tend to be stronger than those whose affections are weakened by satisfaction. By a farther step in the same direction he refused to allow marriages to be contracted at any period of life according to the desire of the parties concerned. Marriage, as he ordained it, must only take place in the prime of bodily strength, this too being, as he believed, a condition important to the production of healthy children. Or again, in the case which might occur of an old man wedded to a young wife. Considering the jealous watch which such husbands usually keep over their wives, he introduced a directly opposite custom; that is to say, he made it incumbent on the aged husband to introduce someone whose qualities, physical and moral, he admired, to have sex with his wife and to beget him children. Or again, in the case of a man who might not desire to live with a wife permanently, but yet might still be anxious to have children of his own worthy his name, the lawgiver [Lycurgus] laid down a law in his behalf. Such a person might select some woman, the wife of another man, well born herself and blest with fair offspring, and the sanction and consent of her husband first obtained, have children for himself by her.... [Thus] at Sparta a wife will not object to bear the burden of a double relationship,[3] or an husband to adopt sons as foster-brothers of his own children with a full share in his family and position, but possessing no claim to his wealth and property.

So opposed to those of the rest of the world are the principles which Lycurgus devised in reference to the production of children. But if they enabled him to provide Sparta with a race of men superior to all in size and strength I leave to the judgment of whomsoever it may concern.

Description:_____

_____

_____

_____

[3] **Double relationship**: A woman who bears children for two different men.

Inference:_____

_____

_____

Questions:

1. What was the goal of Lycurgus's reforms? How did his reforms affect the individual rights of Spartans?

2. Describe the nature of marriage and sex in Sparta.

3. Compare women's standing in Sparta to other sources you have read to this point?

4. According to Xenophon, what was the outcome of Lycurgus's Laws? Did Xenophon consider Lycurgus's reforms a success?

DOCUMENT 4-6

Aristotle

On the Generation of Animals

4TH CENTURY B.C.E.

Aristotle (384-332 BCE) was a Greek philosopher who studied at the Academy under Plato. He was an extraordinarily prolific writer, composing influential texts on physics, biology, zoology, metaphysics, logic, ethics, aesthetics, poetry, music, rhetoric, linguistics, and politics. Taken together, his writings established a comprehensive understanding of the world that exerted a tremendous influence on Western philosophy and science. On the Generation of Animals, excerpted below, is one of many texts that Aristotle devoted to animals and the natural world. He also wrote On the Movement of Animals, On the Parts of Animals, and a History of Animals. In this text, He takes up the question of the human generation. Aristotle argues that male secretions (semen) contribute to the nature of a child directly, whereas female secretions (menstrual fluid) play a supportive, nutritive role. Vital heat also plays an essential role in fetal development. Males are hotter, and as a result, are more developed than females. These texts are important because they offered naturalistic evidence for perceived gender differences from ancient times well into the early modern period.

Themes: heat, gender differences, reproduction

Aristotle, "De Generatione Animalium," trans. Arthur Platt, in *The Works of Aristotle*, eds., J. A. Smith and W. D. Ross (Oxford: Clarendon Press, 1912), 5:716a, 2.1-23; 727a, 1-30; 727b, 34-728a, 8; 728a, 17-31; 765a, 35-765b, 21; 766a, 19-29. Modernized by Andrew Fogleman.

Male and female

Of the generation of animals we must speak to the various questions as they arise according to each case, and we must connect our account with what has already been said. For, as we said above, the male and female principles are the first and foremost origins of generation. Males contain the efficient cause of generation, females possess the material. The most conclusive proof of this is drawn from considering how the semen is formed and where it comes from; for there is no doubt that semen forms those creatures produced in the ordinary course of nature; but we must observe carefully the way in which this semen itself is formed from the male and female. For it is just because the semen is secreted from the two sexes, the secretion taking place *in* them and *from* them, that they are first principles of generation. By a "male" animal we mean one that generates in another, and by "female" that which generates in itself. This is why, when speaking about the macrocosm, one calls the Earth "mother" and describe it as female, but when addressing Heaven and the sun and other like entities call them "fathers," and describe them as causing generation.

Male and female animals differ in their essence[1] in that the power or faculty had by the one differs from that had by the other, they differ anatomically as well; essentially the male is that which is able to generate in another, as said above; the female is that which is able to generate in itself and out of which comes into being the offspring, which previously existed in the parent.

Male and female secretions

It is plain, then, that menstrual fluid[2] is a secretion, and that it is analogous in females to semen in males. Its behavior shows that this view is correct. For semen begins to appear and to be emitted in men

---

[1] **Essence**: or logos (i.e., reason or principle of order).
[2] **Menstrual fluid**: catamenia.

at the same age that menstrual fluid begin to flow in women, when they change their voice and their breasts begin to develop. So, too, as people age the generative power fails in the men and menstrual fluid in the women.

The following signs also indicate that this discharge in females is a secretion. Generally speaking, women neither suffer from hemorrhoids nor bleeding from the nose nor anything else of the sort except when menstrual fluids are ceasing, and if anything of the kind occurs the [menstrual] flow is interfered with because the discharge is diverted to that location.

Further, the veins of women stand out less than those of men, and women are rounder and smoother because the secretions that goes to these vessels in men are drained away with the menstrual fluid in women. We must suppose, too, that the same cause accounts for the fact that the bulk of the body is smaller in females than in males among the vivpara,[3] since this is the only class in which the menstrual fluid is discharged from the body. And in this class the fact is clearest in women, for the discharge is greater in women than in the other animals. Wherefore her skin color and the absence of prominent blood vessels are most apparent, and so the deficient development of her body is obvious compared with a man's....

Now a boy is like a woman in form, and the woman is, as it were, an infertile male; a woman is in fact a woman on account of a certain incapacity, namely that she is incapable of concocting semen out of the final state of nourishment. And this is either blood or that which is analogous to it in animals, which are bloodless owning to the coldness of their nature. As then diarrhea is caused by the insufficient concoction of blood in the bowels, so are all discharges of blood caused in the blood vessels, including that of menstrual fluid....

---

[3] **Vivipara**: animals whose offspring are born live, as mammals.

Thus it is reasonable to suppose that generation comes from this process. For menstrual fluid is semen, though not in a pure state, but it still needs to be acted upon… Thus when menstrual fluid is mixed with semen it causes generation, and when the latter is mixed with pure nourishment the one effects generation, and the other effects nutrition.…[4]

The role of heat

It is not unreasonable then to suppose that heat and cold are the causes of maleness and femaleness, or that sex differences come from the right side and left, since the right side of the body is hotter than the left, and concocted semen is hotter than unconcocted semen. Concocted semen is set and compacted, and the more concocted it is, the more fertile. Yet to put in this way is to seek for the cause from too remote a starting point; we must draw near the immediate causes in so far as that is possible.

We have, then, previously spoken elsewhere of both the body as a whole and its parts, explaining what each part is and for what reason it exists. We have firstly noted that the male and female are distinguished by a certain capacity and incapacity. For the male is that which can concoct blood into semen and which can form, secrete, and discharge semen that imparts the "principle" or "form"—by "principle" I do not mean a material principle out of which comes into being an offspring resembling the parent, but I mean the first moving cause, whether it have power to act as such in the thing itself or in something else. But the female is that which receives semen, but cannot form it, secrete it, or discharge it. And secondly we explained that all concoction works by means of heat. Therefore the males of animals must be hotter than females. For it is by reason her coldness and [resulting] incapacity that the female is more abundant in blood in certain parts of her anatomy,

---

[4] I followed A. L. Peck's rendering of this line, see Aristotle, *Generation of Animals*, tr., A. L. Peck (Cambridge, Harvard University Press, 1949), 105.

and this abundance is an evidence of the exact opposite of what some suppose, namely that the female is hotter than the male because of the discharge of the menstrual fluid....

But if the "principle" fails to gain mastery and cannot [fully] concoct nourishment through a deficiency of heat and thus cannot bring it into its proper form, then of necessity the material must change over into its opposite condition (i.e., the fetus becomes female). Now the female is opposite of the male, and if one is female then and the other male. And since it differs in the ability it possesses, its organ also is different, so that the embryo changes also. And as one vital part changes, the whole system of the animal differs greatly in form along with it. This may be seen in the case of eunuchs, who though mutilated in one part alone, change so much from their original appearance and become like the female form. The reason of this is that some bodily parts are "principle" parts, and once a principle is changed or affected the parts of the body that cohere to it necessarily change with it.

Description:_____

_____

_____

Inference:_____

_____

_____

Questions:

1. Consider the following assertion: "Now a boy is like a woman in form, and the woman is, as it were, an infertile male; a woman is in fact a woman on account of a certain incapacity, namely that she is incapable of concocting semen out of the final state of nourishment." How exactly does Aristotle define a woman?

2. What is Aristotle saying in the following sentence: "But if the "principle" fails to gain mastery and cannot [fully] concoct nourishment through a deficiency of heat and thus cannot bring it into its proper form, then of necessity the material must change over into its opposite condition (i.e., the fetus becomes female)." How might a view like this affect the perception of women in the premodern world?

3. What role does heat play in Aristotle's physiology?

4. How would you explain Aristotle's method of reaching conclusions in this text? Is it theoretical? Is it observational? Is it something in between the two?

Chapter 5: Rome and the Christians

DOCUMENT 5-1

Livy

The History of Rome

27-9 B.C.E.

"Sextus Tarquinius is he that last night returned hostility for hospitality, and armed with force brought ruin on me, and also on himself—if you are men."

-Lucretia

Titus Livius (ca. 59 BCE - 17 CE), popularly known as Livy, was a Roman historian who wrote an extensive account of ancient Rome. His History of Rome begins with origin myths of the city and continues to his day, with the reign of Emperor Augustus (63 BCE - 14 CE). The selection below covers the legendary expulsion of the last King of Rome, Lucius Tarquinius Superbus, and the birth of the Roman Republic in 509 BCE. Written some 480 years after these purported

Livy: Books I and II, trans. B. O. Foster (Cambridge: Harvard University Press, 1919), 197- 209. Modernized by Andrew Fogleman.

events, Livy's account relates 1st-century attitudes toward kingship and Roman family honor.

Themes: kingship, tyranny, family honor

[The town] Ardea[1] belonged to the Rutuli,[2] who were a nation of commanding wealth for that place and period. This very fact was the cause of the war, since the Roman king was eager not only to enrich himself, impoverished as he was by the splendor of his public works, but also to appease with plunder the feeling of the common people. They hated the monarch for his acts of pride and were especially resentful that he had kept them employed so long as artisans and doing the work of slaves. So, an attempt was made to capture Ardea by assault. Having failed in this, the Romans filled the place with entrenchments, and began to harass the enemy. Here in their permanent camp, as is usual with a long drawn out war, leave was rather freely granted, more freely however to the leaders than to the soldiers. The young princes for their part passed their free hours together at dinners and drinking bouts. It chanced, as they were drinking in the quarters of Sextus Tarquinius,[3] where [his cousin] Tarquinius Collatinus, son of Egerius, was also a guest, that the subject of wives came up. Every man fell to praising his own wife with enthusiasm, and, as their rivalry grew hot, Collatinus said that there was no need to talk about it, for it was in their power to know, in a few hours' time, how far the rest [of the wives] were excelled by his own Lucretia. "Come! If we are not old men, let us mount our horses and see for ourselves the nature of our wives. The best test will be how we find our wives when we arrive unexpected." They were heated with wine. "Agreed!" they all cried, and clapping spurs to their horses were off for Rome. Arriving there at early dusk, they thence proceeded to

---

[1] **Ardea**: A town on the Mediterranean coast, 22 miles south of Rome.
[2] **Rutuli**: a legendary Italic tribe.
[3] **Sextus Tarquinius**: the youngest son of the king of Rome, Lucius Tarquinius Superbus.

Collatia,[4] where Lucretia was discovered very differently employed from the daughters-in-law of the king. These [women] were at a luxurious banquet, wasting away the time with their young friends; but Lucretia, though it was late at night, was busily engaged upon her wool, while her maidens toiled about her in the lamplight as she sat in the hall of her house. Lucretia won this contest of womanly virtue. As Collatinus and the Tarquinii approached, they were graciously received, and the victorious husband courteously invited the young princes to his table. It was there that Sextus Tarquinius was seized with a wicked desire to ruin Lucretia by force. Her beauty and her proved chastity provoked him. However, for the present they ended the boyish prank of the night and returned to the camp.

When a few days had gone by, Sextus Tarquinius, without letting Collatinus know, took a single attendant and went to Collatia. He was kindly welcomed, for no one suspected his purpose, and after dinner he was brought to a guest-chamber. Burning with passion, he waited till all was secure and everybody fast asleep. Then, drawing his sword, he came to the sleeping Lucretia. Holding the woman down with his left hand on her breast, he said, "Be still, Lucretia! I am Sextus Tarquinius. My sword is in my hand. Utter a sound, and you die!" In fright the woman was startled out of her sleep. No help was in sight, but only imminent death. Then Tarquinius began to declare his love, to plead, to mingle threats with prayers, to bring every resource to bear upon her woman's heart. When he found her unyielding and not to be moved even by fear of death, he went further and threatened her with disgrace, saying that when she was dead he would kill his slave and lay him naked by her side, that she might be said to have been put to death in adultery with a man of base condition. At this dreadful prospect her resolute modesty was overcome, as if with force, by his victorious lust. Then Tarquinius departed, exulting in his conquest of a woman's honor. Lucretia, grieving at her great disaster, dispatched a message to

---

[4] **Collatia**: A small town in Central Italy, 9 miles east of Rome, from which Tarquinius Collatinus derives his surname.

her father in Rome and to her husband at Ardea: that they should each take a trusty friend and come; that they must do this and do it quickly, for a frightful thing had happened. Spurius Lucretius (Lucretia's father) came with Publius Valerius, Volesus' son. Collatinus brought Lucius Junius Brutus, with whom he chanced to be returning to Rome when he was met by the messenger from his wife.

Lucretia they found sitting sadly in her chamber. The entrance of her friends brought tears to her eyes. Her husband asked, "Is all well?" She replied, "Far from it; for how can it be well with a woman who has lost her honor? The mark of a another man, Collatinus, is in your bed. Yet although my body only has been violated, my heart is faultless; and death shall be my witness. But pledge your right hands and your words that the adulterer shall not go unpunished. Sextus Tarquinius is he that last night returned hostility for hospitality, and armed with force brought ruin on me, and also on himself—if you are men —when he took his pleasure with me." They gave their pledges, every man in turn. They sought to comfort her, sick at heart as she is, by diverting the blame from her who was forced by the doer of the wrong. They told her that it is the mind that sins, not the body; and that where there is no desire, there is no guilt. "It is for you to determine," she answers, "what is due to him; for my own part, though I acquit myself of the sin, I do not absolve myself from punishment; never will an unchaste woman use the example of Lucretia." Taking a knife, which she had concealed beneath her dress, she plunged it into her chest, and sinking forward upon the wound, fell dead. The wail for the dead was raised by her husband and her father.

Brutus, while the others were absorbed in grief, drew out the knife from Lucretia's wound, and holding it up, dripping with blood, exclaimed, "By this blood, most chaste until a prince wronged it, I swear, and I take you gods to witness, that I will pursue Lucius Tarquinius Superbus and his wicked wife and all his children, with sword, with fire, indeed with whatever violence I can; and that I will suffer neither them nor any other to be king in Rome!" The knife he then passed to Collatinus, and from him to Lucretius and Valerius. They were astonished at this declaration. Where did this new spirit in the breast of Brutus come from? As he bade them [good bye], so they also swore oaths. Grief was swallowed up in anger; and when Brutus summoned them to make war from that very moment on the power of the kings, they followed his lead. They carried Lucretia's corpse from the house and bore it to the market place, where men crowded about them, attracted, as they were bound to be, by the amazing character of the strange event and its heinousness. Each man had his own complaint to make of the prince's crime and his violence. They were moved, not only by the father's sorrow, but by the fact that it was Brutus who rebuked their tears and idle lamentations and urged them to take up the sword, as befitted men and Romans, against those who had dared to treat them as enemies.

The boldest of the young men seized their weapons and offered themselves for service, and the others followed their example. Then, leaving Lucretia's father to guard Collatia, and posting sentinels so that no one might announce the uprising to the royal family, the rest, equipped for battle and with Brutus in command, set out for Rome. Once there, wherever their armed band advanced it brought terror and confusion; But when people saw that in the rear were the chief men of the state, they concluded that whatever it was it could be no meaningless disturbance. And in fact there was no less resentment at Rome when this dreadful story was known than there had been at Collatia. So from every quarter of the city men came running to the Forum. No sooner were they there than a crier summoned the people before the Tribune of the Celeres,[5] which office Brutus then happened to be holding. There he made a speech by no means like what might have been expected of the mind and the spirit which he had feigned up to that day. He spoke of the violence and lust of Sextus Tarquinius, of

---

[5] **Tribune of the Celeres**: Commander of the king's bodyguard, who also exercised the right to pass laws and preside over assemblies.

the shameful defilement of Lucretia and her deplorable death, of the bereavement of Tricipitinus, in whose eyes the death of his daughter was not so outrageous and deplorable as was the cause of her death. He reminded them, besides, of the pride of the king himself and the wretched state of the commons, who were plunged into ditches and sewers and made to clear them out. The men of Rome, he said, the conquerors of all the nations round about, had been transformed from warriors into artisans and stone-cutters. He spoke of the shameful murder of King Tullius, and how his daughter had driven her accursed chariot over her father's body, and he invoked the gods who punish crimes against parents. With these and, I imagine, even fiercer reproaches, such as occur to a man in the very presence of an outrage, but are far from easy for an historian to reproduce, he inflamed the people, and brought them to abrogate the king's authority and to exile Lucius Tarquinius, together with his wife and children....

Description:_____

_____

_____

Inference:_____

_____

_____

Questions

1. Lucretia was often celebrated as an ideal Roman woman. What does her story tell us about Roman family honor?

2. Why do you think Brutus's responded to Sextus Tarquinius's actions by swearing to kill the king of Rome, Lucius Tarquinius Superbus?

3. Apart from the outrage committed against Lucretia, what other issue angered the Romans about the Tarquinian king?

DOCUMENT 5-2

The New Testament

The Sermon on the Mount is Jesus of Nazareth's longest continual discourse in the Gospels. It contains his most famous teachings, such as the Beatitudes and the Lord's Prayer. In the excerpts below, Jesus warns his listeners that persecutions will come, emphasizes the importance of remaining faithful, and charges his listeners to love others and reject violent retaliation. In the Epistle to the Galatians, a Christian community in the Roman province of Galatia, Saint Paul links Jesus' ministry to God's promise to the patriarch Abraham and the Jewish Law. Paul explains that the rigors of the Law were meant to drive people to Jesus, an intercessor, for salvation. In so doing, faith in him replaces the specific requirements of the Law, ushering in a spiritual era open to all: Jew, Gentile, male, female, slave, or free.

Themes: faithfulness, moral action, Law, salvation,

Gospel of Matthew 5

ca. 30—ca. 70 C.E.

When Jesus saw the crowds, he went up the mountain; and after he sat down, his disciples came to him. ² Then he began to speak, and taught them, saying:

³ "Blessed are the poor in spirit, for theirs is the kingdom of heaven.

---

[4] "Blessed are those who mourn, for they will be comforted.

[5] "Blessed are the meek, for they will inherit the earth.

[6] "Blessed are those who hunger and thirst for righteousness, for they will be filled.

[7] "Blessed are the merciful, for they will receive mercy.

[8] "Blessed are the pure in heart, for they will see God.

[9] "Blessed are the peacemakers, for they will be called children of God.

[10] "Blessed are those who are persecuted for righteousness' sake, for theirs is the kingdom of heaven.

[11] "Blessed are you when people revile you and persecute you and utter all kinds of evil against you falsely on my account. [12] Rejoice and be glad, for your reward is great in heaven, for in the same way they persecuted the prophets who were before you.

Salt and Light

[13] "You are the salt of the earth; but if salt has lost its taste, how can its saltiness be restored? It is no longer good for anything, but is thrown out and trampled under foot.

[14] "You are the light of the world. A city built on a hill cannot be hid.

[15] No one after lighting a lamp puts it under the bushel basket, but on the lamp stand, and it gives light to all in the house. [16] In the same way, let your light shine before others, so that they may see your good works and give glory to your Father in heaven.

The Law and the Prophets

[17] "Do not think that I have come to abolish the law or the prophets; I have come not to abolish but to fulfill....

Concerning Anger

[21] "You have heard that it was said to those of ancient times, 'You shall not murder'; and 'whoever murders shall be liable to judgment.' [22] But I say to you that if you are angry with a brother or sister, you will be liable to judgment; and if you insult a brother or sister, you will be liable to the council; and if you say, 'You fool,' you will be liable to the hell of fire. [23] So when you are offering your gift at the altar, if you remember that your brother or sister has something against you, [24] leave your gift there before the altar and go; first be reconciled to your brother or sister, and then come and offer your gift. [25] Come to terms quickly with your accuser while you are on the way to court with him, or your accuser may hand you over to the judge, and the judge to the guard, and you will be thrown into prison. [26] Truly I tell you, you will never get out until you have paid the last penny.

Concerning Adultery

[27] "You have heard that it was said, 'You shall not commit adultery.' [28] But I say to you that everyone who looks at a woman with lust has already committed adultery with her in his heart. [29] If your right eye causes you to sin, tear it out and throw it away; it is better for you to lose one of your members than for your whole body to be thrown into hell. [30] And if your right hand causes you to sin, cut it off and throw it away; it is better for you to lose one of your members than for your whole body to go into hell.

Concerning Oaths

[33] "Again, you have heard that it was said to those of ancient times, 'You shall not swear falsely, but carry out the vows you have made to

the Lord.' [34] But I say to you, Do not swear at all, either by heaven, for it is the throne of God, [35] or by the earth, for it is his footstool, or by Jerusalem, for it is the city of the great King. [36] And do not swear by your head, for you cannot make one hair white or black. [37] Let your word be 'Yes, Yes' or 'No, No'; anything more than this comes from the evil one.

Concerning Retaliation

[38] "You have heard that it was said, 'An eye for an eye and a tooth for a tooth.' [39] But I say to you, Do not resist an evildoer. But if anyone strikes you on the right cheek, turn the other also; [40] and if anyone wants to sue you and take your coat, give your cloak as well; [41] and if anyone forces you to go one mile, go also the second mile. [42] Give to everyone who begs from you, and do not refuse anyone who wants to borrow from you.

Love for Enemies

[43] "You have heard that it was said, 'You shall love your neighbor and hate your enemy.' [44] But I say to you, Love your enemies and pray for those who persecute you, [45] so that you may be children of your Father in heaven; for he makes his sun rise on the evil and on the good, and sends rain on the righteous and on the unrighteous. [46] For if you love those who love you, what reward do you have? Do not even the tax collectors do the same? [47] And if you greet only your brothers and sisters, what more are you doing than others? Do not even the Gentiles do the same? [48] Be perfect, therefore, as your heavenly Father is perfect.

Gospel of Matthew 7

Judging Others

[1] "Do not judge, so that you may not be judged. [2] For with the judgment you make you will be judged, and the measure you give will

be the measure you get. [3] Why do you see the speck in your neighbor's eye, but do not notice the log in your own eye? [4] Or how can you say to your neighbor, 'Let me take the speck out of your eye,' while the log is in your own eye? [5] You hypocrite, first take the log out of your own eye, and then you will see clearly to take the speck out of your neighbor's eye.

The Golden Rule

[12] "In everything do to others as you would have them do to you; for this is the law and the prophets.

The Narrow Gate

[13] "Enter through the narrow gate; for the gate is wide and the road is easy that leads to destruction, and there are many who take it. [14] For the gate is narrow and the road is hard that leads to life, and there are few who find it.

A Tree and Its Fruit

[15] "Beware of false prophets, who come to you in sheep's clothing but inwardly are ravenous wolves. [16] You will know them by their fruits. Are grapes gathered from thorns, or figs from thistles? [17] In the same way, every good tree bears good fruit, but the bad tree bears bad fruit. [18] A good tree cannot bear bad fruit, nor can a bad tree bear good fruit. [19] Every tree that does not bear good fruit is cut down and thrown into the fire. [20] Thus you will know them by their fruits.

Concerning Self-Deception

[21] "Not everyone who says to me, 'Lord, Lord,' will enter the kingdom of heaven, but only the one who does the will of my Father in heaven. [22] On that day many will say to me, 'Lord, Lord, did we not prophesy in your name, and cast out demons in your name, and do many deeds of

power in your name?' ^{23} Then I will declare to them, 'I never knew you; go away from me, you evildoers.'

Hearers and Doers

^{24} "Everyone then who hears these words of mine and acts on them will be like a wise man who built his house on rock. ^{25} The rain fell, the floods came, and the winds blew and beat on that house, but it did not fall, because it had been founded on rock. ^{26} And everyone who hears these words of mine and does not act on them will be like a foolish man who built his house on sand. ^{27} The rain fell, and the floods came, and the winds blew and beat against that house, and it fell—and great was its fall!"

^{28} Now when Jesus had finished saying these things, the crowds were astounded at his teaching, ^{29} for he taught them as one having authority, and not as their scribes.

Description:_____

_____

_____

Inference:_____

_____

_____

Epistle to the Galatians 3:15-29

ca. 40—ca. 60 C.E.

The Promise to Abraham

[15] Brothers and sisters, I give an example from daily life: once a person's will has been ratified, no one adds to it or annuls it. [16] Now the promises were made to Abraham and to his offspring; it does not say, "And to offsprings," as of many; but it says, "And to your offspring," that is, to one person, who is Christ. [17] My point is this: the law, which came four hundred thirty years later, does not annul a covenant previously ratified by God, so as to nullify the promise. [18] For if the inheritance comes from the law, it no longer comes from the promise; but God granted it to Abraham through the promise.

The Purpose of the Law

[19] Why then the law? It was added because of transgressions, until the offspring would come to whom the promise had been made; and it was ordained through angels by a mediator. [20] Now a mediator involves more than one party; but God is one.

[21] Is the law then opposed to the promises of God? Certainly not! For if a law had been given that could make alive, then righteousness would indeed come through the law. [22] But the scripture has imprisoned all things under the power of sin, so that what was promised through faith in Jesus Christ might be given to those who believe.

[23] Now before faith came, we were imprisoned and guarded under the law until faith would be revealed. [24] Therefore the law was our disciplinarian until Christ came, so that we might be justified by faith. [25] But now that faith has come, we are no longer subject to a disciplinarian, [26] for in Christ Jesus you are all children of God through faith. [27] As many of you as were baptized into Christ have clothed

yourselves with Christ. [28] There is no longer Jew or Greek, there is no longer slave or free, there is no longer male and female; for all of you are one in Christ Jesus. [29] And if you belong to Christ, then you are Abraham's offspring, heirs according to the promise.

Description:_____

_____

_____

Inference:_____

_____

_____

Questions

1. In a number of instances, Jesus says, "You have heard it said...", "But I say..." According to the text, is there any pattern to how Jesus' teachings differ from what earlier people have said?

2. Matthew 5 culminates in the following imperative: "Be perfect, therefore, as your heavenly Father is perfect." How do you understand this statement given the other sayings in the passage?

3. According to Saint Paul, is faith in Jesus in conflict with Jewish Law?

4. Does Saint Paul suggest that salvation has an equalizing effect on society?

5. According to these texts, does Christianity seem hard or easy?

Document 5-3

Pliny the Younger

Letters to and from Emperor Trajan

112 C.E.

Pliny the Younger (61—113 C.E.) held numerous positions over the course of his long career as a Roman magistrate. He worked as a prosecutor, defender, and judge in the Roman court system, served in the Senate, held various advisory roles for emperors, and served as consul in 100 C.E. He concluded his career as Imperial Governor of Bithynia-Pontus, a Roman province on the southern end of the Black Sea. There he encountered a growing number of Christians even though practicing their religion was illegal. Despite his long career in law and politics, Pliny wrote then Emperor Trajan for advice on dealing with the Christians. Pliny's letter and Trajan's response is one of the earliest non-Christian depictions of Roman attitudes toward Christians.

Themes: Roman attitudes toward Christians, worship of Roman gods, political loyalty

[Pliny to Emperor Trajan]

As is my custom, I refer all doubtful matters to you, for who else is better able to resolve my doubts and instruct my ignorance? I have never attended the trials of Christians, and consequently do not know how inquiries are made, for what reasons, or the extent of punishment

The *Letters of the Younger Pliny*, trans. John Lewis (London: Kegan Paul, Trench Trübner, & Co., Ltd., 1890), 378-380. Modernized by Andrew Fogleman.

usually inflicted in their cases. Nor do I know whether any distinction should be made between them according to age, if young persons should be treated differently than adults; whether pardon should be given to anyone retracting his beliefs, or if a professed Christian gains nothing by renouncing it; and whether simply professing Christianity is punishable, even without other crimes, or if it is rather the crimes attached to the name that matter.

Meanwhile, in the cases of those brought before me on the charge of being Christians, my course has been as follows: I ask them if they are Christians, and if they admit it, I repeat the question a second and a third time, threatening them with death. For those who persist, I order them to be led away for execution. For, indeed, whatever might be the nature of their profession, I am convinced that their stubbornness and unshakable obstinacy should be punished. There have been others afflicted with this madness that are Roman citizens. I included their names on a list of those sent to Rome for trial. As soon as I begun to deal with this matter, as often happens, the charges became more widespread. An anonymous letter was circulated containing the names of many accused persons. I thought it proper to dismiss any who denied that they were now or ever had been Christians, after they offered a formula of prayer to the gods and wine and incense before your statue (which I had brought into the court for this purpose along with the images of the gods), and moreover had them revile the name, Christ—none of which it is said that any true Christian can be compelled to do.

Others named by the report admitted that they were Christians, and then shortly afterwards denied it, adding that they had been Christians, but had ceased to be so, some as many as twenty years before. All these honored your image, the images of the gods, and reviled Christ. They claimed that the sum of their crime (or their delusion) was meeting together on a stated day, before sunrise, to chant verses to Christ, as if to a god. They also bound themselves by an oath, not for any criminal purpose, but to abstain from thefts, robberies, adulteries, breaking their word, and not to deny any deposits when called to restore it. Following these ceremonies they depart, and then meet together again to take food of an ordinary, innocent kind. But they gave up these meetings after my edict, issued on your instructions, which banned all political societies. This made me think it all the more necessary to seek out the truth by torture of two slaves, whom they called "deaconesses." But I discovered nothing more than a degenerate and extravagant superstition.

As a result, I have called off these inquiries until I receive your counsel on the matter. Indeed, it seemed to me worthy of your consideration, on account of the number of persons endangered. For many people of all ages, ranks, and genders are being brought to trial, and this is likely to continue. And it is not only the cities that are affected by the contagion of this superstition, but villages and county parts as well; yet it seems possible to stop and cure it. For indeed the temples, which were almost entirely deserted, have recently begun to be frequented, and the customary religious rites that had long been interrupted are now being resumed, and the food of sacrificial beasts is now on sale, though up till recently scarcely anyone could be found to buy it. Thus it is easy to see that a great number of people may be won back, if granted the opportunity to repent.

[Emperor Trajan to Pliny]

You have followed the right course of action, my dear Pliny, in investigating the cases of those charged as Christians. For, indeed it is not possible to establish any general, fixed rule in these matters. These people should not be hunted out; if they are brought before you and the charge is proven they should be punished. Yet, if any deny being a Christian, and prove it by their actions, namely, by worshiping our gods, they should be given a pardon, regardless of how suspected their past conduct may be. But anonymous information must not be given consideration in any accusation. This would form the worst type of precedents and is quite out of keeping with the spirit of our time.

Description:_____

_____

_____

Inference:_____

_____

_____

Questions:

1. What role does the worship of Roman gods and prayers before the statue of Trajan play in the prosecution of Christians?

2. How would you describe Pliny and Trajan's tone in these letters? How invested are they in stamping out Christianity?

3. What do we learn about the early Christian Church from these letters? What do we learn about Roman civil concerns?

Document 5-4

Tertullian

Apology

197 C.E.

"If the Tiber rises as high as the city walls, if the Nile does not send its waters up over the fields, if the heavens give no rain, if there is an earthquake, if there is famine or pestilence, straightway the cry is, 'Away with the Christians to the lion!'" -Tertullian

Quintus Septimius Florens Tertullianus (ca. 155—ca. 240 C.E.), popularly known to as Tertullian, was a Christian writer from the Roman province of North Africa. He wrote over forty-five books in Latin and Greek on a broad range of Christian topics: apologetics, ethics, church discipline, and theology, to name a few. The text below is an apology (apologia), or formal defense of a position. In it, Tertullian defends Christianity against rumors about their secret meetings, pleads for equal treatment under the law, and claims that Christians are in fact good and useful Roman citizens.

Themes: justice, commerce, Roman identity

Rulers of the Roman Empire, if, seated for the administration of justice on your high tribunal, under the gaze of every eye, and holding all but the highest position in the state, you do not openly inquire into and consider the real truth regarding the charges made against the

---

Tertullian, "The Apology," trans. Rev. S. Thelwall, in *Ante-Nicene Fathers*, ed., Rev. Alexander Roberts (New York: Charles Scribner's Sons, 1918), 3: 17-18, 21, 23, 24, 26, 42-44, 49, 55. Modernized by Andrew Fogleman.

Christians; and if in this case alone you are afraid or ashamed to make an authoritative, careful, and just public inquiry...then you surely cannot forbid the truth to reach your ears by way of this little book....

If it is true [as you say] that we Christians are the most wicked of men, why do you treat us so differently from our fellow citizens, that is, from other criminals? Should not the same crime get the same treatment? When the charges made against us are made against others, they are permitted to speak and hire lawyers to show their innocence. They have full opportunity to respond and debate [the charges against them]; in fact, it is against the law to condemn an accused who is undefended and unheard. Christians alone are forbidden to say anything in defense of themselves, and of the truth, to help the judge to a righteous decision; all that is cared about is what public hatred demands—that they confess a name (i.e., Christian), not an examination of the charge. But at other judicial investigations, if a man confesses to the crime of murder, or sacrilege, or incest, or treason— just to mention a few of the accusation leveled against us—you do not sentence the person immediately. First you thoroughly examine the circumstances of the confession—what is the true character of the crime, how often, where, in what way, when he has done it, who knew about it, and who actually participated with the accused in it.

Nothing like this is done in our cases, though the many lies circulated about us should have the same process of investigation so that it might be discovered how many murdered children each of us has eaten; how many acts of incest each of us have done in the dark; and which cooks or dogs have been witnesses to our deeds. Imagine the popularity of the ruler who should find a Christian who had eaten a hundred infants! But, instead of that, we find that asking about Christians is forbidden. For we read in the letters of Pliny the Younger,[1] when he was ruler of a province, and had condemned some Christians to death, driven others from their faith, and was still annoyed by their large numbers, at last

---

[1] See Source 5-2.

asked the advice of Emperor Trajan about what to do with the rest of the accused Christians. Pliny explained to Trajan that, apart from an obstinate refusal to offer pagan sacrifices, he found nothing noteworthy in Christian religious services but their meetings at early morning for singing hymns to Christ and God, and committing themselves to a pledge to be faithful to their religion, forbidding murder, adultery, dishonesty, and other crimes. Upon this Trajan wrote back that Christians should not be sought out; but if they were brought before Pliny, they should be punished. What a decision! How self-contradictory! He forbids the discovery of their innocence, and commands them to be punished as guilty. It is at once merciful and cruel; this judgement passes over, and it punishes. Judges, why do you play this game of evasion? If you condemn, why do you not also investigate? If you refuse to investigate, why do you not free the accused? Throughout all the provinces, soldiers are assigned to tracking down robbers. Indeed, every private citizen should fight against traitors and public enemies as well as search out their associates and confederates. Christians alone are not supposed to be sought out, though they may be brought forth and accused before judges, as if that was the main reason of the trial. And so you condemn a man that no one wanted to find when he is presented to you, and who even now does not deserve punishment....

"I am a Christian," this man cries out. He declares what he is; but you want to hear him confess what he is not. You try your best to get lies from him, sitting in your seat of judgment, which is meant, ironically to discover the truth. "I am," he says, "what you suspect I am, that is a Christian. Why do you torture me and tempt me to sin by denying it? I confess, and yet you torture me further. What would you do if I denied?" You regularly doubt criminals when they deny. But when we deny, you believe us at once.... It is clear then, that you deal differently with us than with other criminals, obsessed as you are with taking our name from us. And indeed, you will take it, if we do anti-Christian things [such as lie about who we are]. So it seems obvious that our crime is only in our name... And so, with these comments out of the way about the injustice of the public hatred against us, I will now demonstrate our blamelessness....

...We are accused of observing a religious ritual where we kill a little child and then eat it. And after the feast, we engage in incest, in which dogs—as our pimps, put out the lights and provide darkness for our wicked desires. We are constantly accused of this and yet you take no measures to discover the truth. Either discredit the idea through investigation, or, if you believe it, then prove it....

[Next Tertullian ridicules the idea of this rumor by imagining the process of Christian initiation.]

[I suppose it] is common that those wanting initiation into this religious ritual, would first go to the master of the Christians, who would explain the necessary preparations. He would no doubt say, "You must have an innocent child, unaware of death or the meaning of a ritual knife; bread, too, to collect the gushing blood; in addition to these, candlesticks, and lamps, and dogs—with tasty snacks to cause them to turn out the lights.[2] And above all, bring your mother and your sister with you." But what if [one's] mother and sister do not want to come? Or what if someone does not have one or the other? What if there are Christians with no Christian relatives? Surely he will not be counted, I suppose, a true follower of Christ, who has not a brother or a son to share.

You also say, "You do not worship the gods, and you do not offer sacrifices for the emperors." Well, we do not offer sacrifice for others, for the same reason that we do not offer sacrifices for ourselves—namely, that we do not worship your gods, and as a result, we are

---

[2] **Cause them to turn out the lights**: According to these rumors, Christians tied strings from the tails of dogs to candles and then prompted the dogs to move with treats. This movement would apparently put out the light and provide darkness for their incestuous relations.

accused of sacrilege and treason. This is the chief charge against us—in fact, it is the only charge … Indeed, we do not worship your gods, because they do not exist. This, therefore, is what you should ask of us: to demonstrate the non-existence of your gods, and thereby prove that they do not deserve worship; for they would only deserve worship if indeed they exist.…

You also say that we … pretend to pray for emperor to escape persecution. Thank you for your mistake, for it gives us the opportunity of disproving such allegations. If you think we care nothing for the welfare of Cæsar, examine our sacred books, which are not hidden, and are easily available to you. There you will learn that we are ordered to to pray to God for our enemies, and to ask blessings on our persecutors… And Scripture says most clearly, "Pray for kings, and rulers, and powers, that all may be peace with you."[3] For when the empire is disturbed, the commotion is felt by everyone, and surely we too, though not the cause of the disorder, are nevertheless affected by the calamity.…

It is also said that we are a danger to the state for another reason, that we are useless to society. But how in all the world can that be the case, when we living among you, eat the same food, wear the same clothing, have the same habits, and face the same necessities of life? We are not ascetic Indian Brahmins, who live in woods and refuse to participate in ordinary social activities. We do not forget the debt of gratitude we owe to God, our Lord and Creator; we don't reject any of this creation, though certainly we exercise restraint upon ourselves, so that we do not make sinful use of any of His gifts. So we live in this world with you, we reject neither the forum, nor the butcher shop, nor bath, nor workshop, nor inn, nor weekly market, nor any other places of commerce. We sail with you, and fight with you, and farm the ground with you; and likewise sell goods with you—even in the various arts we make public property of our works for your benefit. I cannot

---

[3] *1 Timothy* 2:2.

understand then how we are useless to society, living with you and by you as we do? And if I do not attend your religious ceremonies, I am still a man on that sacred day. I do not bathe myself at dawn at the Saturnalia, yet I do bathe at a decent and healthy hour, preserving my heat and blood. ... I do not buy a crown [of flowers] for my head. If I still buy the flowers, why does it matter to you how I use them? ...We do not go to your spectacles; yet if we need the things sold there, we buy them other places. We certainly buy no frankincense [for sacrifices to the gods]. If the Arabian sellers complain of this, let them be assured that we buy more precious and costly products when burying Christians than when others burn incense to the gods. ... And your tax collectors should give thanks to Christians; for in the faithfulness that forbids us to defraud a brother, we make sure to pay all our dues....

But your cruelty toward us, however great, does not really help your cause, but is simply a kind of temptation to us. The more we are cut down by you, the faster we grow; for the blood of Christians is the seed [of the Church]. Many of your writers celebrate courage in the face of pain and death—as with Cicero in the *Tusculans,* Seneca in his *Chances,* Diogenes, Pyrrhus, and Callinicus—and yet their words do not find as many disciples as Christians do. Christians do not teach by words, but by their deeds. And that very obstinacy you complain about is itself a kind of teacher. For who after seeing it, is not moved to inquire about it? And who, after inquiring about it, does not embrace our doctrines? And when he has embraced them, who among them does not desire to suffer that he may become a partaker of God's full grace, obtaining complete forgiveness of all offenses by God in exchange for his blood? This is why we give thanks on the very spot of our sentencing. As the divine and human are ever opposed to each other, when we are condemned by you, we are acquitted by God.

Description:_____

_____

_____

Inference:_____

_____

_____

Questions:

1. According to Tertullian, how do Roman rulers treat Christians?

2. What are some of the rumors circulating about Christians?

3. In which ways does Tertullian claim that Christians contribute to Roman society?

4. What does Tertullian consider the real cause of tension between Christians and Roman rulers? Is it an insurmountable obstacle to him?

DOCUMENT 5-5

The Martyrdom of Saints Perpetua and Felicitas

203 C.E.

"Neither can I call myself anything else than what I am, a Christian."

-Perpetua

The following selection is the story of the execution (or martyrdom) a group of Christians at games given in honor of Septimius Geta, the son of the Roman Emperor Septimius Severus, at Carthage in 203. One year earlier, Septimius Severus had promulgated a decree forbidding any Roman from converting to Judaism or Christianity. Of the group condemned to death for their association with Christianity, this account focuses on Vibia Perpetua, a 20-year old woman from a distinguished Roman family, and a pregnant slave named Felicitas. Perpetua herself is believed to have written the majority of this text, up to the point of her martyrdom where an un-named editor completes the account. Perpetua's authorship is extraordinary, as the writings of only four Roman women are known from the entire period of 2nd c. B.C.E. to 2nd c. C.E.

Themes: gender, social hierarchy, individualism

A number of young catechumens,[1] Revocatus, [the slave] Felicitas, Saturninus and Secundulus were arrested. Among them also was Vivia Perpetua. She was respectably born, liberally educated, and a married

---

"The Martyrdom of Perpetua and Felicitas," trans. R. E. Wallis, in *Ante-Nicene Fathers*, ed. Alexander Roberts, James Donaldson, and A. Cleveland Coxe (Buffalo, NY: Christian Literature Publishing Co., 1885), 3: 700-702, 704-706. Modernized by Andrew Fogleman.

[1] **Catechumens**: a Christian convert still learning the doctrines of Christianity before baptism.

woman with a father and mother and two brothers. One of her brothers was a catechumen like herself. She was about twenty-two years of age and also had an infant son at the breast. From this point onward, Perpetua will narrate the story of her martyrdom, as she left it described by her own hand and according to her own mind:

"While we were still with our persecutors, my father, for the sake of his love for me, urged me to turn away from the faith. 'Father,' I said, 'do you see, this vessel lying here used as a little pitcher, or for anything else?' And he said, 'Yes.' And I said to him, 'Can it be called by any other name than what it is?' And he said, 'No.' 'Neither can I call myself anything else than what I am, a Christian.' Then my father, enraged by this name, lunged at me, as if he would tear my eyes out. But he left it at that and departed along with his diabolical arguments.

Then a few days after I had been without my father, I gave thanks to the Lord because his absence became a source of consolation to me. In that same interval of a few days we were baptized, and the Spirit made clear to me that nothing else was needed for bodily endurance than the water of baptism. After a few days, we were taken into the dungeon of the prison, and I was very afraid, because I had never experienced such darkness... And I was also distressed and anxious about my baby. But the blessed deacons, Tertius and Pomponius, cared for us and arranged by way of a bribe for our transfer to a better part of the prison for a few hours. As we left the dungeon, we all attended to our own needs. I breast-fed my child, who was now weak with hunger. In my anxiety for my son, I sent for my mother and brother and delivered him into their care...

Then my brother said to me, ' Dear sister, you are already in a position of great dignity, and as such may pray to God for a vision. Please ask whether this imprisonment will result in a martyrdom or an escape.' And I, who knew that I was indeed privileged to speak with the Lord, whose kindnesses I had found to be so great, boldly promised him, and said, 'Tomorrow I will tell you.' And I asked, and this was what was shown me. I saw a golden ladder of marvelous height, reaching up to heaven. The ladder was very narrow, so that those climbing could only ascend it one at a time. And on the sides of the ladder was fixed every kind of iron weapon. There were swords, lances, hooks, and daggers; so that if any one went up carelessly, or not looking upwards, these weapons would hook his flesh and he would be torn to pieces. And under the ladder itself was crouching a enormous dragon, who lay in wait for those who ascended. He tried to scare them as they climbed upward. And Saturus climbed up first, as he had freely handed himself over to the authorities on our account, and thus was not present at the time that we were taken prisoners. And he climbed to the top of the ladder, and turned towards me, and said to me, 'Perpetua, I am waiting for you. But be careful that the dragon does not bite you.' And I said, 'In the name of the Lord Jesus Christ, he shall not hurt me.' And from under the ladder, as if in fear of me, he slowly lifted up his head. And I stepped on his head as though it were the first step of the ladder. And I went up, and I saw an immense garden, and in the midst of the garden a tall, white-haired man clothed as a shepherd and milking a sheep. And standing around him were many thousand of people in white robes. He raised his head, looked upon me, and said, 'You are welcome, daughter.' And he called me, and gave me as it were a little cake, and I received it with folded hands; and I ate it, and all who stood around said, "Amen." And at the sound of their voices I woke up, still tasting a sweetness in my mouth, which I cannot describe. And I immediately shared this experience with my brother, and we understood our captivity would end in martyrdom, and as a result, we put no more hope in this world.

After a few days an announcement went out that we would be given a hearing, and my father came to me from the city, worn out with anxiety. He approached me, trying to convince me to give up my cause, saying, 'Have pity my daughter on my grey head. Have pity on your father, if I am worthy to be called your father. If I have brought you up to the flower of your age with these hands, if I have preferred you to all your brothers, do not give me over to be mocked by men. Think of your brothers, think of your mother and your aunt, think of your son, who will not be able to live after you are gone. Give up your pride! You will destroy us all! None of us will be able to speak freely if anything should happen to you.' My father said these things out of affection for me, kissing my hands, and throwing himself at my feet. With tears in his eyes, he no longer addressed me as his daughter but as a woman.[2] And I felt pity for my father in his old age, especially since he alone of all my family would not rejoice over my martyrdom. I comforted him, saying, 'Father, in the prisoner's dock, whatever God wills will happen. For understand we are not governed by ourselves, but by God's power.' And he departed from me in great sadness.

Another day, while we were at dinner, we were suddenly taken away to a hearing at a town-hall. At once a rumor spread throughout the neighborhood of the gathering, and an immense number of people came to see what would happen. We mounted a platform for the hearing. The others were interrogated, and confessed. Then they came to me, and my father immediately appeared with my child, dragged me from the step, and pleaded, 'Have pity on your baby.' And Hilarianus the governor, who had just received his authority over life and death in the place of the deceased proconsul Minucius Timinianus, said, 'have pity on your father's grey head, and spare your child. Offer the sacrifice for the well-being of the emperors.' And I replied, 'I will not.' Hilarianus said, 'Are you a Christian?' And I replied, 'Yes, I am.' And as my father stood there pleading with me to offer the sacrifice, Hilarianus ordered him thrown down and beaten with rods. And I was grieved for my father's misfortune as if I myself had been beaten, and I grieved his wretched old age. Then the governor delivered judgment on us all, condemning us to the wild beasts. And we went cheerfully back to the dungeon. Then, because my child was used to being fed by me,

---

[2] **As a woman**: the Latin here is *Domina* (the feminine gender of *dominus*), or a women endowed with authority.

and often stayed with me in the prison, I send Pomponius the deacon to my father to ask for my child. But my father would not give him up. But as God willed it, the child no longer had need of my breast, nor were my breasts inflamed....

The day before we were to fight in the arena, I saw a vision. In it, the deacon Pomponius came to our prison gate and knocked loudly. I went out to him, and opened the gate for him. He was clothed in a richly decorated white robe, and he had on manifold *calliculæ*.[3] He said to me, 'Perpetua, we are waiting for you; come to us!' He took my hand, and we walked a rough and winding road until we arrived breathless at an amphitheater. Pomponius led me into the middle of the arena, and said, 'Do not fear, I am here with you, and I am laboring with you;' and he departed. I gazed up and to my surprise saw an immense assembly of people in the stands. And I wondered why the wild beasts were not yet set on me, since I knew that was to be my fate. Then an Egyptian came out to fight me. He was horrible in appearance and surrounded by his backers. And handsome youths came to me as my helpers and encouragers. They stripped off my clothes, and suddenly I was a man. Then my helpers began to rub me with oil, as is the custom in gladiatorial contests. And I looked across the arena and saw the Egyptian rolling in the dust. And a certain man came forth, of wondrous height. He was taller even than the top of the amphitheater. He wore a loose tunic and a purple robe with two bands over the middle of his chest. He had on *calliculæ* of gold and silver of various forms. And he carried a rod, as if he were a trainer of gladiators, and a green branch upon which were apples of gold.

He called for silence, and said, 'If this Egyptian, should overcome this woman, he will kill her with the sword; and if this woman should conquer him, she will receive this branch.' Then he departed. And we drew near to one another, and began punch each other. Then he tried

---

[3] *Calliculæ*: the meaning of this word is unclear. It may refer to small bells worn priestly robes.

to grab hold of my feet, but I kicked him in the face with my heels. And I was lifted up in the air, and began to kick at him without touching the ground. Then there was a break in the fighting and I joined my hands and fingers together and hit him on the head. He fell face-forward to the ground, and I stepped on his head. Then the people began to shout, and my helpers celebrated. I approached the trainer and took the branch. He kissed me, and said to me, 'Daughter, peace be with you:' and I departed victoriously through to the Sanavivarian gate.[4] Then I awoke, and immediately understood that I would not simply fight against beasts in the arena, but rather against the Devil. And yet I knew that I would be victorious. This is what I have written, with several days yet to go before the gladiatorial contest. Someone else may write what happens there." ...

[With Perpetua's narration of her experiences completed, the editor recounts the story of the contest in the amphitheater.]

Now Felicitas was eight-months pregnant when she was arrested. As the day of the contest drew near, she was anxious that her pregnancy might delay her martyrdom, since it is unlawful to publically punish pregnant women. She did not want her holy and innocent blood shed later among common criminals. And her fellow martyrs were also saddened that they should have to leave so excellent a friend and companion behind to walk this path alone. Therefore, joining their voices together, they poured forth prayer to the Lord three days before the exhibition. And immediately after their prayer, birth pains came upon Felicitas. And as she was groaning in pain, one of the soldiers of the prison said to her, "You think you are suffering now? What will you do when you are thrown to the beasts, a fate you have brought upon yourself by refusing to sacrifice [to the emperors]?" And she replied, "At this moment I am suffering alone. But in the arena there will be another in me, who will suffer for me as I suffer for Him."

---

[4] **Sanavivarian Gate:** the gate through which gladiatorial victims spared through popular pity escaped from the amphitheater.

Then she brought forth a little girl, which a certain sister brought up as her daughter....

On the day of their victory, they came forth from the prison into the amphitheater with joyous and radiant countenances, trembling if at all with joy rather than fear. Perpetua followed with a calm look, as the bride of Christ, the beloved of God, putting down everyone's stare with her own intense gaze. Moreover, Felicitas, rejoiced that she had safely brought forth her child, so that she might fight with the wild beasts. In the process, she moved from the blood of birth to [the blood] of the gladiator, ready to wash with a second baptism after childbirth. And when they were brought to the arena gate, the men were ordered to wear costumes of the priests of Saturn, and the women, the priestesses of Ceres.[5] But noble Perpetua resisted this saying, "We have come this far of our own free will, so you should not attempt to force this on us now. For we have given up ourselves provided we do no such thing. You agreed with us to this." Injustice acknowledged the justice in her words, and the tribune agreed and brought them out simply as they were. Perpetua proceeded into the arena singing psalms, already treading under foot the head of the Egyptian; Revocatus, Saturninus, and Saturus uttered threats to the onlookers. When they came within sight of Hilarianus, they gestured to him and said, "You judge us, but God will judge you." At this the people, cried out that they should be tormented with whips as they passed through a line of soldiers.[6] And the Christians rejoiced that they should incur one of their Lord's methods of suffering.

But He who had said, "Ask, and you shall receive,"[7] gave to them what they asked, the death each one had wished for. For when they had spoken among themselves about their martyrdom, Saturninus had said

---

[5] **Ordered to put on costumes**: gladiatorial victims were often made to play specific losing roles in the arena from Roman history or literature.
[6] **A line of soldiers**: a row of men drawn up to whip them as they passed along, a punishment probably similar to what is called "running the gauntlet."
[7] *John* 26:24.

that he wished to be thrown to all the beasts, wishing that he might wear a more glorious crown. In the beginning of the contest he and Revocatus were matched with a leopard. And at the prisoner's dock they were harassed by a bear. Saturus dreaded nothing more than a bear and hoped that he might be killed by a single bite of a leopard. But when a gladiator tied him to a wild boar, it was the gladiator who was rather gored and died shortly after the show. Saturus was only dragged along the floor of the areana. And when he was tied and left on the floor near a bear, the bear would not come out of his cage. And so Saturus was called back unhurt for a second time.

For the young women however the Devil prepared a wild cow. This was an unusual animal for an exhibition, but was chosen according to their sex. And so, stripped and clothed with nets, they were led forth. The crowd however reacted with pity as they looked on at the delicate frame of the one woman and the other with breasts still dripping with milk from her recent childbirth. So, the women were called back and given robes.

Perpetua entered the arena first. She was struck and tossed by the cow to the ground. When she saw that her robe was torn and her body exposed, she drew the robe over her as a veil, thinking rather of modesty than her suffering. She was then called back again, and then thought to fix her her disheveled hair. For she did not think that it was right for a martyr to suffer with disheveled hair, as she might appear to be mourning in her moment of glory. So she got up, and when she saw Felicitas crushed to the ground, she came near and giving her a hand, lifted her up. And both of them stood there together. At that moment the brutality of the audience was appeased, so they were called to the Sanavivarian gate. There Perpetua was tended to by the catechumen, Rusticus, who often saw to her needs; and she, as if just woken up from sleeping, or in the Spirit and in an ecstasy, looked around her, and said to the amazement of all, "When will we be led out to that cow?" And when she was told what had already happened, she did not believe it until she saw her injuries and her torn robe. At that moment she recognized Rusticus and called another brother over and addressed them, saying, "Stand firm in the faith, and love one another, all of you, and do not be afraid at my sufferings." ...

And then the spectators called for the Christians to be killed by the sword. The Christians stood up of their own accord, and walked to the place where they were directed. But first they kissed one another desiring to conclude their martyrdom with the ritual kiss of peace. Then, immoveable and in silence, each of them were cut down by the sword. Now Saturus, who was the first to give up his spirit and climb the ladder, waited for Perpetua. Perpetua then was stabbed with a sword between the ribs and cried out loudly. She then took the shaking right hand of a young gladiator guided it to her throat. It was as though such a woman, feared as she was by unclean spirits, could not be killed unless she willed it.

O most brave and blessed martyrs! O those truly called and chosen to the glory of our Lord Jesus Christ! Those of you who magnify, honor, and adore [God], should surely read these examples—no less than ancient ones—to the Church for its edification. That way, these new manifestations of virtue may also testify that one and the same Holy Spirit has always operated even until now. [Praise be] to God, the Father, Omnipotent, and His Son Jesus Christ our Lord, whose is the glory and infinite power forever and ever. Amen.

Description:_____

_____

_____

Inference:_____

_____

_____

Questions:

1. How did Christianity empower women according to this text?

2. How did 'confessing Christ' in the face of persecution come into conflict with traditional social obligations for women? How did Perpetua deal with these conflicts?

3. What was the meaning of Perpetua's vision in which she fought an Egyptian in the amphitheater?

4. Who was really in control during the arena death scene? Find some specific instances to prove your point.

Chapter 6:
The Spread of
Christianity

DOCUMENT 6-1

Saint Benedict of Nursia

The Rule of Saint Benedict

CA. 530

"Idleness is the enemy of the soul." -St. Benedict

Sometime in his twenties, Saint Benedict of Nursia (ca. 480—547) renounced his Roman status and family expectations to live as a hermit in a cave about forty miles outside of Rome. Eventually, Benedict's reputation for holiness attracted attention and followers. He would go on to found 12 monasteries including the great Benedictine monastery of Monte Cassino, where he likely wrote the Rule excerpted below. The Rule, or guidelines for living in a monastery, sought to balance the administrative necessities of a monastic institution with the Christ-focused life of a Christian hermit. Manual labor, prayer, and reading defended against the sin if idleness, while oversight and obedience to superiors dampened the sins of pride and self-indulgence. Benedict initially meant for his rule to govern individual monasteries,

The Rule of St. Benedict, ed. D. Oswald Hunter Blair (London: Sands & Co., 1907), 3, 11, 13, 15, 17, 19, 27, 31, 99, 101, 129, 131, 133. Modernized by Andrew Fogleman.

but it became the guiding charter of the Benedictine order and is still in use fifteen centuries later.

Themes: obedience, oversight, sin, good works, literacy

Prologue

Hearken, O my son, to the precepts of your master, and incline the ear of your heart; willing receive and faithfully fulfill the advice of your loving Father, that you may return by the work of obedience to Him from whom you have departed through the sloth of disobedience.... We must establish a school for the Lord's service, the likes of which we hope is not too harsh or rigorous. But even if, to correct bad habits and to preserve charity, sound reason dictates anything that turns out somewhat difficult, do not at once become disheartened by fear, and flee from the way of salvation, which cannot be entered upon except by a narrow entrance. But as we go forward in our life and in faith, we should run in the way of God's commandments with hearts enlarged and with an unspeakable sweetness of love; so that never departing from His guidance, but preserving in His teaching in the monastery until death, we may by patience share in the suffering of Christ, that we may deserve to be partakers of His kingdom. Amen.

Of the kinds of monks

It is well known that there are four kinds of monks. The first are the Cenobites: that is those in monasteries, who live under the rule of an Abbot. The second are the Anchorites or Hermits: that is those who, not in the initial fervor of conversion, but after a long time spent in the monastery, have learned by the help and experience of other brothers to fight against the devil; and going forth well armed from the ranks of their brethren to the single-handed combat of solitude, are able, without the support of others, to fight by the strength of their own arm, God Helping them against the failings of the flesh and their evil thoughts.

The third and most disreputable kind of monks are the Sarabites, who have been tested by no rule nor refined as gold in the furnace by the guidance of a master. But rather they are as soft as lead [because] they still serve the world by their works and are known by their tonsure to lie to God.[1] These live without a shepherd in twos or or threes, or even singly, dwelling not in the Lord's sheepfold but in their own. Their law is the gratification of their desires, because what they like or choose, they call holy, but what they dislike they consider unlawful.

The fourth kind of monks are those called Gyratory.[2] These spend all their lives wandering about in various provinces, staying in different cells for three or four days at a time. They are ever roaming, with no stability; they indulge their passions and the cravings of their appetite, and in every way worse than the Sarabites. It is better to say nothing than to speak of their miserable lives. Therefore, passing these over, let us proceed with the help of God to lay down a rule for the best kind of monks, the Cenobites....

Of the character of the abbot

An Abbot who is worthy to rule over the monastery should always remember the origin of his name, and reflect that name by his deeds. For he is believed to hold the place of Christ in the monastery, since he is called by His name, as the Apostle says: "You have received the spirit of the adoption of children, in which we cry Abba, Father."[3] And therefore the Abbot should never (God forbid) teach, ordain, or command anything contrary to the law of the Lord; but let his direction

---

[1] **Tonsure**: the shaved part of the crown of the head for priests and monks. Benedict suggests the Sarabites lie to God because their tonsure suggests a holy life.
[2] **Gyratory**: that which moves about in a circular motion.
[3] *Romans* 8:15.

and his doctrine be infused into the minds of his disciples like the leaven of divine justice.[4]

The Abbot should always be mindful that he will have to give an account both of his own teaching and of the obedience of his disciples at the dreadful judgment of God.... Therefore, when anyone receives the name of Abbot, he ought to direct his disciples by a two-fold teaching: that is, he should reflect goodness and holiness by his deeds more so than his words. He should be able to declare to the intelligent among his disciples the commandments of the Lord by words. But to the simple-minded he should set forth divine precepts by the example of his deeds; lest, while preaching to others, he should himself become a castaway [through his actions], and God should say to him: "why did you declare my Justice, and speak my covenant but hated discipline and cast my words behind you."[5] And again, "you saw the speck of wood in your bother's eye, did you not see the beam of wood in your own [eye]?"[6]

Show no favoritism in the monastery. One [person] should not be loved more than another, unless he excels in good works or obedience. Those of noble birth should not come before former slaves, unless for a reasonable cause. But if upon just consideration such a preference [for one person or the other] seems good to the Abbot, let him arrange people as he pleases; but otherwise, let everyone keep to their own place; because, whether slave or free, we are all one in Christ, and hold an equal rank in the service of the Lord: "for with God there is no respecting of persons."[7] Only those who excel in good works and in humility find preference in His sight. Let the Abbot, then show equal

---

[4] **Leaven of divine justice**: The *Bible* often uses the analogy of leaven (or yeast) to talk about the growth or expansion of something. In this case, the Abbot's leadership causes divine justice spread within the monastery.

[5] *Psalms* 49:16,17.

[6] *Matthew* 7:3.

[7] Ephesians 6:9.

love to all, and apply the same treatment to all according to their merits.

Whether monks ought to have anything of their own

Above all, the vice of private ownership is to be cut off at the root within the monastery. Let none presume to give or receive anything without permission from the Abbot. Let none keep anything as their own, either book or writing-tablet or pen, or anything whatsoever, since monks neither have ownership of their body nor their will. But they receive all that is necessary from the father of the monastery: nor are they allowed to keep anything that the Abbot has not given, or at least permitted them to have. Let all things be [shared in] common with all, as it is written: "Neither did anyone say that the things he possessed were his own."[8] But if anyone should be found to indulge in this most shameful vice, and after one or two warnings does not change his behavior, let him be subject to correction.

Of the daily manual labor

Idleness is the enemy of the soul; and hence at certain seasons the brethren should busy themselves in the work of their hands, and at other [times] in holy reading. We think, therefore, that the times for each may be disposed as follows: from Easter to the first of October, let the brethren work at assigned tasks from from [the office of prayer] *Prime*[9] in the morning, until about the fourth hour.[10] From the fourth hour until near the sixth[11] let them read. And when they rise from [the lunch] table, after the sixth hour, let them rest on their beds in perfect silence; or if anyone would like to read, let him do so in such a way as not to disturb anyone else. Let [the prayer office of] *None*[12] be said in

---

[8] *Acts* 4:32.

[9] *Prime*: A standard hour of prayer at six o'clock in the morning.

[10] **The fourth hour**: Ten o'clock in the morning.

[11] **The sixth [hour]**: Twelve, noon.

[12] *None*: A standard hour of prayer at two o'clock in the afternoon.

good time, at about the middle of the eighth hour; and then let them again work on assigned tasks until *Vespers*.[13] And if on account of poverty or the specific needs of the monastery require it, let them gather the crops. If this is the case, do not be saddened; because then are they truly monks, when they live by the labor of their hands, as did our Fathers and Apostles. And let all [these rules] be kept with consideration, on account of the weaker brethren.

From the first of October to the beginning of Lent,[14] the brethren may read until the end of the second hour.[15] Then let [the prayer office of] *Tierce* be said, and let everyone work according to their assigned tasks until nine. When the first signal of the ninth hour is given, let every one stop their work, and nourish themselves until the second signal is sounded. After their lunch, let them occupy themselves in their reading, or [saying] the *Psalms*. During Lent, let them read from morning until the end of the third hour, and then work at their various tasks until the end of the tenth.

During Lent let each monk borrow a book from the library, and read it all through in order. These books are to be given out at the beginning of Lent. And appoint one or two senior [monks] to go round the monastery at the hours when the brethren are engaged in their reading, and see that there is no slothful brother giving himself to idleness or to foolish talk, and not applying himself to his reading. Such men are not only useless to themselves but are also a distraction to others. If such a monk is found (which God forbid) let him be corrected once and a second time; and if he does not change his behavior, let him be subjected to the chastisement of the Rule, so that the rest may be afraid. And let not one brother associate with another at unreasonable hours.

---

[13] *Vespers*: A standard hour of prayer at sunset.
[14] **Lent**: A liturgical period of six weeks, starting with Ash Wednesday, where Christians identify with the sufferings of Jesus in preparation for the celebration of the Easter.
[15] **Second hour**: eight o'clock in the morning.

On Sunday let all occupy themselves in reading, except those who have been appointed to specific tasks. But if anyone is so negligent and slothful, as to be either unwilling or unable to study or to read, let some task be given him so he is not idle. And give the brethren that are weak or delicate appropriate tasks. Strive to prevent them from being either idle [on the one hand] or so overwhelmed by excessive labor [on the other hand] that they run away. The Abbot must take their weaknesses into account....

Of the instruments of Good works

1. First of all to love the Lord God with all our heart, with all our soul, with all our mind.

2. Then you neighbor as yourself

3. Then not to kill.

4. Not to commit adultery.

5. Not to steal.

6. Not to covet.

7. Not to bear false witness.

8. To honor all men.

9. Not to do to another what we would not have done to ourselves.

10. To deny ourselves, in order to follow Christ.

11. To chastise the body.

12. Not to seek after delights.

13. To love fasting.

14. To relieve the poor.

15. To clothe the naked.

16. To visit the sick.

17. To bury the dead.

18. To help those that are in trouble.

19. To comfort the sad.

20. To withdraw ourselves from worldly ways.

21. To prefer nothing to the love of Christ.

22. Not to give way to anger.

23. Not to harbor revenge in our mind.

24. Not to foster trickery or deceit in our heart.

25. Not to make a false peace.

26. Not to forsake charity.

27. Not to swear at all, lest we forswear ourselves.

28. To speak the truth with heart and mouth.

29. Not to render evil for evil.

30. Not to do any injury; indeed, and patiently to bear any injury done to us.

31. To love our enemies.

32. Not to speak ill of such as speak ill of us, but rather to speak well of them.

33. To suffer persecution for justice's sake.

34. Not to be proud.

35. Not given to wine.

36. Not to over-eat.

37. Not sleepy.

38. Not lazy.

39. Not a murmurer.

40. Not a detractor.

41. To put our trust in God.

42. When we see any good in ourselves, let us attribute it to God and not to ourselves.

43. But let us always know that evil is done by us; therefore let us attribute it to ourselves.

44. To fear the Day of Judgment.

45. To be afraid of hell.

46. To desire life everlasting with spiritual thirst.

47. To have death always before our eyes.

48. To observe at every hour the actions of our life....

Description:_____

_____

_____

Inference:_____

_____

_____

Questions:

1. According to the introduction what is the problem with other kinds of monks? How is Benedict's Cenobite model a solution?

2. Benedict calls idleness the enemy of the soul. Why do you think he says this? What daily activities does he prescribe to resist idleness?

3.   Benedictine monasteries became important centers of learning at a time when civil institutions were failing in medieval Europe. What aspect of the *Rule* support education?

4.   How would you characterize monastic life based on this reading?

DOCUMENT 6-2

Saint Augustine

On Christian Doctrine

397

Saint Augustine (354—430 CE) is arguably the most influential author in Western Christianity. Named one of the four doctors of the Church, he wrote over a hundred separate treatises after converting to Christianity in his early thirties. Augustine wrote On Christian Doctrine *as a guide for understanding Sacred Scripture. In the first three books he explores various aids for interpreting the Bible, such as the use of literal and figurative interpretations, and in the last book he takes up the role of rhetoric in preaching. Along the way, he also addresses the important question of the usefulness of non-Christian literature for interpreting the Bible in particular and for the pursuit of truth in general.*

Themes: truth, logic, non-Christian learning

But let every good and true Christian understand that wherever truth may be found, it belongs to his Master [God]. And while he recognizes and acknowledges the truth, even in Pagan religious literature, let him reject the figments of superstition...

Saint Augustine, "On Christian Doctrine," trans. Rev. J. F. Shaw, in *Nicene and Post-Nicene Fathers*, ed. Philip Schaff (Michigan: WM. B. Eerdmans Publishing Company, 1886), 2: 545, 550-554. Modernized by Andrew Fogleman.

On the use of logic

There are branches of knowledge, which do not deal with bodily senses, but with the mind, and among them, the science of reasoning and mathematics are the most important. The science of reasoning, or logic, is very helpful for inquiring into and solving all sorts of questions that come up in Scripture. But in using logic, we should guard against the love of arguing for the sake of arguing, and the childish vanity produced by trapping an opponent. For there are countless *sophisms*, or inferences in reasoning, that are false, But these seem so true that they not only deceive dull people, but also intelligent men when they are not on their guard. For example, one man might suggest the following proposition: "What I am, you are not." The other man agrees, for the proposition is in part true. Then the first speaker adds: "I am a man;" and when the other has agreed to this also, the first man draws his conclusion: "Then you are not a man." Now Scripture rejects these sorts of deceitful arguments, where it states, "There is one that shows wisdom in words, and is hated."[1] Additionally, ways of speaking that are overly concerned with beautiful language, even when they do not attempt to trap their opponent, are also considered sophistical in nature.

There are also valid ways of reasoning that purposely lead to false conclusions.... These conclusions are sometimes drawn by a good and learned man, in an attempt to cause an opponent to give up his position because it requires him to hold opinions, which he actually condemns. For example, the apostle [Paul] did not draw true conclusions when he said, "Then is Christ not risen,"[2] and again, "Then is our preaching is in vain, and your faith is also vain."[3] For Christ has risen, and the preaching of those who declared this fact is not in vain, nor is their faith in vain who had believed it. But those

---

[1] *Ecclesiasticus* 37:20.

[2] *1 Corinthians* 15:13.

[3] *ibid.*, 15:14.

false conclusions do follow logically from the proposition "there is no resurrection of the dead." These inferences, then, being rejected by us as false, it follows that since they would be true if the dead do not rise, there will be a resurrection of the dead.[4] Thus valid conclusions may be drawn from true and false propositions. These laws of valid reasoning may easily be learnt in secular schools that have nothing to do with the Church. But the truth of propositions must be found in the sacred books of the Church.

Valid reasoning is not created, but only observed by man.

And yet valid reasoning is not created by men, but is observed and noted by them that they may be able to learn and teach it. For [logic] exists eternally in the reason of things, and has its origin with God. For as the man who describes the order of events does not himself create that order; and as he who describes the situations of places, or the natures of animals, or roots, or minerals, does not describe creations of man; and as he who points out the stars and their movements does not point out anything that he himself or any other man has caused to be;—in the same way, he who says, "When the consequent is false, the antecedent must also be false," says what is true; but he did not cause it to be true. He only points out that it is true. And the Apostle Paul's quotation operates according to this rule of logic. For the antecedent is, "There is no resurrection of the dead,"—the position taken up by those whose error the apostle wished to overthrow. Next, from this antecedent, the proposition, namely, that there is no resurrection of the dead, the necessary consequence is, "Then Christ is not risen." But this consequence is false, for Christ has risen; therefore the antecedent is also false. But the antecedent is, that there is no resurrection of the dead. We conclude, therefore, that there is a resurrection of the dead.

---

[4] The form of St. Paul's argument is as follows: "If there is no resurrection, then faith is in vain. Faith is not in vain, therefore there is a resurrection." St. Augustine recognizes in this the following rule of logic: "When the consequent is false, the antecedent must also be false." See St. Augustine's further discussion on Paul's argument below.

Now all this is briefly expressed thus: If there is no resurrection of the dead, then is Christ not risen; but Christ is risen, therefore there is a resurrection of the dead. This rule, then, that when the consequent is negated, the antecedent must also be negated, is not created by man, but only pointed out by him. And this rule refers to the validity of the reasoning, not to the truth of the statements.[5]

False Inferences May Be Drawn from Valid Reasoning

In this passage, however, where the argument is about the resurrection, both the law of the inference is valid, and the conclusion arrived at is true. But in the case of false conclusions, too, there is a validity of inference in some such way as the following. Let us suppose some man admits: If a snail is an animal, it has a voice. This being agreed upon, then, when it is proved that the snail has no voice, it follows (since when the consequent is proved false, the antecedent is also false) that the snail is not an animal. Now this conclusion is false, but it is a true and valid inference from the false statement. Thus, the truth of a statement stands on its own merits; the validity of an inference depends on the statement of the man with whom one is arguing. And thus, as I said above, a false inference may be drawn by a valid process of reasoning, in order that he whose error we wish to correct may be sorry that he has admitted the antecedent, when he sees that its logical consequences are absurd...

We must use whatever the heathens have said that is true

Moreover, if those who are called philosophers, and especially the Platonists, have said anything that is true and in harmony with our faith, we should not reject it, but claim it for our own use from those who have unlawful possession of it. For, the Egyptians had false idols and heavy burdens on the one hand, and vessels and ornaments of gold

---

[5] Augustine is acknowledging here that the form of an argument may be valid, that is the conclusions follow necessarily from the premises, even if the content of the statement is not true.

and silver, and garments on the other. By the command of God, the Israelites took the vessels, ornaments and garments as they left Egypt, designing them for a better use. The Egyptians then, in their ignorance, provided the Israelites with objects that they themselves were not making a good use of.[6] In the same way, every branch of heathen learning has false and superstitious fancies in it, and heavy burdens of unnecessary toil, which every one of us, when leaving fellowship of heathens, should despise and avoid. But they also contain liberal instruction, excellent precepts of morality, and some truths even with regard to the worship of the One God. All of these are better adapted to the use of the truth. Now these are, so to speak, their gold and silver, which they did not create themselves, but dug out of the mines of God's providence which are scattered throughout the world. But they perversely and unlawfully offered them to the worship of devils. Christians then should take these things for themselves as they depart from the unhappy fellowship of these men, and to devote these treasures to their proper use in preaching the gospel. Their garments also—that is to say human institutions, which are indispensable in this life,—we must also take and turn to a Christian use.

Description:_____

_____

_____

Inference:_____

_____

_____

Questions:

1. What is St. Augustine's position on truth? In his view, where does truth come from? How does this position support his

---

[6] *Exodus* 3:21,22 and 12:35,36.

claim that Christians should appropriate non-Christian learning?

2. Augustine distinguishes between arguments that are valid according to logic but false according to the truth (e.g., the snail analogy). Why should this matter to him?

3. Are Augustine's arguments surprising? Or is this just what you would expect from a 5th-century Christian thinker? What impact do you think these views would have on Christians as the Christian Church developed

Chapter 7:
The Expansion of Islam

DOCUMENT 7-1

The Qur'an

Surah 2, The Cow (Al-Baqarah)

609 -632

The Qur'an (lit. "the recitation") is a collection of religious directives, which Muslims believe Allah (God) revealed to Muhammad (ca. 570—632) over the course of his 23-year ministry. Muhammad shared these divine revelations with his followers, who reportedly memorized them or wrote them down.   Following Muhammad's death in 632, and the Caliph Uthman (576—656) established an official version of the Qur'an in 650. Muslims hold Muhammad as part of the same prophetic tradition that produced Abraham and Jesus. As such, they recognize Jewish and Christian scriptures as inspired, but understand the Qur'an as Allah's last and fullest message given to humanity. Although the excerpts of the Qur'an given below are in English, it is important to note that Muslims believe the Qur'an is only properly understood when read in the original Arabic.

The Holy Qur'an, trans. Maulvi Muhammad Ali (Punjab: Ahmadiyya Anjuman Ishaat-i-Islam Lahore, 1920), 11-59, 72-90-95-99.190,135. Please note that I have omitted the parallel Arabic text and footnotes from the original publication for the sake of space.

Themes: mercy, violence, Jews, Christians, Muslims

In the name of God, the Beneficent, the Merciful.

¹ I, God, am the best knower.

² This Book, there is no doubt in it, is a guide to those who keep their duty,

³ Who believe in the Unseen and keep up prayer and spend out of what We have given them,

⁴ And who believe in that which has been revealed to thee and that which was revealed before thee, and of the Hereafter they are sure.

⁵ These are on a right course from their Lord and these it is that are successful.

⁶ Those who disbelieve—it being alike to them whether thou warn them or warn them not—they will not believe.

⁷ God has sealed their hearts and their hearing; and there is a covering on their eyes, and for them is a grievous chastisement.

⁸ And there are some people who say: We believe in God and the Last Day and they are not believers.

⁹ They seek to deceive God and those who believe, and they deceive only themselves and they perceive not.

¹⁰ In their hearts is a disease, so God increased their disease, and for them is a painful chastisement because they lie.

¹¹ And when it is said to them, Make not mischief in the land, they say: We are but peacemakers.

¹² Now surely they are the mischief-makers, but they perceive not.

¹³ And when it is said to them, Believe as the people believe, they say: Shall we believe as the fools believe? Now surely they are the fools, but they know not.

¹⁴ And when they meet those who believe, they say, We believe; and when they are alone with their devils, they say: Surely we are with you, we were only mocking.

¹⁵ God will pay them back their mockery, and He leaves them alone in their inordinacy, blindly wandering on.

¹⁶ These are they who buy error for guidance, so their bargain brings no gain, nor are they guided.

¹⁷ Their parable is as the parable of one who kindles a fire but when it illumines all around him, God takes away their light, and leaves them in darkness—they cannot see.

¹⁸ Deaf dumb, (and) blind, so they return not:

¹⁹ Or like abundant rain from the clouds in which is darkness, and thunder and lightning; they put their fingers into their ears because of the thunder-peal, for fear of death. And God encompasses the disbelievers.

²⁰ The lightning almost takes away their sight. Whenever it shines on them they walk in it, and when it becomes dark to them they stand still. And if God had pleased, He would have taken away their hearing and their sight. Surely God is Possessor of power over all things.

²¹ O men, serve your Lord Who created you and those before you, so that you may guard against evil,

²² Who made the earth a resting-place for you and the heaven a structure, and sends down rain from the clouds then brings forth with

it fruits for your sustenance; so do not set up rivals to God while you know.

[23] And if you are in doubt as to that which We have revealed to Our servant, then produce a chapter like it and call on your helpers besides God if you are truthful.[1]

[24] But if you do (it) not—and you can never do (it) —then be on your guard against the fire whose fuel is men and stones; it is prepared for the disbelievers.

[25] And give good news to those who believe and do good deeds, that for them are Gardens in which rivers flow. Whenever they are given a portion of the fruit thereof, they will say: This is what was given to us before and they are given the like of it. And for them therein are pure companions and therein they will abide.

[26] Surely God disdains not to set forth any parable—a gnat or anything above that. Then as for those who believe, they know that it is the truth from their Lord; and as for those who disbelieve, they say: What is it that God means by this parable? Many He leaves in error by it and many He leads aright by it. And He leaves in error by it only the transgressors.

[27] Who break the covenant of God after its confirmation and cut asunder what God has ordered to be joined, and make mischief in the land. These it is that are the losers.

[28] How can you deny God and you were without life and He gave you life? Again, He will cause you to die and again bring you to life, then you shall be brought back to Him.

---

[1] **Produce a chapter like it**: the artistry of the text itself is presented here as supernatural proof of its truth.

[29] He it is Who created for you all that is in the earth. And He directed Himself to the heaven, so He made them complete seven heavens; and He is Knower of all things.

[30] And when thy Lord said to the angels, I am going to place a ruler in the earth, they said: Wilt Thou place in it such as make mischief in it and shed blood? And we celebrate Thy praise and extol Thy holiness. He said: Surely I know what you know not.

[31] And He taught Adam all the names, then presented them to the angels; He said: Tell Me the names of those if you are right.

[32] They said: Glory be to Thee We have no knowledge but that which Thou hast taught us. Surely Thou art the Knowing, the Wise.

[33] He said: O Adam, inform them of their names. So when he informed them of their names, He said: Did I not say to you that I know what is unseen in the heavens and the earth? And I know what you manifest and what you hide.

[34] And when We said to the angels, Be submissive to Adam, they submitted, but Iblis (did not).[2] He refused and was proud, and he was one of the disbelievers.

[35] And We said: O Adam, dwell thou and thy wife in the garden, and eat from it a plenteous (food) wherever you wish, and approach not this tree, lest you be of the unjust.

[36] But the devil made them slip from it, and caused them to depart from the state in which they were. And We said: Go forth, some of you are the enemies of others. And there is for you in the earth an abode and a provision for a time.

---

[2] **Iblis**: the Devil.

37 Then Adam received (revealed) words from his Lord, and He turned to him (mercifully). Surely He is Oft-returning (to mercy), the Merciful.

38 We said: Go forth from this state all. Surely there will come to you guidance from Me, then whoever follows My guidance, no fear shall come upon them, nor shall they grieve.

39 And (as to) those who disbelieve in and reject Our messages, they are the companions of the Fire in it they will abide.

40 O Children of Israel, call to mind My favor which I bestowed on you and be faithful to (your) covenant with Me, I shall fulfill (My) covenant with you; and Me, Me alone, should you fear.

41 And believe in that which I have revealed, verifying that which is with you, and be not the first to deny it; neither take a mean price for My messages; and keep your duty to Me, Me alone.

42 And mix not up truth with falsehood, nor hide the truth while you know.

43 And keep up prayer and pay the poor-rate and bow down with those who bow down.

44 Do you enjoin men to be good and neglect your own souls while you read the Book? Have you then no sense?

45 And seek assistance through patience and prayer, and this is hard except for the humble ones,

46 Who know that they will meet their Lord and that to Him they will return.

47 O Children of Israel, call to mind My favor which I bestowed on you and that I made you excel the nations.

⁴⁸ And guard yourselves against a day when no soul will avail another in the least, neither will intercession be accepted on its behalf, nor will compensation be taken from it, nor will they be helped.

⁴⁹ And when We delivered you from Pharaoh's people, who subjected you to severe torment, killing your sons and sparing your women, and in this there was a great trial from your Lord.

⁵⁰ And when We parted the sea for you, so We saved you and drowned the people of Pharaoh while you saw.

⁵¹ And when We appointed a time of forty nights with Moses, then you took the calf (for a god) after him, and you were unjust.

⁵² Then We pardoned you after that so that you might give thanks.

⁵³ And when We gave Moses the Book and the Discrimination that you might walk aright.

⁵⁴ And when Moses said to his people: O my people, you have surely wronged yourselves by taking the calf (for a god), so turn to your Creator (penitently), and kill your passions. That is best for you with your Creator. So He turned to you (mercifully). Surely He is the Oft-returning (to mercy), the Merciful.

⁵⁵ And when you said: O Moses, we will not believe in thee till we see God manifestly, so the punishment overtook you while you looked on.

⁵⁶ Then We raised you up after your stupor that you might give thanks.

⁵⁷ And We made the clouds to give shade over you and We sent to you manna and quails. Eat of the good things that We have given you. And they did not do Us any harm, but they wronged their own souls.

⁵⁸ And when We said: Enter this city, then eat from it a plenteous (food) whence you wish, and enter the gate submissively, and make

petition for forgiveness. We will forgive you your wrongs and increase the reward of those who do good (to others).

[59] But those who were unjust changed the word which had been spoken to them, for another saying, so We sent upon the wrongdoers a pestilence from heaven, because they transgressed.

[60] And when Moses prayed for water for his people, We said: March on to the rock with thy staff. So there flowed from it twelve springs. Each tribe knew their drinking-place. Eat and drink of the provisions of God, and act not corruptly, making mischief in the land.

[61] And when you said: O Moses, we cannot endure one food, so pray thy Lord on our behalf to bring forth for us out of what the earth grows, of its herbs and its cucumbers and its garlic and its lentils and its onions. He said: Would you exchange that which is better for that which is worse? Enter a city, so you will have what you ask for. And abasement and humiliation were stamped upon them, and they incurred God's wrath. That was so because they disbelieved in the messages of God and would kill the prophets unjustly. That was so because they disobeyed and exceeded the limits.

[62] Surely those who believe, and those who are Jews, and the Christians, and the Sabians, whoever believes in God and the Last Day and does good, they have their reward with their Lord, and there is no fear for them, nor shall they grieve.

[63] And when We made a covenant with you and raised the mountain above you: Hold fast that which We have given you, and bear in mind what is in it, so that you may guard against evil.

[64] Then after that you turned back; and had it not been for the grace of God and His mercy on you, you had certainly been among the losers.

⁶⁵ And indeed you know those among you who violated the Sabbath, so We said to them: Be (as) apes, despised and hated.

⁶⁶ So We made them an example to those who witnessed it and those who came after it and an admonition to those who guard against evil.

⁶⁷ And when Moses said to his people: Surely God commands you to sacrifice a cow. They said: Dost thou ridicule us? He said: I seek refuge with God from being one of the ignorant.

⁶⁸ They said: Call on thy Lord for our sake to make it plain to us what she is. (Moses) said: He says, Surely she is a cow neither advanced in age nor too young, of middle age between these (two); so do what you are commanded.

⁶⁹ They said: Call on thy Lord for our sake to make it clear to us what her colour is. (Moses) said: He says, She is a yellow cow; her colour is intensely yellow delighting the beholders.

⁷⁰ They said: Call on thy Lord for our sake to make it dear to us what she is, for surely to us the cows are all alike, and if God please we shall surely he guided aright.

⁷¹ (Moses) said: He says: She is a cow not made submissive to plough the land, nor does she water the tilth, sound, without a blemish in her. They said: Now thou hast brought the truth. So they slaughtered her, though they had not the mind to do (it).

⁷² And when you (almost) killed a man, then you disagreed about it. And God was to bring forth that which you were going to hide.

⁷³ So We said: Smite him with it partially. Thus God brings the dead to life, and He shows you His signs that you may understand.

⁷⁴ Then your hearts hardened after that, so that they were like rocks, rather worse in hardness. And surely there are some rocks from which

streams burst forth; and there are some of them which split asunder so water flows from them; and there are some of them which fall down for the fear of God. And God is not heedless of what you do.

[75] Do you then hope that they would believe in you, and a party from among them indeed used to hear the word of God, then altered it after they had understood it, and they know (this).

[76] And when they meet those who believe they say, We believe, and when they are apart one with another they say: Do you talk to them of what God has disclosed to you that they may contend with you by this before your Lord? Do you not understand?

[77] Do they not know that God knows what they keep secret and what they make known?

[78] And some of them are illiterate; they know not the Book but only (from) hearsay, and they do but conjecture.

[79] Woe! then to those who write the Book with their hands then say, This is from God; so that they may take for it a small price. So woe! to them for what their hands write and woe! to them for what they earn.

[80] And they say: Fire will not touch us but for a few days. Say Have you received a promise from God? Then God will not fail to perform His promise. Or do you speak against God. what you know not?

[81] Yea, whoever earns evil and his sins beset him on every side, those are the companions of the Fire therein they abide."

[82] And those who believe and do good deeds, these are the owners of the Garden; therein they abide.

[83] And when We made a covenant with the Children of Israel. You shall serve none but God. And do good to (your) parents, and to the near of kin and to orphans and the needy, and speak good (words) to

(all) men, and keep up prayer and pay the poor-rate. Then you turned back except a few of you, and you are averse.

[84] And when We made a covenant with you: You shall not shed your blood, nor turn your people out of your cities; then you promised and you bear witness.

[85] Yet you it is who would slay your people and turn a party from among you out of their homes, backing each other up against them unlawfully and exceeding the limits. And if they should come to you as captives you would ransom them, whereas their turning out itself was unlawful for you. Do you then believe in a part of the Book and disbelieve in the other? What then is the reward of such among you as do this but disgrace in the life of this world, and on the day of Resurrection they shall be sent back to the most grievous chastisement. And God is not heedless of what you do.

[86] These are they who buy the life of this world for the Hereafter, so their chastisement shall not be lightened, nor shall they be helped.

[87] And We indeed gave Moses the Book and We sent messengers after him one after another and We gave Jesus, son of Mary, clear arguments and strengthened him with the Holy Spirit. Is it then that whenever there came to you a messenger with what your souls desired not, you were arrogant? And some you gave the lie to and others you would slay.

[88] And they say: Our hearts are repositories. Nay, God has cursed them on account of their unbelief so little it is that they believe.

[89] And when there came to them a Book from God verifying that which they have, and aforetime they used to pray for victory against those who disbelieved—but when there came to them that which they recognized, they disbelieved in it; so God's curse is on the disbelievers.

⁹⁰ Evil is that for which they sell their souls—that they should deny that which God has revealed, out of envy that God should send down of His grace on whomsoever of His servants He pleases; so they incur wrath upon wrath. And there is an abasing chastisement for the disbelievers.

⁹¹ And when it is said to them, Believe in that which God has revealed, they say: We believe in that which was revealed to us. And they deny what is besides that, while it is the Truth verifying that which they have. Say: Why then did you kill God's prophets before (this) if you were believers?

⁹² And Moses indeed came to you with clear arguments, then you took the calf (for a god) in his absence and you were wrongdoers.

⁹³ And when We made a covenant with you and raised the mountain above you: Take hold of that which We have given you with firmness and obey. They said: We hear and disobey. And they were made to imbibe (the love of) the calf into their hearts on account of their disbelief. Say: Evil is that which your faith bids you if you are believers.

⁹⁴ Say: If the abode of the Here-after with God is specially for you to the exclusion of the people, then invoke death if you are truthful.

⁹⁵ And they will never invoke it on account of what their hands have sent on before, and God knows the wrongdoers.

⁹⁶ And thou wilt certainly find them the greediest of men for life (greedier) even than those who set gods (with God). One of them love to be granted a life of a thousand years, and his being granted a long life will in no way remove him further off from the chastisement. And God is Seer of what they do.

[97] Say: Whoever is an enemy to Gabriel for surely he revealed it to thy heart by God's command, verifying that which is before it and a guidance and glad tidings for the believers.

[98] Whoever is an enemy to God and His angels and His messengers and Gabriel and Michael, then surely God is an enemy to disbelievers.

[99] And We indeed have revealed to thee clear messages, and none disbelieve in them except the transgressors.

[100] Is it that whenever they make a covenant, a party of them cast it aside? Nay, most of them have no faith.

[101] And when there came to them a messenger from God verifying that which they have, a party of those who were given the Book threw the Book of God behind their backs as if they knew nothing.

[102] And they follow what the devils fabricated against the kingdom of Solomon. And Solomon disbelieved not, but the devils disbelieved, teaching men enchantment. And it was not revealed to the two angels in Babel, Harut and Marut. Nor did they teach (it to) anyone, so that they should have said, We are only a trial, so disbelieve not. But they learn from these two (sources) that by which they make a distinction between a man and his wife. And they cannot hurt with it anyone except with God's permission. And they learn that which harms them and profits them not. And certainly they know that he who buys it has no share of good in the Hereafter. And surely evil is the price for which they have sold their souls, did they but know!

[103] And if they had believed and kept their duty, reward from God would certainly have been better; did they but know!

[104] O you who believe, say not Ra'i-na and say Unzur-na, and listen. And for the disbelievers there is a painful chastisement.

[105] Neither those who disbelieve from among the people of the Book nor the polytheists, like that any good should be sent down to you from your Lord. And God chooses whom He pleases for His Mercy; and God is the Lord of mighty grace.

[106] Whatever message We abrogate or cause to be forgotten, We bring one better than it or one like it. Knowest thou not that God is Possessor of power over all things?

[107] Knowest thou not that God's is the kingdom of the heavens and the earth, and that besides God you have not any friend or helper?

[108] Rather you wish to put questions to your Messenger, as Moses was questioned before. And whoever adopts disbelief instead of faith he indeed has lost the right direction of the way.

[109] Many of the people of the Book wish that they could turn you back into disbelievers after you have believed, out of envy from themselves, after truth has become manifest to them. But pardon and forgive till God bring about His command. Surely God is Possessor of power over all things.

[110] And keep up prayer and pay the poor-rate. And whatever good you send before for yourselves, you will find it with God. Surely God is Seer of what you do.

[111] And they say: None shall enter the Garden except he who is a Jew, or the Christians. These are their vain desires. Say: Bring your proof if you are truthful.

[112] Nay, whoever submits himself entirely to God and he is the doer of good (to others); he has his reward from his Lord, and there is no fear for such nor shall they grieve.

[113] And the Jews say, The Christians follow nothing (good), and the Christians say, The Jews follow nothing (good), while they recite the

(same) Book. Even thus say those who have no knowledge, like what they say. So God will judge between them on the day of Resurrection in that wherein they differ.

¹¹⁴ And who is more unjust than he who prevents (men) from the mosques of God, from His name being remembered therein, and strives to ruin them? (As for) these, it was not proper for them to enter them except in fear. For them is disgrace in this world, and theirs is a grievous chastisement in the Hereafter.

¹¹⁵ And God's is the East and the West, so whither you turn thither is God's purpose. Surely God is Ample-giving, Knowing.

¹¹⁶ And they say: God has taken to Himself a son—glory be to Him! Rather, whatever is in the heavens and the earth is His. All are obedient to Him.

¹¹⁷ Wonderful Originator of the heavens and the earth! And when He decrees an affair, He says to it only, Be, and it is.

¹¹⁸ And those who have no knowledge say: Why does not God speak to us or a sign come to us? Even thus said those before them, the like of what they say. Their hearts are all alike. Indeed We have made the messages clear for a people who are sure.

¹¹⁹ Surely We have sent thee with the Truth as a bearer of good news and as a warner, and thou wilt not be called upon to answer for the companions of the flaming Fire.

¹²⁰ And the Jews will not be pleased with thee, nor the Christians, unless thou follow their religion. Say Surely God's guidance, that is the (perfect) guidance. And if thou follow their desires after the knowledge that has come to thee thou shalt have from God no friend, nor helper.

[121] Those to whom We have given the Book follow it as it ought to be followed. These believe in it. And whoever disbelieves in it, these it is that are the losers.

[122] O Children of Israel, call to mind My favour which I bestowed on you and that I made you excel the nations.

[123] And be on your guard against a day when no soul will avail another in the least, neither will any compensation be accepted from it, nor will intercession profit it, nor will they be helped....

[159] Those who conceal the clear proofs and the guidance that We revealed after We have made it clear in the Book for men, these it is whom God curses, and those who curse, curse them (too),

[160] Except those who repent and amend and make manifest (the truth), these it is to whom I turn (mercifully); and I am the Oft-returning (to mercy), the Merciful.

[161] Those who disbelieve and die while they are disbelievers, these it is on whom is the curse of God and the angels and men, of all (of them):

[162] Abiding therein; their chastisement shall not be lightened nor shall they be given respite.

[163] And your God is one God, there is no God but He! He is the Beneficent, the Merciful.

[164] In the creation of the heavens and the earth, and the alternation of night and day, and the ships that run in the sea with that which profits men, and the water that God sends down from the sky, then gives life therewith to the earth after its death and spreads in it all (kinds of) animals, and the changing of the winds and the clouds made subservient between heaven and earth, there are surely signs for a people who understand.

¹⁶⁵ Yet there are some men who take for themselves objects of worship besides God, whom they love as they should love God. And those who believe are stronger in (their) love for God. And O that the wrongdoers had seen, when they see the chastisement, that power is wholly God's, and that God is severe in chastising!

¹⁶⁶ When those who were followed renounce those who followed (them), and they see the chastisement and their ties are cut asunder.

¹⁶⁷ And those who followed will say: If we could but return, we would renounce them as they have renounced us. Thus will God show them their deeds to be intense regret to them, and they will not escape from the Fire.

¹⁶⁸ O men, eat the lawful and good things from what is in the earth, and follow not the footsteps of the devil. Surely he is an open enemy to you.

¹⁶⁹ He enjoins on you only evil and indecency, and that you speak against God what you know not.

¹⁷⁰ And when it is said to them, 'Follow what God has revealed," they say: "Nay, we follow that wherein we found our fathers. What! Even though their fathers had no sense at all, nor did they follow the right way.

¹⁷¹ And the parable of those who disbelieve is as the parable of one who calls out to that which hears no more than a call and a cry. Deaf, dumb, blind, so they have no sense.

¹⁷² O you who believe, eat of the good things that We have provided you with, and give thanks to God if He it is Whom you serve.

¹⁷³ He has forbidden you only what dies of itself, and blood, and the flesh of swine, and that over which any other (name) than (that of) God has been invoked. Then whoever is driven by necessity, not

desiring, nor exceeding the limit, no sin is upon him. Surely God is Forgiving, Merciful.

[174] Those who conceal aught of the Book that God has revealed and take for it a small price, they eat nothing but fire into their bellies, and God will not speak to them on the day of Resurrection, nor will He purify them; and for them is a painful chastisement.

[175] Those are they who buy error for guidance and chastisement for forgiveness; how bold they are to challenge the Fire!

[176] That is because God has revealed the Book with truth. And surely those who disagree about the Book go far in opposition.

[177] It is not righteousness that you turn your faces towards the East and the West, but righteous is the one who believes in God, and the Last Day, and the angels and the Book and the prophets, and gives away wealth out of love for Him to the near of kin and the orphans and the needy and the wayfarer and to those who ask and to set slaves free and keeps up prayer and pays the poor-rate and the performers of their promise when they make a promise, and the patient in distress and affliction and in the time of conflict. These are they who are truthful; and these are they who keep their duty.

[178] O you who believe, retaliation is prescribed for you in the matter of the slain the free for the free, and the slave for the slave, and the female for the female. But if remission is made to one by his (aggrieved) brother, prosecution (for blood-wit) should be according to usage, and payment to him in a good manner. This is an alleviation from your Lord and a mercy. Whoever exceeds the limit after this, will have a painful chastisement. And there is life for you in retaliation, O men of understanding, that you may guard yourselves.

[180] It is prescribed for you, when death approaches one of you, if he leaves behind wealth for parents and near relatives, to make a bequest in a kindly manner; it is incumbent upon the dutiful.

[181] Then whoever changes it after he has heard it, the sin of it is only upon those who change it. Surely God is Hearing, Knowing.

[182] But if one fears a wrong or a sinful course on the part of the testator, and effects an agreement between the parties, there is no blame on him. Surely God is Forgiving, Merciful.

[183] O you who believe, fasting is prescribed for you, as it was prescribed for those before you, so that you may guard against evil.

[184] For a certain number of days. But whoever among you is sick or on a journey, (he shall fast) a (like) number of other days And those who find it extremely hard may effect redemption by feeding a poor man. So whoever does good spontaneously, it is better for him; and that you fast is better for you if you know.

[185] The month of Ramadan is that in which the Qur'an was revealed, a guidance to men and clear proofs of the guidance and the Criterion. So whoever of you is present in the month, he shall fast therein, and whoever is sick or on a journey, (he shall fast) a (like) number of other days. God desires ease for you, and He desires not hardship for you, and (He desires) that you should complete the number and that you should exalt the greatness of God for having guided you and that you may give thanks.

[186] And when My servants ask thee concerning Me, surely I am nigh. I answer the prayer of the suppliant when he calls on Me, so they should hear My call and believe in Me that they may walk in the right way.

[187] It is made lawful for you to go in to your wives on the night of the fast. They are an apparel for you and you are an apparel for them. God

knows that you acted unjustly to yourselves, so He turned to you in mercy and removed (the burden) from you. So now be in contact with them and seek what God has ordained for you, and eat and drink until the whiteness of the day becomes distinct from the blackness of the night at dawn, then complete the fast till nightfall, and touch them not while you keep to the mosques. These are the limits of God, so go not near them. Thus does God make clear His messages for men that they may keep their duty.

[188] And swallow not up your property among yourselves by false means, nor seek to gain access thereby to the judges, so that you may swallow up a part of the property of men wrongfully while you know.

[189] They ask thee of the new moons. Say: They are times appointed for men, and (for) the pilgrimage. And it is not righteousness that you enter the houses by their backs, but he is righteous who keeps his duty. And go into the houses by their doors; and keep your duty to God, that you may be successful.

[190] And fight in the way of God against those who fight against you but be not aggressive. Surely God loves not the aggressors.

[191] And kill them wherever you find them, and drive them out from where they drove you out, and persecution is worse than slaughter. And fight not with them at the Sacred Mosque until they fight with you in so if they fight you (in it), slay them. Such is the recompense of the disbelievers.

[192] But if they desist, then surely God is Forgiving, Merciful.

[193] And fight them until there is no persecution, and religion is only for Allah. But if they desist, then there should be no hostility except against the oppressors.

[194] The sacred month for the sacred month, and retaliation (is allowed) in sacred things. Whoever then acts aggressively against you, inflict injury on him according to the injury he has inflicted on you and keep your duty to God, and know that God is with those who keep their duty.

[195] And spend in the way of God and cast not yourselves to perdition with your own hands and do good (to others). Surely God loves the doers of good....

[213] Mankind is a single nation. So God raised prophets as bearers of good news and as warners, and He revealed with them the Book with truth, that it might judge between people concerning that in which they differed. And none but the very people who were given it differed of about it after clear arguments had come to them, envying one another. So God has guided by His will those who believe to the truth about which they differed. And God guides whom He pleases to the right path.

[214] Or do you think that you will enter the Garden, while there has not yet befallen you the like of what befell those who have passed away before you. Distress and affliction befell them and they were shaken violently, so that the Messenger and those who believed with him said: When will the help of God come? Now surely the help of God is nigh!

[215] They ask thee as to what they should spend. Say: Whatever wealth you spend, it is for the parents and the near of kin and the orphans and the needy and the wayfarer. And whatever good you do, God surely is Knower of it.

[216] Fighting is enjoined on you, though it is disliked by you and it may be that you dislike a thing while it is good for you, and it may be that you love a thing while it is evil for you; and God knows while you know not.

[217] They ask thee about fighting in the sacred month. Say: Fighting in it is a grave (offence). And hindering (men) from God's way and denying Him and the Sacred Mosque and turning its people out of it, are still graver with God and persecution is graver than slaughter And they will not cease fighting you until they turn you back from your religion, if they can. And whoever of you turns back from his religion, then he dies while an unbeliever—these it is whose works go for nothing in this world and the Hereafter. And they are the companions of the Fire: therein they will abide.

[218] Those who believed and those who fled (their homes) and strove hard in God's way—these surely hope for the mercy of God. And God is Forgiving, Merciful....

[256] There is no compulsion in religion—the right way is indeed dearly distinct from error. So whoever disbelieves in the devil and believes in God, he indeed lays hold on the firmest handle, which shall never break. And God is Hearing, Knowing.

[257] God is the Friend of those who believe—He brings them out of darkness into light. And those who disbelieve, their friends are the devils who take them out of light into darkness. They are the companions of the Fire; therein they abide....

[285] The Messenger believes in what has been revealed to him from his Lord, and (so do) the believers. They all believe in God and His angels and His Books and His messengers. We make no difference between any of His messengers. And they say: We hear and obey; our Lord, Thy forgiveness (do we crave), and to Thee is the eventual course.

[286] God imposes not on any soul a duty beyond its scope. For it is that which it earns (of good) and against it that which it works (of evil). Our Lord, punish us not if we forget or make a mistake. Our Lord, do not lay on us a burden as Thou didst lay on those before us. Our Lord, impose not on us (afflictions) which we have not the strength to bear.

And pardon us! And grant us protection! And have mercy on us! Thou art our Patron, so grant us victory over the disbelieving people.

Description:_____
_____
_____

Inference:_____
_____
_____

Questions:

1. What do you make of the juxtaposition of the language of mercy with that of violence in this surah (chapter)? For example, 2:160-163.

2. Verses 47-86 recount examples of Jewish disobedience to God. How do these stories factor into the point of this surah?

3. What role does belief play in this surah?

4. What does the following verse mean: "Whatever message We abrogate or cause to be forgotten, We bring one better than it or one like it. Knowest thou not that God is Possessor of power over all things?" Why does it matter?

5. What are the rules of fighting according to verses 190-194?

6. If you have not read any portion of the *Qur'an* before, what stood out to you?

DOCUMENT 7-2

The Pact of Umar

CA. 637

The Pact of Umar is a treaty of limitations and privileges purportedly negotiated between conquered Syrian Christians and Umar I (584-644). This influential texts exists in a number of variations but probably took its present form sometime in the 9th century. Muslim political leaders later extended the pact to other conquered "people of the book," including Jews.

Themes: hierarchy, protection, religion, power

In the name of God, the Merciful, the Compassionate!

This is a writing to Umar from the Christians of such and such a city. When You [Muslims] marched against us [Christians], we asked of you protection for ourselves, our posterity, our possessions, and our co-religionists; and we made this stipulation with you:

We will not erect in our city or the suburbs any new monastery, church, cell or hermitage; we will not repair any of such buildings that may fall into ruins, or renew those that may be situated in the Muslim quarters of the town.

We will not refuse the Muslims entry into our churches either by night or by day.

We will open the gates wide to passengers and travellers.

Jacob Marcus, *The Jew in the Medieval World: A Sourcebook, 315-1791* (New York: JPS, 1938), 13-15.

We will receive any Muslim traveller into our houses and give him food and lodging for three nights.

We will not harbor any spy in our churches or houses, or conceal any enemy of the Muslims.

We will not teach our children the Qur'an.

We will not make a show of the Christian religion nor invite any one to embrace it.

We will not prevent any of our kinsmen from embracing Islam, if they so desire.

We will honor the Muslims and rise up in our assemblies when they wish to take their seats.

We will not imitate them in our dress, either in the cap, turban, sandals, or parting of the hair; that we will not make use of their expressions of speech, nor adopt their surnames.

We will not ride on saddles, or gird on swords, or take to ourselves arms or wear them, or engrave Arabic inscriptions on our rings; we will not sell wine.

We will shave the front of our heads.

We will keep to our own style of dress, wherever we may be.

We will wear girdles round our waists.

We will not display the cross upon our churches or display our crosses or our sacred books in the streets of the Muslims, or in their market places.

We will strike the clappers in our churches lightly.

We will not recite our services in a loud voice when a Muslim is present.

We will not carry Palm branches [on Palm Sunday] or our images in procession in the streets.

At the burial of our dead we will not chant loudly or carry lighted candles in the streets of the Muslims or their market places.

We will not take any slaves that have already been in the possession of Muslims, nor spy into their houses.

And we will not strike any Muslim.

All this we promise to observe, on behalf of ourselves and our co-religionists, and receive protection from you in exchange; and if we violate any of the conditions of this agreement, then we forfeit your protection and you are at liberty to treat us as enemies and rebels.

Description:_____

_____

_____

Inference:_____

_____

_____

Questions

1. How would you characterize the limitations on the Christians (and later Jews) in this text?

2. What sort of existence are "the people of the book" allowed given these rules?

3. Do any of these restrictions surprise you? If so, which ones?

Chapter 8:
The Middle Ages

Document 8-1

Feudal Homage

13ᵀᴴ AND 14ᵀᴴ CENTURY

The accounts below depict various commendation ceremonies, in which a vassal does homage to a lord by extending his hands in a sign of humility and swearing an oath of fealty to him. These ceremonies were understood as formal and binding contracts between the two parties involved. Vassals received a fief, generally a grant of land, in exchange for their service, usually military, whenever called upon by the Lord. These relationships, based on mutual benefit, became particularly necessary to the security of Europe during the 9th and 10th centuries when weak kings ruled Europe. Ties of homage created a wide-ranging and decentralized defense system in Europe that protected against invasions of Vikings from the West, Magyars from the East, and Muslims from the South. The tradition of lord and vassal relationships also established the conceptual framework of the Chivalric Romances of the 12ᵗʰ and 13ᵗʰ centuries, with their celebrated ideals of defense and absolute loyalty.

Theme: hierarchy, loyalty

"Homage," in *A Source Book for Mediaeval History*, ed. Oliver J. Thatcher and Edgar Holmes McNeal (New York: Charles Scribner's Sons: 1905), 363-365.

Boutillier, Somme rurale, I, 18.[1]

The man (vassal) should put his hands together as a sign of humility, and place them between the two hands of his lord as a token that he vows everything to him and promises faith to him; and the lord should receive him and promise to keep faith with him. Then the man should say: "Sir, I enter your homage and faith and become your man by mouth and hands (i.e., by taking the oath and placing his hands between those of the lord), and I swear and promise to keep faith and loyalty to you against all others, and to guard your rights with all my strength."

Coutume de la Marche

The manner of doing homage to another is as follows: the man who wishes to enter the homage and fealty of a lord should humbly request the lord to receive him into his faith; his head should be uncovered, and the lord may be seated if he wishes; the vassal should take off his belt and sword, and should kneel and say the words of homage...

Tabularium Campaniae

I, John of Toul, make known that I am the liege man of the Lady Beatrice, Countess of Troyes, and of her son, Theobald, Count of Champagne, against every creature, living or dead, saving my allegiance to Lord Enjorand of Coucy, Lord John of Areis, and the Count of Grandpré. If it should happen that the Count of Grandpré should be at war with the Countess and Count of Champagne on his own quarrel, I will aid the Count of Grandpré in my own person, and will send to the Count and the Countess of Champagne the knights whose service I owe to them for the fief which I hold of them. But if the Count of Grandpré shall make war on the Countess and the Count of Champagne on behalf of his friends and not in his own quarrel, I will

---

[1] An account of French customary law

aid in my own person the Countess and Count of Champagne, and will send one knight to the Count of Grandpré for the service which I owe him for the fief which I hold of him, but I will not go myself into the territory of the Count of Grandpré to make war on him.

Description:_____

_____

_____

Inference:_____

_____

_____

Question:

1. How did the rituals of commendation ceremonies reinforce differences in social hierarchy?

2. What sort of resources did John of Toul have at his disposal? What does this mean about the status of some vassals?

3. What sort of complexity does John of Toul's account reveal about lord and vassal relationships in the Middle Ages?

DOCUMENT 8-2

Fulcher of Chartres

Speech of Pope Urban II at the Council of Clermont

1095

"I say this to those who are present, it is meant also for those who are absent. Moreover, Christ commands it." -Fulcher of Chartres

Fulcher of Chartres (1059—1128) was a priest who served the crusader king, Baldwin I, as a chaplain during the First Crusade (1095—1099). He later wrote a chronicle of the crusade in three books. The excerpt below is Fulcher's first-hand account of Pope Urban II's speech at the Council of Clermont (1095), generally accepted as the beginning of the crusade movement in Europe. There Urban addressed both Catholic prelates and secular lords. Urban had received envoys from the Byzantine emperor, Alexius I Comnenus (1056—1118), requesting military assistance against the Seljuk Turks who had conquered most of Asia Minor (Asiatic Turkey) and threatened Constantinople. Rather than send Alexius mercenary soldiers directly, Urban encouraged European leaders to travel to the East under their own leadership to battle the Turks and liberate the Holy Land.

Themes: peace, violence, sin, church influence

Fulcher of Chartres, "The Speech of Urban II at the Council of Clermont, 1095," in *A Source Book for Mediaeval History*, ed. Oliver J. Hatcher (New York: Charles Scribner's Sons, 1905), 512-517. Modernized by Andrew Fogleman.

Most beloved brethren: Urged by necessity, I, urban, by the permission of God, chief bishop and prelate over the whole world, have come into these parts as an ambassador with a divine warning for you, the servants of God. I hoped to find you as faithful and as zealous in the service of God as I had supposed you to be. But if there is in you any deformity or crookedness contrary to God's law, with divine help I will do my best to remove it. For God has put you as overseers over his family to minister to it. Happy indeed will you be if he finds you faithful in your work. You are called shepherds; see that you do not act merely as a hired hand.[1] But be true shepherds, with your crooks always in your hands. Do not go to sleep, but guard the flock committed to you on all sides. For if through your carelessness or negligence a wolf carries away one of your sheep, your will surly lose the reward laid up for you with God. And after you have been bitterly afflicted with guilt for your faults, you will be fiercely overwhelmed in hell, the abode of death. For according to the gospel you are the salt of the earth.[2] But if you fall short in your duty, how, it may be asked, can it be salted? And O how great is the need of salting! It is indeed necessary for you to correct with the salt of wisdom this foolish people so devoted to the pleasures of this world, lest the Lord, when He may wish to speak to them, find them decayed by their sins, unsalted and foul-smelling. For if He shall find worms, that is sins, in them, because you have been negligent in your duty, He will command them as worthless to be thrown into the place of the unclean things. And because you cannot restore to Him His great loss, He will surely condemn you and drive you from His loving presence.

---

[1] John 10:11-14: "I am the good shepherd. The good shepherd lays down his life for the sheep. The hired hand, who is not the shepherd and does not own the sheep, sees the wolf coming and leaves the sheep and runs away—and the wolf snatches them and scatters them. The hired hand runs away because a hired hand does not care for the sheep. I am the good shepherd."

[2] *Gospel of Matthew* 5:13, Document 5-4.

But the man who applies this salt should be prudent, sensible, modest, learned, peaceable, watchful, pious, just, equitable and pure. For how can the ignorant teach others? How can the shameful person make other modest? And how can the impure make others pure? If anyone hates peace, how can he make others peace loving? Or if anyone has dirtied his hands with filthy things, how can he cense the impurities of another? We read also that if the blind lead the blind, both will fall into the ditch.[3] So first correct yourself, in order that, free from blame, you many be able to correct those who are subject to you. If you wish to be the friends of God, gladly do the things that you know will please Him.

You must especially let all matters that pertain to the church be controlled by the law of the church. And be careful that simony does not take root among you, lest both those who buy and those who sell [church offices] be beaten with the scourges of the Lord through narrow streets and driven into the place of destruction and confusion.[4] Keep the church and the clergy in all its parts entirely free from the control of secular power. See that the tithes that belong to God are fitfully paid from all the produce of the land; let them not be sold or withheld. If anyone seizes a bishop let him be treated as an outlaw. If anyone seizes or robs monks, or clergymen, or nuns, or their servants, or pilgrims, or merchants, let him be anathema.[5] Let robbers, incendiaries, and all their accomplices be expelled from the church and anathematized. If a man who does not give a part of his goods as alms is punished with the damnation, how should one be punished who robs another of his goods? For thus it happened to the rich man in the Gospel;[6] for he was not punished because he had stolen the goods of another, but because he had not used the things that were his for good.

---

[3] *Gospel of Matthew* 15:14.

[4] **Simony**: paying money to obtain a position in the church or offering a church position for money.

[5] **Anathema**: a formal condemnation of a pope or church council, cutting a believer off from the sacraments of the church.

[6] *Gospel of Luke* 16:19.

You have seen for a long time the great disorder in the world caused by such crimes. Some of your provinces, I am told, are so weak in the administration of justice that one can hardly travel the road by day or night without being attacked by robbers; and whether at home or abroad, one is in danger of being despoiled either by force or fraud. Therefore it is necessary to reenact the truce, as it is commonly called, which was proclaimed a long time ago by our holy fathers.[7] I exhort and demand that each of you try hard to have the truce kept in your diocese. And if anyone shall be led by greed or arrogance to break this truce, by the authority of God and with the sanction of the council he shall be anathematized."

After these and various other matters had been attended to, all who were present, clergy and people, gave thanks to God and agreed to the pope's proposition. They all faithfully promised to keep the decrees. Then the pope said that in another part of the world Christianity was suffering from a state of affairs that was worse than the [European] one just mentioned. He continued:

"Although, O sons of God, you have promised more firmly than ever to keep the peace among yourselves and to preserve the rights of the church, there remains still an important work for you to do. Freshly inspired by the divine correction, you must apply the strength of your righteousness to another matter that concerns you, as well as God. For your brethren who live in the East are in urgent need of your help, and you must hasten to give them the aid, which has often been promised. For, as most of you have heard, the Turks and Arabs have attacked them and have conquered the territory of Romania [the Greek empire] as far west as the shore of the Mediterranean and the Hellespont, which is call the Arm of St. George. They have occupied more and more of the land of those Christians, and have overcome them in seven

---

[7] **The truce**: This likely refers to the Peace of God movement beginning in the 10th century. Starting with the Synod of Charroux in 989, clergy sought to limit violence in regions, especially against non-combatants.

battles. They have killed and captured many, and have destroyed the churches and devastated the empire. If you permit them to continue in this manner with impunity, the faithful of God will be much more widely attacked by them. On this account, I, or rather the Lord, beg you as Christ's messengers to publish this [request] everywhere and to persuade all people of whatever rank, foot-soldiers, and knights, poor and rich, to carry aid promptly to those Christians and to destroy that vile people from the lands of our friends. I say this to those who are present, it is meant also for those who are absent. Moreover, Christ commands it.

All who die by the way, either by land or by sea, or in battle against these non-believers, shall have immediate forgiveness of sins. This I grant them through the power of God with which I am invested. O what a disgrace if such a despised and base people, which worships demons, should conquer a people which has the faith of the omnipotent God and is made glorious with the name of Christ! With what accusations will the Lord overwhelm us if you do not aid those who, with us, profess the Christian religion!

Let those who have been accustomed unjustly to wage private warfare against the faithful now go against the non-believers and end with victory this war, which should have been begun long ago. Let those who, for a long time, have been robbers, now become knights. Let those who have been fighting against their brothers and relatives now fight in a proper way against the barbarians. Let those who have been serving as mercenaries for small pay now obtain the eternal reward. Let those who have been wearing themselves out in both body and soul now work for a double honor. Behold on this side will be the sorrowful and the poor, on that, the rich; on this side, the enemies of the Lord, on that, his friends. Let those who choose to go not put off the journey. Rather rent your lands and collect money for expenses; and as soon as winter is over and spring comes, set out eagerly on the way with God as your guide."

Description:_____

_____

_____

Inference:_____

_____

_____

Questions:

1. According to Pope Urban II's first speech, what role does the Church play in local justice? What tools does the Church employ for affecting local justice?

2. What is the connection between the first part of this sermon and the second?

3. Consider the following injunction: " Let those who have been accustomed unjustly to wage private warfare against the faithful now go against the non-believers ... Let those who, for a long time, have been robbers, now become knights. Let those who have been fighting against their brothers and relatives now fight in a proper way against the barbarians." Is Urban simply getting rid of troublesome people, or is he helping sinners find redemption?

4. What types of people does Urban encourage to go East? Do you think this is what Alexius I Comnenus wanted?

DOCUMENT 8-3

Magna Carta

1215

Magna Carta Libertatum, or Great Charter of Liberties, was a document drawn up by the Archbishop of Canterbury to make peace between King John of England (1166-1216) and a group of dissident barons. The charter limited royal taxation, secured legal justice for the barons, and defended the independence of the English Church against royal control. The charter also established a council of 25 barons to oversee the implementation of these rights and privileges. Later rejected by John and annulled by Pope Innocent III, the document never had continuous enforcement in England, though various kings periodically renewed it. Magna Carta nonetheless played an important symbolic and philosophical role in discussions of individual rights for English citizens and influenced the conception of individual rights in the American Constitution.

Themes: rights, liberties, checks and balances, oversight, rule of law

John, by the grace of God king of England, lord of Ireland, duke of Normandy and Aquitaine, count of Anjou: to the archbishops, bishops, abbots, earls, barons, justices, foresters, sheriffs, prevosts, serving men, and to all his bailiffs and faithful subjects, greetings. Know that we, by the will of God and for the safety of our soul, and of the souls of all our predecessors and our heirs, to the honor of God and or the exalting of the Holy Church and the bettering of our realm: by the counsel of our venerable fathers Stephen archbishop of Canterbury,

"Magna Carta," in *Select Historical Documents of the Middle Ages*, ed. Ernest F. Henderson (London: George Bell and Sons, 1892), 135-148. Modernized by Andrew Fogleman.

primate of all England and cardinal of the holy Roman church... and others of our faithful subjects.

First that we have granted to God, and by this present charter have confirmed for us and for our heirs forever, that the English church shall be free and shall have its rights intact and its liberties uninfringed upon. And thus we will that it be observed. As is apparent from the fact that we, spontaneously and of our own free will, before discord broke out between ourselves and our barons, did grant and by our charter confirm—and did cause the lord pope Innocent III to confirm—freedom of elections, which is considered most important and most necessary to the church of England. Which charter both we ourselves shall observe, and we will that it be observed with good faith by our heirs forever. We have also granted to all free men of our realm, on the part of ourselves and our heirs forever, all the subjoined liberties, to have and to hold, to them and to their heirs, from us and from our heirs: ...

8. No widow will be forced to marry when she prefers to live without a husband; But she will give security that she will not marry without our [royal] consent, if she hold from us, or the consent of the lord from whom she holds, if she hold from another.

11. If any one shall have taken any sum, great or small as a loan from the Jews, and shall die before that debt is paid,—that debt shall not bear interest so long as the heir, from whomever he may hold, shall be under age. And if the debt fall into our hands, we shall take nothing save the chattel contained in the deed.

11. And if any one dies owing a debt to the Jews, his wife shall have her dowry, and shall restore nothing of that debt. But if there shall remain children of that dead man, and they shall be under age, the necessaries shall be provided for them according to the nature of the dead man's holding; and, from the residue, the debt shall be paid,

saving the service due to the lords. In like manner shall be done concerning debts that are due to others besides Jews.

12. No scutage[1] or aid shall be imposed in our realm unless by the common counsel of our realm; except for redeeming our body, and knighting our eldest son, and marrying once our eldest daughter. And for theses purposes there shall only be given a reasonable aid. In like manner shall be done concerning the aids of the city of London.

13. And the city of London shall have all its old liberties and free customs as well by land as by water. Moreover we will and grant that all other cities and boroughs, and towns and ports, shall have all their liberties and free customs.

14. And, in order to have the common counsel of the realm in the matter of assessing an aid otherwise than in the aforesaid cases, or of assessing a scutage, —we shall cause, under seal through our letters, the archbishops, bishops, abbots, earls, and greater barons to be summoned for a fixed day—for a term, namely, at least forty days distant,—and for a fixed place. And, moreover, we shall cause to be summoned in general, through our sheriffs and bailiffs, all those who hold of us in chief. And in all those letters of summons we shall express the cause of the summons. And when a summons has thus been made, the business shall be proceeded with on the day appointed according to the counsel of those who shall be present, even though not all shall come who were summoned.

17. Common lawsuits shall not follow our court but shall be held in a certain fixed place.

21. Earls and barons shall not be fined but through their peers, and only according to the measure of the offense.

---

[1] **Scutage**: a tax paid by a vassal instead of military service.

23. Neither a town nor a man shall be forced to make bridges over the rivers, with the exception of those who, from of old and of right ought to do it.

26. If any one holding from us a lay fee shall die, and our sheriff or bailiff can show our letters patent containing our summons for the debt which the dead man owed to us,—our sheriff or bailiff may be allowed to attach and enroll the chattels of the dead man to the value of that debt, through view of lawful men; in such way, however that nothing shall be removed thence until the debt is paid which was plainly owed to us. And the residue shall be left to the executors that they may carry our the will of the dead man. And if nothing is owed to us by him all the chattels shall go to the use prescribed by the deceased, saving their reasonable portions to his wife and children.

27. If any free man shall have died intestate[2] his chattels shall be distributed through the hands of his near relatives and friends, by view of the church; saving to any one the debts which the dead man owed him.

28. No constable or other bailiff of ours shall take the corn or other chattels of any one except he straightway give money for them, or can be allowed a respite in that regard by the will of the seller...

30. No sheriff nor bailiff of ours, nor any one else, shall take the horses or carts of any freeman for transport, unless by the will of that freeman.

32. We shall not hold the lands of those convicted of felony longer than a year and a day and then the lands shall be restored to the lords of the fiefs.

---

[2] **Intestate**: without a will.

35. There shall be one measure of wine throughout our whole realm, and one measure of ale and one measure of corn[3]—namely, the London quart;—and one width of dyed and russet and hauberk cloths— namely, two ells below the selvage. And with weights, moreover, it shall be as with measures.

38. No bailiff, on his own simple assertion, shall henceforth put any man on trial without producing faithful witnesses in evidence.

40. To none will we sell, to none deny or delay, right or justice.

45. We will not make men justices, constables, sheriffs, or bailiffs, unless they are such as know the law of the realm, and are minded to observe it rightly.

52. If anyone shall have been taken by us, or removed, without a legal sentence of his peers, from his lands, castles, liberties or lawful right, we shall straight way restore them to him. And if a dispute shall arise concerning this matter it shall be settled according to the judgment of twenty-five barons who are mentioned below as sureties for the peace...

55. All fines imposed by us unjustly and contrary to the law of the land, and all punishments made unjustly and contrary to the law of the land, shall be altogether remitted, or it shall be done with regard to them according to the judgment of the twenty-five barons mentioned below as sureties for the peace, or according to the judgment of the majority of them together with the aforesaid Stephen archbishop of Canterbury...

60. Moreover all the subjects of our realm, clergy as well as laity, shall, as far as pertains to them, observe with regard to their vassals, all these aforesaid customs and liberties which we have decreed shall as far as pertains to us, be observed in our realm with regard to our own.

---

[3] **Corn**: grain.

In as much as, for the sake of God, and for the bettering of our realm, and for the more ready healing of the discord which has arisen between us and our barons, we have made all these aforesaid concessions,—wishing them to enjoy forever entire and firm stability, we make and grant to them the following security; that the barons may elect at their pleasure twenty-five barons from the realm, who ought, with all their strength, to observe, maintain and cause to be observed, the peace and privileges which we have granted to them and confirmed by this our present charter. In such wise, namely, that if we, or our justice, or our bailiffs, or any one of our servants shall have transgressed against any one in any respect, or shall have broken some one of the articles of peace or security, and our transgression shall have been shown to four barons of the aforesaid twenty-five: those four barons shall come to us, or if we are abroad, to our justice, showing to us our error; and they shall ask us to cause that error to be amended without delay. And if we do not amend that error, or, we being abroad, if our justices do not amend it within it within a term of forty days from the time when it was shown to us or, we being abroad, to our justice: the aforesaid four barons shall refer the matter to the remainder of the twenty-five barons, and those twenty-five barons, with the whole land in common, shall seize our property and oppress us in every way in their power,—namely, by taking our castles, lands and possessions, and in every other way that they can, until amends shall have been made according to their judgment, saving the persons of ourselves our queen and our children....

And if any one of the twenty-five barons shall die, or leave the country, or in any other way be prevented from carrying out the aforesaid measures,—the remainder of the aforesaid twenty-five barons shall choose another in his place, according to their judgment who shall be sworn in the same way as the others. Moreover, in all things entrusted to those twenty-five barons to be carried out, if those twenty-five shall be present and chance to disagree among themselves with regard to some matter, or if some of them having been summoned, shall be unwilling or unable to be present; that which the majority of those present shall decide or decree shall be considered binding and valid, just as if all the twenty-five had consented to it...

Wherefore we will and firmly decree that the English church shall be free, and that the subjects of our realm shall have and hold all the aforesaid liberties, rights and concessions, duly and in peace, freely and quietly, fully and entirely, for themselves and their heirs, from us and our heirs, in all matters and in all places, forever, as has been said. Moreover it has been sworn, on our part as well as on the part of the barons, that all these above-mentioned provisions shall be observed with good faith and without evil intent. The witnesses being the above mentioned and many others. Given through our hand, in the plain called Runnimede between Windsor and Stanes, on the fifteenth day of June, in the seventeenth year of our reign.

Description:_____

_____

_____

Inference:_____

_____

_____

Questions:

1. *Magna Carta* is generally remembered as a charter granting democratic rights and the rule of law, but the first liberties acknowledged by the charter go to the English church. Why might this have been necessary?

2. This text is a list of rights. If this document was produced to check abuses, make a list of abuses that the document seems to address.

3. What is the function of the twenty-five barons in this document?

4. What provisions does *Magna Carta* make for delays in justice?

Peter Abelard

Sic et non

CA. 1125

"By doubting we come to examine, and by examining we reach the truth." -Abelard

Peter Abelard (1079—1142) was a brilliant philosopher, theologian, and logician. Following a sexual affair with one of his students, Heloise d'Agenteuil, Heloise's vengeful uncle castrated Abelard. Abelard interpreted his castration as the judgment of God for his sins and became a monk, seeking a life of penance. Despite this devastating moment for Abelard, he went on to have a long academic career writing and teaching. The excerpts below come from his treatise Sic et non, which translates to "Yes and No." In this work, Abelard presents 158 yes-or-no type statements on topics of Christian theology. He then supplies quotations from Church authorities, which seem either to agree with the statement or argue contra (or against it). It is the task of the reader to reconcile these apparently contradictory authoritative sayings, as Abelard did not include any solutions to the provocative questions he posed. This work reveals the culture of debate and open discussion that characterized early scholastic learning in the West and informed the teaching methods of later medieval Universities.

Themes: debate, truth, medieval education

Peter Abelard, "Sic et Non," in *Readings in the History of Education: Medieval Universities*, ed. Arthur O. Norton (Cambridge: Harvard University: 1909), 20-24. Modernized by Andrew Fogleman.

[Prologue:]

Questions ought to serve to excite tender readers to a zealous inquiry into truth and so sharpen their minds. The master key of knowledge is, indeed, a persistent and frequent questioning. Aristotle, the most clear-sighted of all the philosophers, was desirous above all else to arouse this questioning spirit, for in his *Categories* he exhorts a student as follows: "It may well be difficult to reach a positive conclusion in these matters unless they be frequently discussed. It is by no means fruitless to be doubtful on particular points." By doubting we come to examine, and by examining we reach the truth.[1]

[Table of Contents:]

1. That faith is based upon reason, *et contra* (and against)

5. That God is not single, *et contra.*

6. That God is tripartite, *et contra.*

8. That in the Trinity it is not to be stated that there is more than one Eternal being, *et contra.*

11. That the Divine Persons mutually differ, *et contra.*

12. That in the Trinity, each is one with the other, *et contra.*

13. That God the Father is the cause of the son, *et contra.*

14. That the Son is without beginning, *et contra.*

27. That God judges with foreknowledge, *et non.*

28. That the providence of God is the cause of things happening, *et non.*

32. That to God all things are possible, *et non.*

36. That God does whatever he wishes, *et non.*

---

[1] Peter Abelard, "Prologue," in *Readings in European History*, ed. James Harvey Robinson (Boston: Ginn, 1904): 1: 451.

37. That nothing happens contrary to the will of God, *et contra*.

38. That God knows all things, *et non*.

84. That man's first sin did not begin through the persuasion of the devil, *et contra*.

55. That Eve only, not Adam, was tricked [by the Devil], *et contra*.

56. That by sinning man lost free will, *et non*.

69. That the Son of God was predestinated, *et contra*.
    79. That Christ was a deceiver, *et non*.

116. That the sins of the fathers are visited upon [their] children, *et contra*.

122. That everybody should be allowed to marry, *et contra*.

141. That works of sanctity do not justify a man, *et contra*.

153. That a lie is never permissible, *et contra*.

154. That a man may [kill] himself for some reason, *et contra*.

155. That Christians may not for any reason kill a man, *et contra*.

156. That it is lawful to kill a man, *et non*.

Jerome on *Isaiah*, Bk. 5. "He who cuts the throat of a man of blood, is not a man of blood."

Idem (next), On the *Epistle to the Galatians*: "He who attacks the wicked because they are wicked and whose reason for the murder is that he may slay an evildoer, is a servant of the Lord."

Idem, on *Jeremiah*: "For the punishment of murderers, impious persons, and poisoners is not bloodshed, but serving the law."

Cyprian, from the *Ninth Kind of Abuse*: "The King ought to restrain theft, punish deeds of adultery, cause the wicked to perish from off the face of the earth, [and] refuse to allow parricides and perjurers to live."

Augustine: Although it is manslaughter to slaughter a man, a person may sometimes be slain without sin. For both a soldier in the case of an enemy and a judge or his official in the case of a criminal—and the man from whose hand, perhaps without his will or knowledge, a weapon has flown—do not seem to me to sin, but merely to kill a man.

Likewise: "The soldier is ordered by law to kill the enemy and if he refrains from such slaughter, he pays the penalty at the hands of his commander. Should we not call these laws unjust or rather not laws at all? For that which was not just does not seem to me to be a law."

Idem, on *Exodus* Ch. 27: "The Israelites committed no theft in spoiling the Egyptians,[2] but rendered a service to God at his bidding, just as when the servant of the judge kills a man whom the law hath ordered to be killed; certainly if he does it of his own volition he is a murderer, even though he knows that the man whom he executes ought to be executed."

Idem, on *Leviticus* Ch. 75: "When a man is justly put to death, the law puts him to death, not you."

Idem, Bk. I of the *City of God*: "Thou shalt not kill, except in the case of those whose God ordered, or else when a law has been passed to suit the needs of the time and express command has been laid upon a person. But he does not kill who owes service to the person who gives him his order, for he is as it were a mere sword for the person who employs his assistance."

---

[2] **Spoiling the Egyptians**: After years of servitude, God ordered Moses to instruct the Hebrews to take clothing and items of silver and gold from the Egyptians as a form of payment for their service. See Book of Exodus 12:35, 36.

Idem, to *Publicola*: Counsel concerning the slaying of men doesn't please me, that none may be slain by them, unless perhaps a man is a soldier or in a public force, so that he does the deed not in his own behalf but for others and for the state, accepting power legitimately conferred, if it is consonant with the task imposed on him."

Likewise: it has been said: "Let us not resist the evil man, let not vengeance delight us, which feeds the mind on other's ill; let us not neglect the warning of men."

Idem, to *Marcella*: "If that earthly commonwealth of yours keep to the teachings of Christ, even wars will not be waged without goodwill, so that the lusts of desire may be subdued and those faults destroyed which ought under just rule to be either rooted out or chastised. For if Christians training condemned all wars, this should rather be the advice given in the gospel for their safety to the soldier who ask for it, namely to throw aside their arms and retire altogether from the field [of battle]. For this is word spoken to them: Do violence to no man, neither accuse any falsely; and be content with your wages (*Luke* 3:14). He warns them that the wages that belong to them should satisfy them, but he by no means forbids them to take the field [of battle]."

Idem, *To his Comrade Boniface*: "I will give you and yours useful advice: Take arms in your hands; let prayer strike the ears of the creator; because in battle the heavens are opened, God looks forth and awards the victory to the side he sees to be the righteous one."

Idem: 'The wars to be waged we undertake either at the command of God or under some lawful rule or else John, when the soldiers to be baptized came to him saying, "And what shall we do?" would make answer [the following] to them: "Cast aside your arms, leave the service; attack no man; kill no man." Bet because he knew that they did these things because they were in the service, that they were not [simply] slayers of men, but servants of law; and not avengers of their own injuries, but guardians of the public safety, his answers to them was: "Do violence to no man," etc."

Pope Nicolas, from *The Questions on the Bulgarians*: If there is no urgent need, not only in Lent but at all times, men should abstain from battles. If however there is an unavoidable and urgent occasion, and it is not Lent, beyond all doubt preparation for wars should be sparingly made in one's own defense or in that of one's country or the laws of one's fathers; lest indeed this word be said: A man if he has an attack to make, does not carefully take counsel beforehand for his own safety and that of others, nor does he guard against the injury to holy religion."

Description:_____
_____
_____

Inference:_____
_____
_____

Questions:

1. What kinds of subjects are open for discussion in Abelard's table of contents? Does it surprise you that any of these are up for discussion?

2. After reading the list of authorities, what is your conclusion to the question? Within the Christian tradition (as defined by the list of authorities above), is it lawful to kill a man or not?

3. What is the range of concerns expressed by these authors on the topic of lawful killing or its rejection?

4. Although the title of Abelard's work is *Yes and No*, do these topics yield straightforward yes or no answers?

DOCUMENT 8-5

Saint Thomas Aquinas

Summa Theologica

1268

"Therefore it is necessary to go back to some first mover, which is itself moved by nothing—and this all men know as God." -St. Thomas Aquinas

Saint Thomas Aquinas (1225-1274) was an Italian Dominican friar and Doctor of the Church known for his immense learning. It is hard to overstate his enduring influence on Catholic theology up to the present. He is best known for his compendiums of theology, the Summa Theologica (below) and his Summa Contra Gentiles, as well as his commentaries on Scripture and Aristotle. For Aquinas, there existed two immediate sources of knowledge: revelation (or the supernatural truths revealed in the Bible) and reason (which included things known through observation). He saw no conflict between these two types of knowledge since he understood God as the author of both.

This short excerpt from Aquinas's immense Summa Theologica is meant to supply a taste of the intellectual culture of the medieval university. Medieval professors wrote in a highly structured manner called the Scholastic (or Dialectic) method. It was meant to be systematic and exhaustive. Here is how it worked: A professor started with a question to be determined, for example: "Whether the existence of God is

St. Thomas Aquinas, "Summa Theologicae," in *The Library of Original Sources: The Early Medieval World*, ed. Oliver J. Thatcher (Milwaukee: University Research Extension Co., 1907), 4:359-363.

demonstrable." He then presented arguments for a contrary position on the question ("God existence is not demonstrable because of arguments A, B, and C") and next gave reasons for a positive position on the question ("God's existence is demonstrable because of arguments X, Y, and Z"). Following the presentation of the best arguments for both sides of the issue, he gave a "determination" of the question ("I answer that..."). After revealing his position in the determination, he then gave replies to the arguments opposing his view, or disputed both sets of arguments if he took a neutral position.

The scholastic method was meant to present a question, and the various opinions on it, as clearly as possible. Below Aquinas first asks whether the existence of God is demonstrable at all. Then concluding that it is, he offers possible arguments in favor of God's existence.

Themes: faith, reason, eternity, cause and effect

Article 2. Whether the Existence of God is Demonstrable

It is objected (1) that the existence of God is not demonstrable: that God's existence is an article of faith, and that articles of faith are not demonstrable, because the office of demonstration is to prove, but faith pertains (only) to things that are not to be proven, as is evident from the Epistle to the Hebrews, 11.[1] Hence God's existence is not demonstrable.

Again, (2) that the subject matter of demonstration is that something exists, but in the case of God we cannot know what exists, but only

---

[1] *Hebrews* 11:1 "Now faith is the assurance of things hoped for, a conviction of things not seen."

what does not, as Damascus[2] says (*Of the Orthodox Faith*, I., 4.). Hence we cannot demonstrate God's existence.

Again, (3) that if God's existence is to be proved it must be from what he causes, and that what He effects is not sufficient for His supposed nature, since He is infinite, but the effects finite, and the finite is not proportional to the infinite. Since, therefore, a cause cannot be proved through an effect not proportional to itself, it is said that god's existence cannot be proved.

But against this argument the apostle says, (Rom. I., 20), "The unseen things of God are visible through His manifest works." But this would not be so unless it were possible to demonstrate God's existence through His works. What ought to be understood concerning anything is first of all, whether it exists.

Conclusion. It is possible to demonstrate God's existence, although not a priori (by pure reason), yet a posteriori[3] from some work of his more surely known to us.

In answer I must say that the proof is double. One is through the nature of a cause and is called *propter quid*:[4] this is through the nature of

---

[2] **Damascus**: John of Damascus (ca. 676-749) was a Christian Theologian. Regarding knowing God's essence he writes, "But even this gives no true idea of [God's] essence, to say that He is unbegotten, and without beginning, changeless and imperishable, and possessed of such other qualities as we are wont to ascribe to God and His environment. For these do not indicate what He is, but what He is not.... In the case of God, however, it is impossible to explain what He is in His essence, and it befits us the rather to hold discourse about His absolute separation from all things. For He does not belong to the class of existing things: not that He has no existence, but that He is above all existing things, nay even above existence itself."

[3] **A priori...a posteriori**: *a priori* refers to conclusions that are reached from deduction, not observation or experience. *a posteriori* deals with conclusions drawn from observation or experience, not deduction.

[4] *Propter quid...quid*: This is a reference to Aristotle treatise on logic, Posterior Analytics, Bk 1, Ch 13. A *propter quid* argument demonstrates an effect from a known cause, and a *quia* argument reasons from a known effect to a cause. Aquinas will use the *quia* version, arguing that God (as a cause) can be known from the things he creates (effects).

preceding events. The other is through the nature of the effect, and is called *quia*, and is through the nature of preceding things as respects us. Since the effect is better known to us than the cause, we proceed from the effect to the knowledge of the cause. From any effect whatsoever it can be proved that a corresponding cause exists, if only the effects of it are sufficiently known to us, for since effects depend on causes, the effect being given, it is necessary that a preceding cause exists. Whence, that God exists, although this is not itself known to us, is provable through effects that are known to us.

To the first objection above, I reply, therefore, that God's existence, and those other things of this nature that can be known through natural reason concerning God, as is said in Romans I., are not articles of faith, but preambles to these articles. So faith presupposes natural knowledge, so grace [presupposes] nature, and perfection [presupposes] a perfectible thing. Nothing prevents a thing that is in itself demonstrable and knowable, from being accepted as an article of faith by someone that does not accept the proof of it.

To the second objection, I reply that, since the cause is proven from the effect, one must use the effect in the place of the definition of the cause in demonstrating that the cause exists; and that this applies especially in the case of God, because for proving that anything exists, it is necessary to accept in this method what the name signifies, not however that anything exists, because the question *what it is* is secondary to the question *whether it exists at all*. The characteristics of God are drawn from His works as shall be shown hereafter (Question XIII), we are able by this very method to see what the name of God signifies.

To the third objection, I reply that, although a perfect knowledge of the cause cannot be had from inadequate effects, yet that from any effect manifest to us it can be shown that a cause does exist, as has been said. And thus from the works of God His existence can be proved, although we cannot in this way know Him perfectly in accordance with His own essence.

Article III. Whether God Exists

It is objected (1) that God does not exist because ... implied in the name God is a certain infinite goodness; if then God existed, no evil would exist. But evil is found in the world; therefore it is objected that God does not exist.

Again, that what can be accomplished through a less number of principles will not be accomplished through more. It is objected that all things that appear on the earth can be accounted for through other principles, without supposing that God exists, since what is natural can be traced to a natural principle, and what proceeds from a proposition can be traced to the human reason or will. Therefore there is no necessity to suppose that God exists.

But as against this note what is said of the person of God (Exodus III, 14) *I am that I am.*

Conclusion. There must be found in the nature of things one first immovable Being, a primary cause, necessarily existing, not created; existing in the most perfect way possible; the first ruler through the intellect, and the ultimate end of all things, which is God.

I answer that it can be shown in five ways that God exists. The first and plainest is the method that proceeds from the point of view of motion. It is certain and in accord with experience, that things on earth undergo change. Now everything that is moved is moved by something; nothing, indeed is changed, except it is changed to something which it is in potentiality. Moreover, anything moves in accordance with something actually existing; change itself, is nothing else than to bring forth something from potentiality into actuality. Now, nothing can be brought from potentiality to actual existence except through some thing actually existing; thus heat in action, as fire, makes wood burn, which is potentially hot, to be actually hot, and through this process, changes itself. The same thing cannot at the same time be actually and potentially the same thing, but only in regard to different things. What is actually hot cannot be at the same time potentially hot, but it is possible for it at the same time to be potentially cold. It is impossible, then, that anything should be both mover and the thing moved, in regard to the same thing and in the same way, or that it should move itself. Everything, therefore, is moved by something else. If, then, that by which it is moved, is also moved, this must be moved by something still different, and this, again, by something else. But this process cannot go on to infinity because there would not be any first mover and therefore nothing else in motion, as the succeeding things would not move except because of what is moved by the first mover, just as a stick does not move except by a hand [or something external to it]. Therefore it is necessary to go back to some first mover, which is itself moved by nothing—and this all men know as God.

The second proof is from the nature of the efficient cause.[5] We find in our experience that there is a chain of causes: it is not possible for anything to be the efficient cause of itself, since it would have to exist before itself, which is impossible. Nor in the case of efficient causes can the chain go back indefinitely, because in all chains of efficient causes, the first is the cause of the middle, and these of the last, whether they be one or many. If the cause is removed, the effect is removed. Hence if there is no first cause there will be no last cause, nor a middle cause. But if the chain were to go back infinitely, there would be no first cause, and thus no ultimate effect, which is obviously false [because many effects exist]. Hence we must presuppose some first efficient cause—which all men call God...

---

[5] **Efficient cause**: Aristotle suggested that there were four types of causes. One of these, the efficient cause, was a cause outside of the thing changed or moved. So for example, the efficient cause of a chair is a carpenter.

The fifth proof arises from the ordering of things for we see that some things which lack reason, such as natural bodies, are operated in accordance with a plan. It appears from this that they are operated always or the more frequently in the same way the closer they follow what is the Highest; whence it is clear that they do not arrive at the result by chance but because of a purpose. The things, moreover, that do not have intelligence do not tend toward a result unless directed by some one knowing and intelligent by which all natural things are arranged in accordance with a plan—and this we call God.

In response to the first objection, then, I reply what Augustine says; that since God is entirely good, He would permit evil to exist in His works only if He were so good and omnipotent that He might bring forth good even from the evil. It therefore pertains to the infinite goodness of God that he permits evil to exist and from this bring forth good.

My reply to the second objection is that since nature is ordered in accordance with some defined purpose by the direction of the same superior agent, those things that spring from nature must be dependent upon God, just as upon a first cause. Likewise, what springs from a proposition must be traceable to some higher cause which is not the human reason or will, because this is changeable and defective and everything changeable and liable to non-existence is dependent upon some unchangeable first principle that is necessarily self-existent as has been shown.

Description:_____

_____

_____

Inference:_____

_____

_____

Questions:

1. Aquinas concludes that God's existence is demonstrable because "from any effect whatsoever it can be proved that a corresponding cause exists, if only the effects of it are sufficiently known to us, for since effects depend on causes, the effect being given, it is necessary that a preceding cause exists. Whence, that God exists, although this is not itself known to us, is provable through effects that are known to us." Put this argument in your own words.

2. Aquinas mentions two Bible verses in Article 2: Hebrews 1, which states that faith deals with things unseen, and Romans 1, which suggests that God can be known through nature. How does Aquinas reconcile these passages? What does this means about Aquinas's use of the Bible?

3. Explain the argument of the following passage: "Everything, therefore, is moved by something else. If, then, that by which it is moved, is also moved, this must be moved by something still different, and this, again, by something else. But this process cannot go on to infinity because there would not be any first mover and therefore nothing else in motion..."

4. How would you describe theses argument? Are they religious? philosophical? scientific? And why do you thinks so?

DOCUMENT 8-6

Student Drinking Songs

13TH CENTURY

As in modern times, medieval students sought amusement and temporary relief from the pressures of schoolwork in local taverns. The two songs below give us a feel for the sense of humor of medieval students and reminds us that alcohol has always brought together unlikely members of society. But it could also lead to conflicts. "Town and gown" violence was the inevitable outcome of the highly privileged university students mixing with local townsfolk. Such conflicts were numerous and could have serious consequences. A dispute over a tavern bill led to physical violence and the death of a number of students in Paris in 1228. When the city's justice failed to satisfy masters of the university, they disbanded the school and left Paris for two years. The University of Oxford similarly disbanded their university after town-gown violence in 1209, returning some five years later.

(1)

Some are gaming, some are drinking,
Some are living without thinking;
And of those who make the racket,
Some are stripped of coat and jacket;
Some get clothes of finer feather,
Some are cleaned out altogether;

A Source Book of Mediaeval History, ed. Frederic Austin Ogg (New York: American Book Company, 1908), 359.

No one there dreads death's invasion,
But all drink in emulation[1]

(2)

The Lady drinks, the Lord drinks,
The soldier drinks, the priest drinks,
He drinks, she drinks,
The manservant drinks with the maidservant,
The quick man drinks, the dull man drinks,
The white man drinks, the black man drinks,
The steadfast man drinks, the wavering man drinks,
The simple man drinks, the wise man drinks[2]

Bibit hera, bibit herus
Bibit miles, bibit clerus,
Bibit ille, bibit illa,
Bibit servus cum ancilla,
Bibit velox, bibit piger,
Bibit albus, bibit niger,
Bibit constans, bibit vagus
Bibit rudis, bibit magus

Description:_____

_____

_____

Inference:_____

_____

_____

---

[1] Emulation: the desire to equal or excel others.
[2] My translation. This song is considerably more entertaining in the Latin version that follows.

Chapter 9:
The Americas

DOCUMENT 9-1

Bernal Díaz del Castillo

The True History of the Conquest of New Spain

CA. 1570

"All of us soldiers who were present when this happened cried out that he did right in taking possession of the land in His Majesty's name."
-Bernal Díaz

The following excerpt comes from the memoires of Bernal Díaz del Castillo (ca. 1496—1584), a conquistador who participated in the conquest of the Mexica (Aztec) capital of Tenochtitlan under the leadership of Hernán Cortés. Díaz was a seventy-year-old encomendero and governor in Guatemala when he composed this account. He claims he was driven to relate the "true" account of Cortés's mission in place of the apparent misinformation of Francisco López de Gomara's history of the conquest. The selection below reveals a number of interesting details about the voyage: Cortes's election as captain of the mission, the transition from an authorized trade mission to one of conquest, and Cortés's interaction with the indigenous communities he meets along the way to Mexico.

The True History of the Conquest of New Spain by Bernal Díaz Del Castillo, ed. Genaro García, trans. Alfred Percival Maudslay (London: The Hakluyt Society, 1908), 69, 70, 107-133, 122-126, 134, 135, 158-160. Modernized by Andrew Fogleman.

Themes: violence, technology, European unity, indigenous alliances

After the return of the Captain Juan de Grijalva to Cuba, governor Diego Velásquez understood the richness of these newly discovered lands; he ordered another fleet, much larger than the former one to be sent off, and he had already collected in the Port of Santiago, where he resided, ten ships, four of them were those in which we had returned with Juan de Grijalva, which had at once been careened, and the other six had been got together from other ports in the Island. He had them furnished with provisions consisting of Cassava bread and salt pork, for at the time there were neither sheep nor cattle in the Island of Cuba, as it had been only recently settled. These provisions were to last until we arrived at Havana, for it was at that port that we were to take in our stores, as was afterward done.

I must cease talking of the provisions and tell about the disputes that arose over the choice of a captain for the expedition. There were many debates and much opposition, for some gentlemen said that Vasco Porcallo, a near relation of the Conde de Feria, should be captain, but Diego Velásquez feared that he would rise against him with the fleet, for he was very daring; others said that Agustin Bermudez or Antonio Velásquez Borrejo, or Bernadino Velásquez, kinsman of Diego Velásquez should go in command.

Most of us soldiers who were there said that we should prefer to go again under Juan de Grijalva, for he was a good captain, and there was no fault to be found either with his person or his capacity for command.

While things were going on in the way I have related, two great favorites of Diego Velásquez named Andrés de Duero, the Governor's secretary, and Amador de Lares, His Majesty's accountant, secretly formed a partnership with a gentleman named Hernando Cortés, a native of Medellin, who held a grant of Indians in the Island. A short while before Cortés had married a lady named Catalina Juarez la

Marcayda; this lady was sister of a certain Juan Juarez who after the conquest of New Spain was a settler at Mexico. As far as I know, and from what other say, it was a love match. On this matter of the marriage other persons who saw it have had much to say, and for that reason I will not touch any more on this delicate subject.

I will go on to tell about this partnership, it came about in this manner: These two great favorites of Velásquez agreed that they would get him to appoint Cortés Captain General of the whole fleet, and that they would divide between the three of them, the spoil of gold, silver and jewels which might fall to Cortés share. For secretly Diego Velásquez was sending to trade and not to form a settlement, as was apparent afterwards from the instructions given about it, although it was announced and published that the expedition was for the purpose of founding a settlement.

When this arrangement had been made, Duero and the accountant went to work in such a way with Diego Velásquez, and addressed such flattering words to him, praising Cortés highly, as the very man for the position of Captain, as in addition to being energetic he knew how to command and ensure respect, and as one who would be faithful in everything entrusted to him, both in regard to the fleet and in everything else, pointing out too, that he was his godson, for Velásquez was his sponsor when Cortés married Doña Catalina Juarez, that they persuaded him to choose [Cortés] as Captain General...

[With Cortés selected as captain, Velásquez's fleets depart in search of Mexico.]

On the 12th March, 1519, we arrived with all the fleet at the Rio de Grijalva, which is also called Tabasco, and as we already knew from our experience with Grijalva that vessels of large size could not enter into the river, the larger vessels were anchored out at sea, and from the smaller vessels and boats all the soldiers were landed at the Cape of the Palms (as they were in Grijalva's time) which was about half a league distant from the town of Tabasco. The riverbanks and the mangrove thickets were swarming with Indians, at which those of us who had not been here in Grijalva's time were much astonished.

In addition to this there were assembled in the town more than twelve thousand warriors all prepared to make war on us, for at this time that town was of considerable importance and other large towns were subject to it and they had all made preparations for war and were well supplied with the arms which they are accustomed to use.

The reason for this was that the people of Potonchan and Lazaro and the other towns in that neighborhood had looked upon the people of Tabasco as cowards, and had told them so to their faces, because they had given Grijalva the gold and jewels which I have spoken about in an earlier chapter, and they said that they were too faint hearted to attack us although they had more towns and more warriors than the people of Potonchan and Lazaro. This they said to annoy them and added that they in their towns had attacked us and killed fifty-six of us. So on account of these taunts which had been uttered, the people of Tabasco had determined to take up arms.

When Cortés saw them drawn up ready for war he told Aguilar the interpreter, who spoke the language of Tabasco well, to ask the Indians who passed near us, in a large canoe and who looked like chiefs, what they were so much disturbed about, and to tell them that we had not come to do them any harm, but were willing to give them some of the things we had brought with us and to treat them like brothers, and we prayed them not to begin a war as they would regret it, and much else was said to them about keeping the peace. However, the more Aguilar talked to them the more violent they became, and they said that they would kill us all if we entered their town, and that it was fortified all round with fences and barricades of large trunks of trees.

Aguilar spoke to them again and asked them to keep the peace, and allow us to take water and barter our goods with them for food, and permit us to tell the Calachones things which would be to their advantage and to the service of God our Lord, but they still persisted in saying that if we advanced beyond the palm trees they would kill us.

When Cortés saw the state of affairs he ordered the boats and small vessels to be got ready and ordered three cannon to be placed in each boat and divided the crossbowmen and musketeers among the boats. We remembered that when we were here with Grijalva we had found a narrow path which ran across some streams from the palm grove to the town, and Cortés ordered three soldiers to find out in the night if that path ran right up to the houses, and not to delay in bringing the news, and these men found out that it did lead there. After making a thorough examination of our surroundings the rest of the day was spent in arranging how and in what order we were to go in the boats.

The next morning we had our arms in readiness and after hearing mass Cortés ordered the Captain Alonzo de Avila and a hundred soldiers among whom were ten crossbowmen, to go by the little path which led to the town, and, as soon as he heard the guns fired, to attack the town on one side while he attacked it on the other. Cortex himself and all the other Captains and the soldiers went in the boats and light draft vessels up the river. When the Indian warriors who were on the banks and among the mangroves saw that we were really on the move, they came after us with a great many canoes with intent to prevent our going ashore at the landing place, and the whole river bank appeared to be covered with Indian warriors carrying all different arms which they use, and blowing trumpets and shells and sounding drums. When Cortés saw how matters stood he ordered us to wait a little and not to fire any shots from guns or crossbows or cannon, for as he wished to be justified in all that he might do he made another appeal to the Indians through the interpreter Aguilar, in the presence of the King Notary, Diego de Godoy, asking the Indians to allow us to land and take water and speak to them about God and about His majesty, and adding that should they make war on us, that if in defending ourselves some should be killed and others hurt, theirs would be the fault and the burden and it would not lie with us, but they went on threatening that if we landed they would kill us.

Then they boldly began to let fly arrows at us, and made signals with their drums, and like valiant men they surrounded us with their canoes, and they all attacked us with such a shower of arrows that they kept us in the water in some parts to our waists. As there was much mud and swamp at that place we could not easily get clear of it, and so many Indians fell on us, that what with some hurling their lances with all their might and others shooting arrows at us, we could not reach the land as soon as we wished.

While Cortés was fighting he lost a shoe in the mud and could not find it again, and he got on shore with one foot bare. Presently someone picked that shoe out of the mud and he put it on again.

While this was happening to Cortés, all of us Captains as well as soldiers, with the cry of "Santiago," fell upon the Indians and forced them to retreat, but they did not fall back far, as they sheltered themselves behind great barriers and stockades formed of thick logs until we pulled them apart and got to one of the small gateways of the town. There we attacked them again, and we pushed them along through a street to where other defenses had been erected, and there they turned on us and met us face to face and fought most valiantly making their greatest efforts, shouting and whistling and crying out "al calacheoni," "al calacheoni," which in their language meant an order to kill or capture our Captain. While we were thus surrounded by them, Alonzo de Avila and his soldiers came up.

As I have already said they came from the Palm grove by land and could not arrive sooner on account of the swamps and creeks. Their delay was really unavoidable, just as we also had been delayed over the summons of the Indians to surrender, and in breaking openings in barricades, so as to enable us to attack them. Now we all joined together to drive the enemy out of their strongholds, and we compelled them to retreat, but like brave warriors they kept on shooting showers of arrows and fire-hardened darts, and never turned their backs on us until [we gained] a great court with chambers and large halls, and three Idol houses, where they had already carried all the goods they possessed. Cortés then ordered us to halt, and not to follow on and overtake the enemy in their flight.

There and then Cortés took possession of that land for His Majesty, performing the act in His Majesty's name. It was done in this way; he drew his sword and as a sign of possession he made three cuts in a huge tree called a *Ceiba*, which stood in the court of that great square, and cried that if any person should raise objection, that he would defend that right with the sword and shield which he held in his hands.

All of us soldiers who were present when this happened cried out that he did right in taking possession of the land in His Majesty's name, and that we should aid him should any person say otherwise. This act was done in the presence of the Royal Notary. The partisans of Diego Velásquez chose to grumble at this act of taking possession.

I call to mind that in that hard fought attack which the Indians made on us, they wounded fourteen soldiers, and they gave me an arrow wound in the thigh, but it was only a slight would; and we found eighteen Indians dead in the water where we disembarked. We slept there [in the great square] that night with guards and sentinels on alert.

…I have already said that we captured five Indians during the battle of whom two were captains. When Aguilar spoke to these men he found out from what they said that they were fit persons to be sent as messengers, and he advised Cortés to free them, so that they might go and talk to the caciques[1] of the town and any other they might see. These two messengers were given green and blue beads, and Aguilar spoke many pleasant and flattering words to them, telling them that

---

[1] **Caciques**: native chiefs.

they had nothing to fear as we wished to treat them like brothers, that it was their own fault that they had made war on us and that now they had better collect together all the caciques of the different towns as we wished to talk to them, and he gave them much other advice in a gentle way as to gain their good will. The messengers went off willingly and spoke to the caciques and chief men, and told them all we wished them to know about our desire for peace.

When our envoys had been listened to, it was settled among them that fifteen Indian slaves, all with stained faces and ragged cloaks and loin cloths, should at once be sent to us with fowls and baked fish and maize cakes. When these men came before Cortés he received them graciously, but Aguilar the interpreter asked them rather angrily why then had come with their faces in that state, that it looked more as though they came to fight than to settle for peace; and he told them to go back to the caciques and inform them that if they wished for peace in the way we offered it, chieftains should come to obtain it, as was always the custom, and that they should not send slaves. But even these painted-faced slaves were treated with consideration by us and blue beads were sent by them in sign of peace, and to soothe their feelings.

They next day thirty Indian Chieftains, clad in good cloaks, came to visit us and brought fowls, fish, fruit and maize cakes, and asked leave from Cortés to burn and bury the bodies of the dead who had fallen in the recent battles, so that they should not smell badly or be eaten by lions and tigers. Permission was at once given them and they hastened to bring many people to bury and burn the bodies according to their customs.

Cortés learnt from the caciques that over eight hundred men were missing, not counting those who had been carried off wounded. They said that they could not stay with us either to discuss the matter or make peace, for on the morrow the chieftains and leaders of all the towns would have assembled, and that then they would agree about a peace.

As Cortés was very wise about everything, he said laughing, to us soldiers who happened to be in his company, "Do you know, gentlemen, that it seems to me that the Indians are terrified at the horses and may think that they and the cannon alone make war on them. I have thought of something which will confirm this belief, and that is to bring the mare belonging to Juan Sedeno, which foaled the other day on board ship, and tie her up where I am now standing also to bring the stallion of Ortiz the musician, which is very excitable, near enough to scent the mare, and when he has scented her to lead each of them off separately so that the caciques who are coming shall not hear the horses neighing as they approach, not until they are standing before me and are talking to me." We did just as Cortés ordered and brought the horse and mare, and the horse soon detected the scent of her in Cortés's quarters. In addition to this Cortés ordered the largest cannon that we possessed to be loaded with a large ball and a good charge of powder.

About mid-day forty Indians arrived, all of them caciques of good bearing, wearing rich mantles such as are used by them. They saluted Cortés and all of us, and brought incense and fumigated all of us who were presented, and they asked pardon for their past behavior, and said that henceforth they would be friendly.

Cortés, through Aguilar the Interpreter, answered them in a rather grave manner, as though he were angry, that they well knew how many times he had asked them to maintain peace, that the fault was theirs, and that now they deserved to be put to death, they and all the people of their towns, but that as we were the vassals of a great King and Lord named the Emperor Don Carlos, who had sent us to these countries, and ordered us to help and favor those who would enter his royal service, that if thy were now as well disposed as they said they were, that we could take this course, but that if they were not, some of those *Tepustles* (cannons) would jump out and kill them. For they call iron *Tepustle* in their language. Cortés continued saying that some of the *Tepustles* were still angry because they had made war on us. At this moment the order was secretly given to put a match to the cannon which had been loaded, and it went off with such a thunderclap as was wanted, and the ball went buzzing over the hills, and as it was mid-day and very still it made a great noise, and the caciques were terrified on hearing it. As they had never seen anything like it they believed what Cortés had told them was true. Then Cortés told them, through Aguilar, not to be afraid for he had given orders that no harm should be done to them.

Just then the horses that had scented the mare was brought and tied up not far distant from where Cortés was talking to the caciques, and, as the mare had been tied up at the place where Cortés and the Indians were talking, the horse began to paw the ground and neigh and become wild with excitement, looking all the time toward the Indians and the place whence the scent of the mare had reached him, and the caciques thought that he was roaring at them and they were terrified. Then Cortés observed their state of mind, he rose from his seat and went to the horse and told two orderlies to lead it far away and said to the Indians that he had told the horse not to be angry as they were friendly and wished to make peace.

While this was going on there arrived more than thirty Indian carriers, whom the natives call *Tamenes*, who brought a meal of fowls and fish and fruits and other food, and it appears that they had lagged behind and could not reach us at the same time as the caciques. Cortés had a long conversation with these chieftains and caciques and they told him that they would all come on the next day and would bring a present and would discuss other matters, and then they went away quite contented.

Early the next morning, the 15th March, 1519, many caciques and chiefs of Tabasco and the neighboring towns arrived and paid great respect to us all, and they brought a present of gold, consisting of four diadems and some gold lizards, and two [ornaments] like little dogs, and earrings, and five ducks, and two masks with Indian faces and two gold soles for sandals, an some other things of little value. I do not remember how much the things were worth; and they brought cloth, such as they make and wear which was quilted stuff. My readers will have heard from those who know those provinces that there is nothing of much value in it.

This present, however, was worth nothing in caparison with the twenty women that were given us, among them was one very excellent woman called Doña Marina, for so she was named when she became a Christian....

... Doña Marina knew the language of Coatzacoalcos, which is that common to Mexico, and she knew the language of Tabasco, as did also Geronimo de Aguilar,[2] which spoke the language of Yucatan and Tabasco, which is one and the same. As a result, these two could understand one another clearly, and Aguilar translated into Castilian for Cortés.

This was the great beginning of our conquests and thus, thanks be to God, things prospered with us. I have made a point of explaining this matter, because without the help of Doña Marina we could not have understood the language of New Spain and Mexico....

When the partisans of Diego Velásquez realized the fact that we had chosen Cortés for our Captain and Chief Justice, and had founded a town and chosen the Alcaldes and Regidores, and appointed Pedro de

---

[2] **Geronimo de Aguilar**: a Spanish friar who had been captured and enslaved by the Maya. During his captivity he learned to speak the languages of Yucatan and Tabasco. Once freed by Cortés, his language skills played an essential role in the conquest of Mexico.

Alvarado as captain [of expeditions] and named the Alguacil Mayor and Maestro de Campo and had done all that I have narrated, they were angry and furious and they began to excite factions and meetings and to use abusive language about Cortés and those of us who had elected him, saying that it was not right to do these things unless all the captains and soldiers who had come on the expedition had been parties to it; that Diego Velásquez had given Cortés no such powers, only authority to trade, and that we partisans of Cortés should take care that our insolence did not so increase as to bring us to blows. Then Cortés secretly told Juan de Escalante that we should make him produce the instructions given him by Diego Velásquez. Upon this Cortés drew them from his bosom and gave them to the King's scribe to read aloud. In these instructions were the words: "As soon as you have gained all you can by trading, you will return" and the document was signed by Diego Velásquez and countersigned by his Secretary, Andres de Duero. We begged Cortés to cause this document to be attached to the deed recording the power we had given him, as well as the proclamation which he issued in the Island of Cuba. And this was done so that his Majesty in Spain should in his royal service, and that he should not bring against us anything but the truth; and it was a good precaution, seeing how we were treated in Spain by Don Juan Rodriguez de Fonseca, Bishop of Burgos and Archbishop of Rosano (for such were his titles) who we knew for certain, took steps to destroy us as I shall tell later on.

After this was done, these same friends and dependents of Diego Velásquez returned to Cortés to say that it was not right that he should have been chosen Captain without their consent and that they did not wish to remain under his command, but to return at once to the Island of Cuba. Cortés replied that he would detain no one by force, and that to anyone who came to ask leave to return he would willing grant it, even although he were left alone. With this some of them were quieted, but not Juan Velásquez de Leon who was a relation of Diego Velásquez, and Diego de Ordas, and Escobar, whom we called the

Page, for he had been brought up by Diego Velásquez, and Pedro Escudero and other friends of Diego Velásquez; and it came to this, that they refused all obedience to Cortés. With our assistance, Cortés determined to make prisoners of Juan Velásquez de Leon, and Diego de Ordas, and Escobar the Page, and Pedro Escudero and others whose names I do not remember, and we took care that the others should create no disturbance. These men remained prisoners for some days, in chains and under guard....

Being in Cempoala, as I have stated, and discussing with Cortés questions of warfare, and our advance into the country, and going on from one thing to another, we, who were his friends, counseled him, although others opposed it, not to leave a single ship in the port, but to destroy them all at once, so as to leave no source of trouble behind, lest, when we were inland, others of our people should rebel like the last; besides, we should gain much additional strength from the masters, pilots and sailors who numbered nearly one hundred men, and they would be better employed helping us to watch and fight than remaining in port.

As far as I can make out, this matter of destroying the ships which we suggested to Cortés during our conversation, had already been decided on by him, but he wished it to appear as though it cam from us, so that if any one should ask him to pay for the ships, he could say that he had acted on our advice and we would all be concerned in their payment. Then he sent Juan de Escalante (who was chief Alguacil[3] and person of distinguished bravery and a great friend of Cortés, and an enemy of Diego Velásquez, because he had not given him good Indians in the Island of Cuba) to Villa Rica with orders to bring on shore all the anchors, cables, sails, and everything else on board which might prove useful, and then to destroy the ships and preserve nothing but the boats, and that the pilots, sailing masters, and sailors, who were old and no use for war, should stay at the town, and with the two nets they

---

[3] **Chief Alguacil**: A Spanish law officer similar to a sheriff or chief constable.

possessed should undertake the fishing for there was always fish in that harbor, although they were not very plentiful. Juan de Escalante did all that he was told to do, and soon after arrived at Cempoala with the company of sailors, whom he had brought from the ship, and some of them turned out to be very good soldiers.

When this was done, Cotes sent to summon all the caciques of the hill towns who were allied to us and in rebellion against Montezuma, and told them how they must give their service to the Spaniards who remained in Villa Rica, to finish building the church, fortress and houses, and Cortés took Juan de Escalante by the hand before them all, and said to them: "This is my brother" and told them to do whatever he should order them, and that should they need protection or assistance against Mexicans, they should go to him and he would come in person to their assistance.

All the caciques willingly promised to do what might be asked of them, and I remember that they at once fumigated Juan de Escalante with incense, although he did not wish it done. I have already said that he was a man well qualified for any post and a great friend of Cortés, so he could place him in command of the town and harbor with confidence, so that if Diego Velazquez should send an expedition there, it would meet with resistance. I must leave him here and go on with my story.

It is here that the historian Gomara says that when Cortés ordered the ships to be scuttled[4] that he did not dare to let the soldiers know that he wished to go to Mexico in search of the great Montezuma. It was not as he states, for what sort of Spaniards would we be, not to wish to go ahead, but to linger in places where there was neither profit nor fighting? This same Gomara also says that Pedro de Ircio remained as captain in Vera Cruz; he was misinformed. I repeat that it was Juan de Escalante who remained there as Captain and chief Alguacil of New

---

[4] **Scuttled**: to cut a hole or holes in a ship's hull, thus making it inoperable.

Spain, and that so far, Pedro de Ircio had not been given any position whatever—not even charge of a company....

Description:_____

_____

_____

Inference:_____

_____

_____

Questions:

1. In the middle of the fight at Tobasco, Cortés took possession of the land for his majesty. Why was this a controversial act on his part?

2. How did Cortés use European animals and technologies to his advantage when fighting and negotiating with the Indians?

3. How would you characterize Cortés's treatment of the Indians he encountered?

4. Was Cortés's party unified or divided? Find examples to support your answer.

5. Doña Marina and Geronimo de Aguilar were chance acquisitions by Cortés. Why were they so important to the mission? What would the mission have been like had they not been there?

Chapter 10:
Renaissance Humanism and the Reformation

DOCUMENT 10-1

Desiderius Erasmus

To Cornelius Gerard

CA. 1492

Desiderius Erasmus of Rotterdam (1466—1536) was a priest, social critic, and Dutch Renaissance humanist. In true humanist fashion, Erasmus labored to make ancient texts available to contemporary readers. He edited the writings of Church Fathers, such as St. Jerome, St. Hilary, St. Augustine, Irenaeus, Origin, and St. Chrysostom; as well as secular Roman writers, including Cato, Plutarch, Seneca, and Cicero. Erasmus also made critical versions New Testament available. His Novum Instrumentum (New Testament) was the first published Latin-facing-Greek edition of the New Testament, allowing readers to compare Erasmus's Latin version of the New Testament to the Greek original. He was a merciless social and religious critic, exposing the foibles of his contemporaries and the failings of the Church in numerous popular writings. Erasmus, however, remained a committed Catholic and hoped to reform the Church from within. He recoiled from the actions

---

Desiderius Erasmus, "Erasmus to Cornelius," in *The Epistles of Erasmus*, Trans. Francis Morgan Nichols (New York, Longmans, Green, and Co., 1901), 1:65-68.

of Luther and other Protestant contemporaries, despite corresponding with them through letters. Indeed, letter writing as a whole was a critical part of the humanist movement's success. The selection below, primarily dealing with poetry, shows how like-minded humanists circulated texts, advertised authors, and reinforced the negative idea of a "middle age" between the ancient period and their own. The letters themselves were also an exercise in writing in the ancient literary forms and expressions they cherished.

Themes: letter writing, Greek and Latin, pursuit of ancient literature

To Cornelius Gerard,[1]

Having already, as I think, sufficiently answered your letter, I am induced by the excess of my love for you to write something for you to answer in return.... I find it most difficult to say, how much pleasure both your *Apologeticus* and your letters have given me. I pray you therefore, to make me always a partner in your studies; and moreover, if there are any others where you are, not unskilled in the poetic art, be so good as to give us some notice of them. It will be a pleasure to us in the first place, and we also shall be able to make their praised know here.

I see that in your poem you mention a certain Hieronymus, who has passed five and twenty years in Italy and Paris in poetical studies, and take pains to comment on an Epitaph of his, but too briefly to give us a clear conception of man's ability. I shall be obliged if you will send us some larger and more striking proof of his genius. But I am surprised when you say that he is the only writer who has kept to the footprints of the Ancients. For, not to speak of yourself, I think I see a great many most learned men of our own time who make no slight approach to the ancient eloquence. The first that occurs to me is Rodolphus Agricola the preceptor of my school-master, Alexander Hegius, a man

---

[1] **Cornelius Gerard**: A Dutch priest (Augustinian Canon) who began corresponding with Erasmus by sending him some of his poetry.

eminently learned in all the liberal arts, and specially skillful in rhetoric and poetry, and finally expert in Greek as well as Latin. Alexander is himself no degenerate disciple of such a master; and represents with so much elegance the style of the ancients, that if his verse were before you without title, you might easily mistake the author [for them]. He too is not altogether ignorant of Greek. Again, Antony Gang and his ally Frederick Morman have dignified Westphalia by their scholarship and are both worthy in my judgment to be remembered by posterity. Moreover I am far from thinking that Bartholomew of Cologne should be excluded from the list of men of letters. Neither should I pass over over in silence our own William of Gouda, your kinsman, if it were not for his close union with myself both as a friend and as a student. But I prefer to hear his praises from you, as I might be supposed to be misled by my personal feelings. All these are seen or have been seen by our own age, and produced by our own Germany. If you are curious about their poems I will undertake that they shall fly to you forthwith.

But if we come to Italy, where do you find more observance of ancient elegance than in Laurentius Valla, or Philephus, where more eloquence than in Aeneas Silvius, Augustinus Dathus, Guarino, Poggio or Gasperino? And all these as everybody knows, lived almost down to our own times.

But the revolution in literature seems to me to be the same as that which has taken place in the more mechanical arts. For we have the testimony of almost all the poets, that in early times there were famous artist of every kind; but if you look at the pictures, sculptures, buildings, or monuments of any craft beyond the last two or three hundred years, you will, I think, be surprised and amused at the excessive rudeness of the work, whereas again in our own age there is no sort of art that has not been produced by the industry of the craftsman. In like manner it is certain that in early ages the study of eloquence, as of other arts, was most flourishing, and afterwards, as the obstinacy of barbarians[2] increased, it disappeared.... Our Thalia[3] was well nigh extinct when Laurentius and Philelphus by their admirable erudition saved her from perishing. The books of the former, which are called *Elegantiae*, will show you with what zeal he exerted himself both to expose the absurdities of the Barbarians and to bring back into use the observances of Orators and Poets long covered with the dust of oblivion. If you have already read them, as I suspect, there is no need of my advising you to do so; if not, I not only exhort but entreat you to begin their perusal. You will never regret the pains you spend upon them. If you wish to see them, ask John, who is devoted to you....

Farewell, most reverend father. You will see by William's letter what is his feeling towards you. If there are any persons in your company who will join with your in love for me, I beg you to salute them in my name. Farewell.

Description:_____

_____

_____

Inference:_____

_____

_____

Questions:

1. Based on this letter, how did humanism spread?

2. What literary genres and languages were important to humanists like Erasmus?

---

[2] **Obstinacy of the barbarians**: This refers to the "fall of Rome" or the Germanic migrations that humanists associated with the beginning of the Middle Ages and an end of the Ancient Roman period.
[3] **Thalia**: Greek muse of poetry.

3. Humanists invented the idea of a negative "middle age" between their day and the ancient period. Does Erasmus suggest such an idea in his letter?

DOCUMENT 10-2

Niccolò Machiavelli

The Prince

1513

"It is necessary for a prince to understand how to avail himself of the beast and the man." -Machiavelli

Niccolò Machiavelli (1469—1527) was a Florentine diplomat, humanist, and political theorist. He witnessed the expulsion of the Medici family from his city in 1494 and the return of the Florentine Republic. Following the Medici ouster, Machiavelli served in the office of the Florentine chancery, drawing up official government documents and participating in diplomatic missions for the republic. When the Medici returned to power in 1512, Machiavelli lost his post and was temporarily imprisoned and tortured for his association with the Republic. He then retired to his villa outside of Florence in exile and composed The Prince, a political treatise presenting strategies for new Princes on how to keep power. He dedicated The Prince to Lorenzo de Medici, a member of the ruling Florentine Medici family, in hopes of gaining a position at the Medici court. It is unclear if Lorenzo ever read The Prince but contemporaries who did read it were shocked and intrigued by its originality.

Themes: power, leadership, morality,

The Prince by Nicolo Machiavelli, trans. W. K. Marriott (New York: E. P. Dutton, 1908), 54, 58, 59, 133-137, 141-145. Modernized by Andrew Fogleman.

Concerning new principalities which are acquired either by the arms of others or by good fortune

It is hard for states that rise unexpectedly to have foundations and relations with other states that are not easily overturned; unless, as is said, those who unexpectedly become princes are men of so much ability that they know they have to be prepared at once to hold that which fortune has thrown into their laps, and that those foundations, which others have laid before they became princes, they must lay afterwards....

When Duke [Cesare Borgia] occupied the Romagna he found it under the rule of weak masters, who rather plundered their subjects than ruled them, and gave them more cause for disunion than for union, so that the country was full of robbery, quarrels, and every kind of violence; and so, wishing to bring back peace and obedience to authority, he considered it necessary to give it a good governor. Thereupon he promoted Messer Ramiro d'Orco [de Lorqua], a swift and cruel man, to whom he gave the fullest power. This man in a short time restored peace and unity with the greatest success. Afterwards the duke considered that it was not advisable to confer such excessive authority, for he had no doubt but that he would become odious, so he set up a court of judgment in the country, under a most excellent president, wherein all cities had their advocates. And because he knew that the past severity had caused some hatred against himself, so, to clear himself in the minds of the people, and gain them entirely to himself, he desired to show that, if any cruelty had been practiced, it had not originated with him, but in the natural sternness of the minister. Under this pretense he took Ramiro, and one morning caused him to be executed and left on the piazza at Cesena with the block and a bloody knife at his side. The barbarity of this spectacle caused the people to be at once satisfied and dismayed.

But let us return whence we started. The duke, had now become sufficiently powerful and partly secured from immediate dangers by having armed himself in his own way, and in a great measure had crushed those forces in his vicinity that could injure him....

Concerning cruelty and clemency, and whether it is better to be loved than feared

Coming now to the other qualities mentioned above, I say that every prince ought to desire to be considered clement and not cruel. Nevertheless he ought to take care not to misuse this clemency. Cesare Borgia was considered cruel; notwithstanding, his cruelty reconciled the Romagna, unified it, and restored it to peace and loyalty. And if this be rightly considered, he will be seen to have been much more merciful than the Florentine people, who, to avoid a reputation for cruelty, permitted Pistoia to be destroyed. Therefore a prince, so long as he keeps his subjects united and loyal, ought not to mind the reproach of cruelty; because with a few examples he will be more merciful than those who, through too much mercy, allow disorders to arise, from which follow murders or robberies; for these are wont to injure the whole people, whilst those executions which originate with a prince offend the individual only.

And of all princes, it is impossible for the new prince to avoid the imputation of cruelty, owing to new states being full of dangers.... He ought to be slow to believe and to act, nor should he himself show fear, but proceed in a temperate manner with prudence and humanity, so that too much confidence may not make him incautious and too much distrust render him intolerable.

Upon this a question arises: whether it be better to be loved than feared or feared than loved? It may be answered that one should wish to be both, but, because it is difficult to unite them in one person, is much safer to be feared than loved, when, of the two, either must be dispensed with. Because this is to be asserted in general of men, that they are ungrateful, fickle, false, cowardly, covetous, and as long as you succeed they are yours entirely; they will offer you their blood, property, life and children, as is said above, when the need is far distant; but when it approaches they turn against you. And that prince who, relying entirely on their promises, has neglected other precautions, is ruined; because friendships that are obtained by payments, and not by greatness or nobility of mind, may indeed be earned, but they are not secured, and in time of need cannot be relied upon; and men have less scruple in offending one who is beloved than one who is feared, for love is preserved by the link of obligation which, owing to the baseness of men, is broken at every opportunity for their advantage; but fear preserves you by a dread of punishment which never fails.

Nevertheless a prince ought to inspire fear in such a way that, if he does not win love, he avoids hatred; because he can endure very well being feared whilst he is not hated, which will always be as long as he abstains from the property of his citizens and subjects and from their women. But when it is necessary for him to proceed against the life of someone, he must do it on proper justification and for manifest cause, but above all things he must keep his hands off the property of others, because men more quickly forget the death of their father than the loss of their patrimony. Besides, pretexts for taking away the property are never wanting; for he who has once begun to live by robbery will always find pretexts for seizing what belongs to others; but reasons for taking life, on the contrary, are more difficult to find and sooner lapse. But when a prince is with his army, and has under control a multitude of soldiers, then it is quite necessary for him to embrace a reputation for cruelty, for without it he would never hold his army united or disposed to its duties.

Among the wonderful deeds of Hannibal this one is enumerated: that having led an enormous army, composed of many various races of men, to fight in foreign lands, no dissensions arose either among them or against the prince, whether in his bad or in his good fortune. This arose from nothing else than his inhuman cruelty, which, with his boundless valor, made him revered and terrible in the sight of his soldiers, but without that cruelty, his other virtues were not sufficient to produce this effect. And shortsighted writers admire his deeds from one point of view and from another condemn the principal cause of them....

Returning to the question of being feared or loved, I come to the conclusion that, men loving according to their own will and fearing according to that of the prince, a wise prince should establish himself on that which is in his own control and not in that of others; he must endeavor only to avoid hatred, as is noted.

Concerning the way in which princes should keep faith

Every one admits how praiseworthy it is in a prince to keep faith, and to live with integrity and not with deceit. Nevertheless our experience has been that those princes who have done great things have held good faith of little account, and have known how to circumvent the intellect of men by craft, and in the end have overcome those who have relied on their word. You must know there are two ways of contesting, the one by the law, the other by force; the first method is proper to men, the second to beasts; but because the first is frequently not sufficient, it is necessary to have recourse to the second. Therefore it is necessary for a prince to understand how to avail himself of the beast and the man. This has been figuratively taught to princes by ancient writers, who describe how Achilles and many other princes of old were given to the Centaur Chiron to nurse, who brought them up in his discipline; which means solely that, as they had for a teacher one who was half beast and half man, so it is necessary for a prince to know how to make use of both natures, and that one without the other is not durable. A prince, therefore, being compelled knowingly to adopt the beast, ought to choose the fox and the lion; because the lion cannot defend himself against snares and the fox cannot defend himself against wolves. Therefore, it is necessary to be a fox to discover the snares and a lion to terrify the wolves. Those who rely simply on the lion do not understand what they are about. Therefore a wise lord cannot, nor ought he to, keep his word when keeping it may be turned against him, and when the reasons that caused him to give it no longer exist. If men were entirely good this advice would not hold, but because they are bad, and will not keep faith with you, you too are not bound to observe it with them. Nor will a prince ever lack a legitimate reason to excuse this nonobservance. Of this endless modern examples could be given, showing how many treaties and engagements have been made void and of no effect through the faithlessness of princes; and so he who has known best how to employ the fox has succeeded best.

But it is necessary to know well how to disguise this characteristic, and to be a great pretender and trickster; and men are so simple, and so subject to present necessities, that he who seeks to deceive will always find someone who will allow himself to be deceived. One recent example I cannot pass over in silence. Pope Alexander VI did nothing else but deceive men, nor ever thought of doing otherwise, and he always found victims; for there never was a man who had greater power in asserting [one thing], or who with greater oaths would affirm a thing, yet would observe it less; nevertheless his deceits always succeeded according to his wishes, because he well understood this side of mankind.

Therefore it is unnecessary for a prince to have all the good qualities I have enumerated, but it is very necessary to appear to have them. And I shall dare to say this also, that to have them and always to observe them is injurious, and that to appear to have them is useful; to appear merciful, faithful, humane, religious, upright, and to be so, but with a mind so framed that should you require not to be so, you may be able and know how to change to the opposite.

And you have to understand this, that a prince, especially a new one, cannot observe all those things for which men are esteemed, being often forced, in order to maintain the state, to act contrary to faith, friendship, humanity, and religion. Therefore it is necessary for him to have a mind ready to turn itself accordingly as the winds and variations of fortune force it, yet, as I have said above, not to diverge from the good if he can avoid doing so, but, if compelled, then to know how to set about it.

For this reason a prince ought to take care that he never lets anything slip from his lips that is not replete with the above-named five qualities, that he may appear to him who sees and hears him altogether merciful, faithful, humane, upright, and religious. There is nothing more necessary to appear to have than this last quality, inasmuch as men judge generally more by the eye than by the hand, because it belongs to everybody to see you, to few to come in touch with you. Every one sees what you appear to be, few really know what you are, and those few dare not oppose themselves to the opinion of the many, who have the majesty of the state to defend them; and in the actions of all men, and especially of princes, which it is not prudent to challenge, one judges by the result.

For that reason, let a prince have the credit of conquering and holding his state, the means will always be considered honest, and he will be praised by everybody because the people are always taken by what a thing seems to be and by what comes of it.

Description:_____

_____

_____

Inference:_____

_____

_____

Questions:

1. Borgia's use of Messer Ramiro d'Orco caused the people of the Romagna to be both "satisfied and dismayed." what was Borgia's strategy here, and was it effective?

2. What is man's nature according to Machiavelli? How does this view influence his advice to the Prince?

3. Machiavelli states that it is much safer to be feared than loved. Why?

4. Is being feared the same thing as being hated?

5. Machiavelli claims that it is important for a prince to have good qualities and to appear to have them. Why this distinction? According to Machiavelli, what is the most important quality to appear to have?

6. Consider the following recommendation: "Therefore a prince, so long as he keeps his subjects united and loyal, ought not to mind the reproach of cruelty; because with a few examples he will be more merciful than those who, through too much mercy, allow disorders to arise, from which follow murders or robberies." Does this seem like good advice?

DOCUMENT 10-3

Martin Luther

Ninety-Five Theses on the Power of Indulgences

1517

No event is more popularly associated with the Protestant Reformation than the posting of Martin Luther's ninety-five theses on indulgences at All Saints' Church in Wittenberg. Whether or not this event took place, Luther's call for a debate on the power of indulgences is often presented in textbooks as the brash and defiant act that set the Reformation in motion. And yet as we have seen, debate at medieval universities was a standard, indeed one might say formulaic, part of medieval educational culture. As a professor of Theology at the University of Wittenberg, Luther used an expected method for probing controversial ideas among his academic peers. But if the venue was common, the content was charged with real animus. Luther's theses reveal rage over the corrosive spiritual effects of the practice of indulgences. According to Luther, indulgences separated sinners from the care of their local priests, encouraged the evasion of just punishment for wrongdoing, and set up material goals (such as the building St. Peter's Basilica) over spiritual ones.

Themes: sin, penance, mortification of the flesh, money, spiritual hierarchy

Disputation of Doctor Martin Luther on the Power and Efficacy of Indulgences October 31, 1517. Out of love for the truth and the desire to bring it to light, the following propositions will be discussed at

Martin Luther, "95 Theses on the Power of Indulgences," in *Works of Martin Luther*, trans. & Eds. Adolph Spaeth, L.D. Reed, Henry Eyster Jacobs, et al. (Philadelphia: A. J. Holman Company, 1915), 1: 29-38. Modernized by Andrew Fogleman.

Wittenberg, under the presidency of the Reverend Father Martin Luther, Master of Arts and of Sacred Theology, and Lecturer in Ordinary[1] on the same at that place. Wherefore he requests that those who are unable to be present and debate orally with us, may do so by letter. In the Name our Lord Jesus Christ. Amen.

1. Our Lord and Master Jesus Christ, when He said, "Repent" (Mt. 4:17), willed that the whole life of believers should be one of repentance.

2. This word cannot be understood to mean sacramental penance, that is, confession and satisfaction, which is administered by the priests.

3. Yet it does not mean only inward repentance; such inward repentance is worthless unless it produces various mortifications of the flesh.[2]

5. The pope does not desire, and indeed cannot remove, any penalties other than those imposed by him or by that of the Canons.

7. God removes guilt from no one unless he also humbles him in all things and brings him into subjection to His vicar, the priest.

20. Therefore when the pope uses the words "full remission of all penalties" he does not actually mean "of all," but only of those he imposed.

21. Therefore those preachers of indulgences are wrong, who say that by the pope's indulgence a man is freed from every penalty, and saved.

22. As a matter of fact, the pope removes from souls in purgatory no penalty, which, according to canon law, they should have paid in this life.

---

[1] **Ordinary**: the term for a medieval university's core courses taught by regular faculty.

[2] **Mortifications of the flesh**: the suppression of bodily desires.

36. Every truly repentant Christian has a right to full remission of penalty and guilt, even without indulgence letters.

37. Every true Christian, whether living or dead, participates in all the blessings of Christ and the Church; and this is granted him by God, even without indulgence letters.

40. A Christian who is truly sorry [for his wrong-doing] seeks and loves penalties for their sin, the bounty of indulgences, however, relaxes penalties and causes men to hate them, or at least, offers an occasion [for hating them].

43. Christians should be taught that he who gives to the poor or lends to the needy does a better work than he who buys indulgences.

44. Love increases through works of love, and man becomes better; but men do not grow better through indulgences, only freer from penalties.

67. Indulgences, which the preachers proclaim as the "greatest graces" are truly such, in so far as they promote gain.

68. Yet they are in truth the very smallest of graces compared with the grace of God and the piety of the Cross.

75. It is madness to think that papal indulgences are so great that they could absolve a man even if he had done the impossible and had violated the Mother of God.

76. We say, on the contrary, that papal indulgences cannot remove the most minor of sins, so far as its guilt is concerned.

82. Tell me this. Why does not the pope empty purgatory, for the sake of holy love and of the dire need of the souls that are there, if he could redeem an infinite number of souls for the sake of miserable money

used to build a Church? The former reason (i.e., to save souls) would be most just; the latter (i.e., to build a church) is most trivial.

86. Also, why does not the pope, whose wealth today is greater than the most wealthy, build this church of St. Peter with his own money, rather than with the money of poor believers?"

Description:_____

_____

_____

Inference:_____

_____

_____

Questions:

1. Given the disputation announcement at the beginning of the text and what you know about the medieval university, what was the purpose of this text?

2. According to Luther, how should true Christians view penalties for their sins?

3. Luther claims that " inward repentance... is worthless unless it produces various mortifications of the flesh." How is this related to the issue of indulgences?

4. Based on this sample of his 95 theses, what does Luther seem most upset about?

DOCUMENT 10-4

Martin Luther

Sermon for Pentecost Tuesday: Of Preachers and Hearers

1522

"It belongs to the sheep to judge, not the preachers." - Luther

Although Luther's posting of the ninety-five theses (Document 10-3) is often presented as a revolutionary act in popular historical accounts of the Sixteenth Century, it was a relatively common event as church history goes. Like many reformers before him, Luther aired grievances about the Church's actions and called for change. Luther's view of the Bible in the lives of believers, however, was revolutionary. Traditionally, the Catholic Church was thought to preserve the authoritative interpretation of Scripture. But Luther argued that anyone with knowledge of the original biblical languages and common sense could grasp the truths of the Bible directly. This meant that parishioners were obligated to test preachers' sermons against their own understanding of the Gospel. In the following sermon, Luther highlights the role of individual conscience in assenting to religious truths and addresses the extent to which the rejection of church authorities could also extend to civil ones.

Themes: conscience, individual judgment, theological truth, church hierarchy

---

Martin Luther, "Sermon for Pentecost Tuesday: Of Preachers and Hearers," in *Luther's Epistle Sermons*, ed. and trans. John Nicholas Lenker et al. (Minneapolis: Luther Press, 1909), 3: 373, 376-377, 378-381. Modernized by Andrew Fogleman.

[Gospel Reading for the Service]

John 10: 1-11: [Jesus said:] Verily, verily, I say unto you, He that enters not by the door into the sheepfold, but climbs up some other way, the same is a thief and a robber. But he that enters in by the door is the shepherd of the sheep. To him the porter opens; and the sheep hear his voice: and he calls his own sheep by name, and leads them out. And when he leads forth his own sheep, he goes before them, and the sheep follow him: for they know his voice. And a stranger will they not follow, but will flee from him: for they know not the voice of strangers. This parable spoke Jesus unto them: but they understood not what things they were which he spoke unto them. Then said Jesus unto them again, Verily, verily, I say unto you, I am the door of the sheep. All that ever came before me are thieves and robbers: but the sheep did not hear them. I am the door: by me if any man enter in, he shall be saved, and shall go in and out, and find pasture. The thief cometh not, but for to steal, and to kill, and to destroy: I am come that they might have life, and that they might have it more abundantly. I am the good shepherd: the good shepherd gives his life *for the sheep.*

[Sermon begins]

"This Gospel treats the office of ministry, how it is constituted, what it accomplishes and how it is misused. It is indeed very necessary to know these things, for the office of preaching is extremely important for Christendom. St. Paul highly esteemed this office for the reason that through it the Word of God was proclaimed which brings about the salvation of all who believe it. He says to the Romans (1:16): "I am not ashamed of the Gospel, for it is the power of God unto salvation to everyone that believeth." We must now consider this theme, since our Gospel lesson presents it...

The doctrines of men, however admirable, fall to the ground, and with them the conscience that has built upon them. There is neither help nor remedy for them. But the Word of God is eternal and must endure forever; no devil can overthrow it. On this foundation the conscience may be established forever. The words of men however must perish and everything that cleaves to them. Those who enter not by the door—that is, those who do not speak the true and pure Word of God, without any addition—do not lay the right foundation; they destroy and torture and slaughter the sheep. Therefore, Christ says further in this Gospel: "But he that enters in by the door is the shepherd of the sheep. To him the porter opens; and the sheep hear his Voice."...

In this text there are two thoughts worthy of note: the liberty of faith, and the power to judge. You know that our soul-destroyers[1] have proposed to us that what the councils and the learned doctors decide and decree, that we should accept, and not judge for ourselves whether it is right or not. They have become so certain of the infallibility of the councils and doctors that they have now established the edict, publicly seen, that if we do not accept what they say, we are put under the ban. Now, let us take a spear in hand and make a hole in their shield; indeed, their resolution is but a spider's web. And you should, moreover, use upon them the spear, which until now they have used upon us, and hold before them its point.

Remember well that the sheep have to pass judgment upon that which is placed before them. They should say: We have Christ as our Lord and prefer his Word to the words of any man or to those of the angels of darkness. We want to examine and judge for ourselves whether the pope, the bishops and their followers do right or not. For Christ says here that the sheep judge and know which is the right voice and which is not. Now let them come along. Have they decreed anything? We will examine whether it is right, and according to our own judgment interpret that which is a private affair for each individual Christian, knowing that the authority to do this is not human, but divine. Even the real sheep flee from a stranger and hold to the voice of their shepherd.

---

[1] **Soul-destroyers**: leaders of the Catholic Church.

Upon this authority, the Gospel dethrones all the councils, all the papal laws, urging us not to receive anything without judging it, because we have the power to judge, and that judgment endures until the present day. The papists[2] have taken from us the sword [of judgment], so that we have not been able to repel any false doctrine, and, moreover, they have by force introduced false teachings among us. If now we take the sword [of judgment] from them they will be sorry. And we must truly take it, not by force, but by means of the Word,[3] letting go all else that we have, saying: I am God's sheep, whose Word I wish to appropriate to myself. If you will give me that, I will acknowledge you to be a shepherd. If you, however, add another Gospel to this one, and do not give me the pure Gospel, then I will not consider you a shepherd, and will not listen to your voice; for the office of which you boast extends no farther than the Word goes. If we find one to be a shepherd, we should receive him as such: if he is not, we should remove him; for the sheep shall judge the voice of the shepherd. If he does not give us the right kind of pasture, we should bid farewell to such a shepherd, that is, to the bishop; for a hat of pearls and a staff of silver do not make a shepherd or a bishop, but rather does the office depend upon his care of the sheep and their pasture.

Now the papists object to judgment being passed upon any of their works; for this reason they have intruded and taken from us the sword [of judgment], which we might use for such a purpose. Also, they dictate that we must accept, without any right of judgment, whatever they propose. And it has almost come to such a pass that whenever the pope breathes they make an article of faith out of it, and they have proclaimed that the authorities have the right to pass such laws for their subjects as they desire, independent of the judgment of the people. These conditions mean ruin to the Christians, so much so that a hundred thousand swords should be desired for one pope. This they know very well, and they cling hard to their laws. If they would permit

---

[2] **Papists**: supporters of the pope.
[3] **The Word**: Bible.

unbiased judgment, their laws would be set aside and they would have to preach the pure Word; but such a course would reduce the size of their stomachs and the number of their horses.

Therefore, be aroused by this passage of Scripture to chop to pieces and cut through everything that is not in harmony with the Gospel, for it belongs to the sheep to judge, and not to the preachers. You have the authority and power to judge everything that is preached; that and nothing less. If we have not this power, then Christ vainly said to us in Mt. 7:15: "Beware of false prophets, who come to you in sheep's clothing, but inwardly are ravening wolves." We could not beware if we had not the power to judge, but were obliged to accept everything they said and preached.

The second thought is, no one shall be forced to believe; for the sheep follow him whom they know and flee from strangers. Now, Christ's wish is that none be forced, but that they be permitted to follow from willing hearts and of their own desire; not out of fear, shame or strife. He would let the Word go forth and accomplish all. When their hearts are taken captive, then they will surely come of themselves. Faith does not go forth from the heart unless it has the Word of God.

Our civic leaders are now mad and foolish in that they undertake to drive people to believe by means of force and the sword. Christ here wishes the sheep to come of themselves, from their knowledge of his voice. The body may be forced, as the pope, for example, has by his laws coerced people to go to confession and to the Lord's Supper, but the heart cannot be taken captive. Christ wants it to be free. Although he had power to coerce men, he wished to win them through his pleasing, loving preaching. Whoever lays hold of Christ's word follows after him and permits nothing to tear him from it. Civic leaders wish to drive the people to believe by means of the sword and fire; that is nonsense. Then let us see to it that we allow the pure Word of God to take its course, and afterward leave them free to follow, whom it has taken captive; indeed, they will follow voluntarily.

By this I do not wish to abolish the civil sword (i.e., state authority); for the hand can hold it within its grasp so that it does no one any harm, but it holds it inactive. It must be retained because of wicked people who have no regard at all for the Word; but the sword cannot force the heart and bring it to faith. In view of its inability, it must keep silent in matters of faith; here one must enter by the door, and preach the Word and make the heart free. Only in this way are men led to believe. These are the two expedients—for the pious and the wicked: the pious are to be drawn by the Word, and the wicked to be driven by the sword to observe order..."

Description:_____

_____

_____

Inference:_____

_____

_____

Questions:

1. What is conscience? And what role does it play in Luther's version of Christianity?

2. What role does personal interpretation of Scripture play in Luther's Christianity?

3. Luther insists that civil government stay out of matters of faith. Why?

4. Who is the final arbiter of the meaning of the Bible according to Luther? And why does that matter in the sixteenth century?

5. How might this discussion of spiritual liberty inform debates about political liberty?

DOCUMENT 10-5

Saint Ignatius of Loyola

The Spiritual Exercises

CA. 1548

"The white which I see, is black if the Hierarchical Church so decides it." -Ignatius of Loyola

The spiritual life of Ignatius of Loyola (1491—1556) began with an injury that ended his military career. Fighting as a soldier of fortune in northern Spain, Loyola's legs were struck by a cannon ball at the Battle of Pamplona in 1521. Over the course of his long recovery, Loyola read the Bible and devotional literature. Following a night vigil in 1522 in which Loyola experienced a religious vision of the Virgin Mary and Jesus, he gave up his sword and pursued a life of Christian poverty modeled after Saint Francis of Assisi. Practicing asceticism in a cave near Catalonia, Loyola developed a method of spiritual life based on prayer and meditation later popularized by his book The Spiritual Exercises. In 1539, Loyola formed the Society of Jesus. Its members, known as Jesuits, committed themselves to poverty, chastity, and obedience and quickly became distinguished for their institutions of learning. Like Luther, Loyola believed that the Catholic Church needed reform. But unlike Protestant thinkers Loyola believed that the Catholic Church as a whole (led by the Holy Spirit) was in a better place to discover theological truths than any one individual. Thus Loyola encouraged a profound spiritual obedience to Church leadership as a solution to the religious division of his age.

Ignatius of Loyola, "The Spiritual Exercises," trans. Father Elder Mullan, S.J., in *The Spiritual Exercises of St. Ignatius of Loyola* (New York: P. J. Kennedy & Sons, 1914), 39.

Themes: spiritual obedience, hierarchy, theological truth

Let the following Rules be observed.

First Rule: All judgment laid aside, we ought to have our mind ready and prompt to obey, in all, the true Spouse of Christ our Lord, which is our holy Mother the Church Hierarchical.

Second Rule: Praise confession to a Priest, and the reception of the most Holy Sacrament of the Altar once in the year...

Third Rule. Praise the hearing of Mass often, likewise hymns, psalms, and long prayers, in the church and out of it; likewise the hours [of prayer] set at the time fixed for each Divine Office and for all prayer and all Canonical Hours.

Fourth Rule: Praise much Religious Orders, virginity and continence, and not so much marriage as any of these.

Fifth Rule: Praise vows of Religion, of obedience, of poverty, of chastity and of other perfections of supererogation....[1]

Sixth Rule: Praise relics of the Saints, giving veneration to them and praying to the Saints; and praise to Stations, pilgrimages, Indulgences, pardons, Crusades, and candles lighted in the churches...

Eighth Rule: Praise the ornaments and the buildings of churches; likewise images, and to venerate them according to what they represent.

Ninth Rule: Finally, to praise all precepts of the Church, keeping the mind prompt to find reasons in their defense and in no manner against them.

---

[1] **Supererogation**: the act of performing more than is required by duty, obligation or need.

Tenth Rule: We ought to be more prompt to find good and praise the ways of our Superiors. Because, although some are not or have not been such, to speak against them, whether preaching in public or discoursing before the common people, would rather give rise to fault-finding and scandal than profit; and so the people would be incensed against their Superiors, whether temporal or spiritual. So that, as it does harm to speak evil to the common people of Superiors in their absence, so it can make profit to speak of the evil actions to the persons themselves who can remedy them.

Eleventh Rule: Praise positive and scholastic learning.... it is more proper to the Scholastics, as St. Thomas, St. Bonaventure, and to the Master of the Sentences, etc., to define or explain for our times the things necessary for eternal salvation; and to combat and explain better all errors and all fallacies.... they being enlightened and clarified by the Divine virtue, help themselves by the Councils, Canons and Constitutions of our holy Mother the Church.

Thirteenth Rule: To be right in everything, we ought always to hold that the white which I see, is black, if the Hierarchical Church so decides it, believing that between Christ our Lord, the Bridegroom, and the Church, His Bride, there is the same Spirit which governs and directs us for the salvation of our souls. Because by the same Spirit and our Lord Who gave the ten Commandments, our holy Mother the Church is directed and governed.

Description:_____

_____

_____

Inference:_____

_____

_____

Questions:

1. The thirteenth rule, or course, is a provocative one. It demands submission to the church even in the face of apparent counter evidence. What is the logic behind this type of obedience?

2. Compare Loyola's *Spiritual Exercises* to Luther's *Of Preachers and Hearers*. Both texts are concerned with laying hold of theological truth. But how does each author pursue it?

Chapter 11: Exploration and the Global Economy

DOCUMENT 11-1

Christopher Columbus

Letter from the First Voyage

1493

Christopher Columbus's encounter with the Indies could have been lost forever. After making the perilous seven-month trip to the Americas and back, Columbus faced a deadly storm off of the Azores islands. Hoping to preserve the legacy of his discovery, he dashed off the following letter to Luis de Santángel, one of the financial backers of his trip. Printed within the month of his return, Columbus's letter gained a wide circulation for the time thanks to the printing press. In it, he describes the topography, natural resources, communities, and inhabitants he found in the Americas and what they might mean to the Spanish monarchs.

Themes: trade, conversion, character of indigenous

Christopher Columbus, "Letter from the First Voyage," in John Boyd Thacher, *Christopher Columbus: His Life, His Works, His Remains* (New York: G. P. Putnam's Sons, 1903), 2: 21-26. Modernized by Andrew Fogleman.

Spanish Letter to Luis de Santángel[1]

Sir: As I know that you will be pleased by the great victory that our Lord has given me in my voyage, I write you this letter, by which you shall learn that, in twenty days, I passed over to the Indies with the fleet that the most Illustrious King and Queen, our Lords, gave me. I found there very many islands inhabited with people beyond number. And I have taken possession of all of them for their Highnesses, with proclamation and the royal standard displayed; and I was not resisted.

On the first island that I found, I put the name Saint Salvador, in commemoration of His High Majesty, who marvelously supplied our trip. The Indians call it Guanahani. The second I named the island of Saint Maria de Concepcion, the third Ferrandina, the fourth Fair Island,[2] the fifth La Isla Juana; and so for each one a new name. When I reached Juana, I followed its coast westerly, and found it so large that I thought it might be the mainland province of Cathay (or China). I did not find however any towns and villages on the seacoast, save small clusters of homes with the people who fled so quickly I was not able to speak with them. So I went on farther in the same direction, thinking I would not miss any great cities or towns. And at the end of many leagues seeing that there was no change, and that the coast was bearing me northwards, though my desire was to go southward, and since the winter was already confronting us, I turned back to the South, and as the wind also blew against me, I determined not to wait for different weather and and sailed back to an earlier port.

From there I sent two men into the country to learn if there was a king, or any great cities. They travelled for three days, and found numerous small villages and a numberless population, but they did not find any

---

[1] **Luis De Santángel** (d. 1498): A supporter and financial backer of Columbus's expedition.
[2] The Catalonian printer who prepared this edition wrote *La Isla Bella*, instead of *La Ysabella*, as it is in the Spanish edition of the letter. Columbus wished to honor Queen Isabella, His patroness.

ruling authority; wherefore they returned. I understood sufficiently from other Indians whom I had already taken, that this land was an island; and so I followed its coast eastward for a hundred and seven leagues to where it terminated. From there I saw another island to the east, ten or eight leagues distant from this, which I named La Spañola. And I passed over to it and followed the northern coast, as with La Juana, eastwardly for a hundred and seventy-eight great leagues in a direction easterly course. This island, and all the others, are extremely large. In them there are many seacoast harbors, incomparable with any others that I know in Christendom, and plenty of rivers so good and great that it is marvelous to behold. The lands there are high, and in them are very many ranges of hills, and lofty mountains incomparably to the Island of Centrefrei; they are all most beautiful and formed in thousands of shapes. They are accessible, and full of trees of a thousand kinds, so lofty that they seem to reach the sky. And I am assured that the trees never lose their foliage; as may be imagined, since I saw them as green and as beautiful as they are in Spain during May. And some of them were in flower, some in fruit, some in another stage according to their kind. The nightingale was singing, and other birds of a thousand sorts, round about the way that I was going in the month of November. There are palm-trees of six or eight species, wondrous to see for their beautiful variety; but so are the other trees, fruits, and plants. There are wonderful pine groves, and very large plains of vegetation, and there is honey, and many kinds of birds, and many various fruits.

There are many mines of metals in the earth, and there is a population of incalculable number. Spañola is a marvel; the mountains, hills, plains, fields, and land are so beautiful and suitable for planting and sowing, for breeding cattle of all sorts, and for building towns and villages. There could be no believing, without seeing, such harbors as are here, as well as the many and great rivers, and excellent waters, most of which contain gold. In the trees, fruits and plants, there are great differences from those of Juana. There are many spices, and great mines of gold and other metals. The people, men and women, of this island, and of all the others that I have found and seen or not seen, all go naked just as their mothers brought them forth. Some women cover a single place with the leaf or a plant, or a cotton something made for that purpose.

The people there have no iron or steel, nor any weapons; nor would it be expected of them. This is not because they are misshapen or unduly small,[3] but because they are wondrously timid. They have no other weapons than the stems of reeds in their seeding state. And on the end, they attach little sharpened stakes. Even these, they dare not use; for on many occasions I sent two or three men ashore to some village to make contact, and countless numbers of them came out, but as soon as they saw our men approach, they fled away so quickly that even fathers did not not wait for their sons. And this was not because our men injured any of them:—on the contrary, at every landing where I have gone and been able to speak with them, I gave them everything I had, cloth and many other things, without accepting anything in return. And yet, they are, incurably timid. But they have become more assured, and are losing their initial fear. They are simple and generous with what they have, to such a degree, as no one would believe it unless they had seen it. They never say no if asked for anything they have, but rather invite the person to accept it. In this they show so much loving kindness that it would seem they would give their very hearts. They are so immediately content with any little trifle given them in return for their objects, be they of great value or of little worth, that I forbade that worthless objects, such as fragments of broken platters, pieces of broken glass, or buckles and straps, should be given them. But when they were able to get such things, they seemed to think they had the best jewels in the world. Sailors became accustomed to exchange a strap or other things of lesser value, for gold weighing two and a half *castellanos*. For new *blancas* the Indians gave everything they had, even

---

[3] **Unduly small**: or "lacking a fair stature."

though it was [the worth of] two or three gold *castellanos*, or one or two arrobas of spun cotton. They even took pieces of broken barrel-hoops, and gave whatever they had, like senseless brutes;[4] so that it seemed wrong to me. I forbade it. Rather I gave freely a thousand useful thing that I possessed, in order that these might generate affection [between us], and furthermore that they might become Christians. For they are already inclined to the love and service of our Highnesses and of all the Castilian nation. They strive to give us things that we need and they have in abundance. And there is no sect or idolatry among them, save that they all believe that power and goodness come from the sky. They believe firmly that I, with my ships and crew, came from the sky. They received me this way at every place I landed, once they ceased to be afraid of us.

They did not receive us this way because they are ignorant. On the contrary, they are men of very subtle intelligence, who navigate all their seas, and who give a marvelously good account of everything, but rather because they have never seen men wearing clothes or anything like of our ships. And as soon as I arrived in the Indies, in the first island that I found, I took some of the Indians by force, intending that they should learn our language and inform me about the area. And so it was, that very soon they understood us and we them either by speech or by signs. Those [Indians] have proved very valuable, and to this day I carry them [with me]. They still hold the opinion that I come from heaven, [as it appears] from much conversation that they have had with me. And they are the first to proclaim it wherever I arrived; and the others in those regions go running from house to house and to the neighboring villages with loud crises of "Come! Come to see the people from heaven!" Then, as soon as they felt comfortable with us, each one came, men as well as women, so that there remained none behind, big or little. They all brought something to eat and drink, which they gave with wondrous affection.

---

[4] **Like senseless brutes**: *commo bestias* in the Spanish edition.

They have very many canoes in all the islands, similar to our rowing-galleys, some larger, some smaller. In fact many are larger than a galley of eighteen benches. They are not as wide though, because they are made of a single log of timber. However, a galley of ours could not keep up with them in rowing, for their motion is a thing beyond belief. They navigate by these canoes through the numberless islands of the area and conduct their traffic. I have seen some of those canoes with seventy or eighty men in them, each one with his oar.

In all these islands, I did not see much diversity in the looks of the people, or in their manners and languages. They all understand each other, which is encouraging for what I hope our Highnesses will determine—to make them familiar with our holy faith, as they are well disposed to it. I have already told how I had gone a hundred and seven leagues, in a straight line from West to East, along the seacoast of the Island of Juana; and declare that that island is larger than England and Scotland combined! In addition to those hundred and seven leagues, there remains also the western side two provinces where I did not go. One of these islands they call Anan, where the people are born with tails. According to what may be understood from the Indians with me, who know all the islands, these provinces cannot be less in length than fifty or sixty leagues. This other, Española, has a greater circumference than the whole of Spain from Colibre in Catalunya, by the seacoast, as far as Fuente Ravia in Biscay; since along one of its four sides, I went for a hundred and eighty-eight great leagues in a straight line from West to East.

This is [a land] to be desired, and once seen never to be relinquished! I have taken possession of them all for our Highnesses, and all are more richly endowed than I have skill and power to say. I hold them all in the name of our Highnesses who can dispose thereof as much and as completely as of the kingdoms of Castile. Española is a particularly suitable location because of its proximity to gold mines and traffic with the continent on the one side, and the possibility of great commerce and profit on the further side of the Great khan.[5] I took possession of a large town, which I named the city of Navidad. I have made fortifications there and a fort, which by this time will have been completely finished. I left enough men there for that task, with arms, artillery, and provisions for more than a year. I have also left a boat and a master shipbuilder for making others. I have established a great friendship with the King of that land, to such a degree that he prides himself on calling me his brother. And even though this might change and he may attack the men I left behind, neither he nor his people know what weapons are, and go naked. As I have already said, they are the most timid creatures in the world, so that the men who remain there are sufficient to destroy all that land. Thus the island is without danger for them if they know how to behave themselves.

It seems to me that in those islands, all the men are content with a single wife; but to their chief or king they give as many as twenty. The women, it appears to me, do more work than the men. I have not been able to learn whether they hold personal property, for it seemed to me that whatever one had, they all took shares of, especially of eatable things. Down to the present, I have not found in those islands any monstrous men, as many expected, but on the contrary all the people are very attractive. Nor are they black like those in Guinea, but have flowing hair. They are not born where there is excessive heat from the rays of the sun. It is true that the sun is there very strong there, despite the fact that it is twenty-six degrees distant from the equator. It was very cold this winter in the areas where there were lofty mountains, but the Indians endure it by being accustomed to the weather, and by the help of the meats, which they eat with many extraordinarily hot spices. Thus I have not found, and do not have any information of monsters, except of an island, which is the second in the approach to the Indies, which is inhabited by a people whom the Indians regard as very ferocious. They eat human flesh, and have many canoes with which

---

[5] **Great Khan**: the title Europeans used for the Emperor of China.

they run throughout all the islands of India, and plunder and take as much as they can. They have the same form as the others, but have the custom of wearing their hair long, like women. They use bows and arrows of the same reed-stems, with a point of wood at the top, because they lack iron. Among the other tribes who are excessively cowardly, these are [considered] ferocious; but I hold them as nothing. These are they who have to do with the women of Matremonio—which is the first island that is encountered in the passage from Spain to the Indies—in which there are no men. Those women practice no female occupations, but have bows and arrows of reeds such as those mentioned above; and they cover themselves with plates of copper of which they have much. In another island, which they assure me is larger than Española, the people have no hair. There is incalculable gold there, and I bring Indians with me as witnesses to the fact.

In conclusion, to speak only of what has been done on this voyage, which has been so hastily performed, our Highnesses may see that I shall give them as much gold as they may need, with very little aid which our Highnesses will give me. Also I will give spices and cotton at once, as much as our Highnesses will order to be shipped, and Mastic, too—which till now has never been found except in Greece, at the island of Xio.[6] There the Signori sell it for what he likes. Also, aloe-wood as much as they shall order to be shipped, and slaves as many as they shall order—and these shall be gathered from idolaters. And I believe that I have discovered rhubarb and cinnamon. Additionally, the men whom I left there will discover a thousand other things of value; since I did not stay long at any point, so long as the wind gave me an opportunity of sailing. The only exception was the town of Navidad, where I stayed till I had left things safely arranged and well established. And in truth I could have done much more if the ships had served me as well as might reasonably have been expected.

---

[6] **Mastic**: an aromatic gum or resin used as a varnish or waterproof filler and sealant in building.

This is enough; [thanks to the] eternal God our Lord who gives to all those who walk in His way, victory over things which seem impossible! And this was notably one such [seemingly impossible endeavor], for although men have talked or written of those lands, it was all by speculation, without confirmation from eyesight, taking in just so much that the hearers for the most part listened and believed that there was more fable in it than anything actual. Since thus our Redeemer has given to our most illustrious King and Queen, and to their famous kingdoms, this victory in so high a matter, Christendom should be glad, make great festivals, and give solemn thanks to the Holy Trinity for the great acclaim they shall have by the conversion of so many people to our Holy faith. And next [should give thanks] for the earthly benefits which will bring refreshment and profit here, not only to Spain, but to all Christians. This briefly, in accordance with the facts, dated on the caravel, off the Canary Islands, the 15 February of the year 1493.

At your command,
The Admiral

[Postscript contained in the letter]

After having written this [letter], and being in the sea of Castile, there rose so much wind from the South and South-West, that I had to lighten my vessels. However, I sailed today to the port of Lisbon, which is the greatest wonder in the world, and I decided to write to our Highnesses. I sailed to the Indies in thirty-three days, and returned in twenty-eight. I always found the Indies as the season of May [here]. But the storms here have delayed me twenty-three days, running about this sea. All the seamen here say that there has never been a winter this bad, nor so many shipwrecks.

Dated 14th of March.

Description:_____

_____

_____

Inference:_____

_____

_____

Questions:

1. The original goal of Columbus's voyage was to establish trade with the East by way of a western route. Although he failed to find the old, established trading communities of China and India, how did Columbus nonetheless present his voyage as a "great victory" to his benefactors?

2. How does Columbus describe the inhabitants of the Indies? Why might the nature and character of these inhabitants interest the King and Queen of Spain?

3. This letter was copied and circulated widely throughout Europe immediately after Columbus's return. What parts of this letter do you think Europeans would have found most interesting and why?

DOCUMENT 11-2

Pope Paul III

Sublimis Deus

1537

"We... consider, however, that the Indians are truly human." -Pope Paul III

A papal bull is an official letter written by the pope of the Roman Catholic Church on matters pertaining to the Catholic faith or its administration. The word "bull" refers to the lead seal (bulla) that authenticated them, and the titles of these documents come from the first few words of the letter. Sublimis deus was issued in the wake of on-going debates between church leaders and colonists in the Americas about the intellectual capacity of the Indians. By 1536, a number of Dominican friars including Bernardino de Minaya, Bartolomé de Las Casas, and Julián Garcés had contacted Pope Paul III to complain about the harsh treatment of the Indians and the philosophical theories that supported such behavior. The trio of Dominicans particularly rejected the view that Indians had a sub-human intellectual capacity that hindered their appreciation of the Gospel message and therefore cut them off from salvation. If they were not human enough for salvation, so went the theory, then colonists could take their property and treat them like animals. Paul III responded in 1537 with Sublimis deus, which upheld their human status and their right to property.

Themes: slavery, reason, conversion

Pope Paul III, "Sublimis Deus," in Francis MacNutt, *Bartholomew de Las Casas* (New York: G. P. Putnam's Sons, 1909), 427, 429, 431. Modernized by Andrew Fogleman.

Pope Paul III: To all faithful Christians to whom this writing may come, health in Christ our Lord and the apostolic benediction. The Sublime God so loved the human race that He created man in such wise that he might participate, not only in the good that other creatures enjoy, but endowed him with capacity to attain to the inaccessible and invisible Supreme Good and behold it face to face; and since man, according to the testimony of the sacred scriptures, has been created to enjoy eternal life and happiness, which none may obtain save though faith in our Lord Jesus Christ, it is necessary that he should possess the nature and faculties enabling him to receive that faith; and that whoever is thus endowed should be capable of receiving that same faith. Nor is it credible that any one should possess so little understanding as to desire the faith and yet be destitute of the most necessary faulty to enable him to receive it. Hence Christ, who is the Truth itself, that has never failed and can never fail, said to the preachers of the faith whom He chose for that office "Go ye and teach all nations." He said all, without exception, for all are capable of receiving the doctrines of the faith.

The enemy of the human race, who opposes all good deeds in order to bring men to destruction, beholding and envying this, invented a means never before heard of, by which he might hinder the preaching of God's word of Salvation to the people: he inspired his followers who, to please him, have not hesitated to publish abroad that the Indians of the West and the South, and other people of whom we have recent knowledge should be treated as dumb brutes[1] created for our service, pretending that they are incapable of receiving the catholic faith.

We, who, though unworthy, exercise on the earth the power of our Lord and seek with all our might to bring those sheep of His flock who are outside, into the fold committed to our charge, consider, however, that the Indians are truly human[2] and that they are not only capable of

---

[1] **Dumb brutes**: *muta animalia.*
[2] **Truly human**: *veros homines.*

understanding the catholic faith but, according to our information, they desire exceedingly to receive it. Desiring to provide ample remedy for these evils, we define and declare by these our letters, or by any translation thereof signed by any notary public and sealed with the seal of any ecclesiastical dignitary, to which the same credit shall be given as to the originals, that, notwithstanding whatever may have been or may be said to the contrary, the said Indians and all other people who may later be discovered by Christians, are by no means to be deprived of their liberty or the possessions of their property, even though they be outside the faith of Jesus Christ; and that they may and should, freely and legitimately, enjoy their liberty and the possession of their property; nor should they be in any way enslaved; should the contrary happen, it shall be null and of no effect.

By virtue of our apostolic authority, We define and declare by these present letters, or by any translations thereof signed by any notary public and sealed with the seal of any ecclesiastical dignitary, which shall thus command the same obedience as the originals, that the said Indians and other peoples should be converted to the faith of Jesus Christ by preaching the word of God and by the example of good and holy living.

Given in Rome in the year of our Lord 1537. The fourth of June and of our Pontificate, the third year.

Description:_____

_____

_____

Inference:_____

_____

_____

Questions:

1. According to Pope Paul III, who is behind the idea that the Indians were "dumb brutes created for ... service?"

2. What role does the "nature and faculties" of the Indians play in Pope Paul III's letter?

3. How should the Indians be converted to Christianity according the Pope?

DOCUMENT 11-3

Bartolomé de Las Casas

A Brief Account of the Destruction of the Indies

1542

"I have been an eyewitness of all these cruelties, and an infinite number of others that I pass over in silence." -Bartolomé de Las Casas

Born in Spain, Bartolomé de Las Casas (1484—1566) traveled to the Americas with his father on a colonial expedition in 1502. He participated in the subjugation of the native Taíno people on the Island Hispaniola. There he acquired land, which he worked with indigenous slaves. He became a priest in 1510 and served as a chaplain in the conquest of Cuba by Diego Velásquez de Cuéllar. Velásquez rewarded him for his efforts with an encomienda. A group of Dominican friars challenged Las Casas and his fellow colonists, claiming that their treatment of the native Indians was inhumane, and denied all encomenderos the sacrament of reconciliation (confession). Years later, while studying the Bible in preparation for a sermon, Las Casas also became convinced of the injustice of the Spanish colonizing mission, as well as the role he played in it. Las Casas freed his slaves, gave up his encomienda, and encouraged others to do likewise. From this point on, he traveled between Spain and the Americas as an advocate for the rights of the Indians. He petitioned Spanish monarchs directly, participated in public debates about the injustice of the encomienda system, and wrote numerous books popularizing their plight.

Bartolomé de Las Casas, "A Relation of the Voyages and Cruelties of the Spaniard in the West Indies," in *An Account of the First Voyages and Discoveries Made by the Spaniards in America* (London: F. Darby, 1699), 1-9. Modernized by Andrew Fogleman.

Themes: justice, greed, violence, religion

The West Indies were discovered in the year 1492; the year after, the Spaniards settled there, and inhabited this new world. But for the space of these past 49 years, an infinite number of people have left Spain to dwell in these countries. They generally touch at Hispaniola,[1] which is a very fertile and large island, and has become very famous. The extent of it is above 600 leagues. It is surrounded with a multitude of small islands and abounds with inhabitants, such that there is no country in the world with more people. The continent, which is more than 250 leagues distant from Hispaniola, is very large. A significant part of it has been already explored, and fresh discoveries are made every day. Such great numbers of people inhabit all these countries, that it seems as if providence had amassed together the greatest part of mankind in this part of the world.

All these people are naturally simple, they are free from all trickery, artifice, ill will, and hostility; they are very obedient and faithful to their rightful governors. They are humble, patient, and submissive, even to the Spaniards who have subdued and enslaved them. They love to live quietly, and are enemies of disputes and quarrels. They hardly know what it is to be malicious, and seldom plot revenge.

They are weak and effeminate people, not capable of enduring great fatigue. They care not to be exposed to toil and labor, and they do not live long. Their constitution is so tender, that a small bout of sickness kills them. The children of their princes and nobility are in all respects treated like the lowest subjects. In this way they differ much from our Europeans, among whom the children of kings and great men, are brought up with all delicacy and tenderness imaginable.

---

[1] **Hispaniola**: the Island containing the modern-day nations of Haiti and Dominican Republic.

The people of this island are so very poor, that they lack almost everything. They are very indifferent to the pursuit of worldly advantages, and seem not to be inclined to pride or ambition. Their way of living is so prudent, that the ancient Hermits in the wilderness were scarcely more sober and ascetic. All the Indians in general go naked, with only the modesty to wear a sort of apron about their waist. They sometimes use a king of shaggy covering, or a piece of cloth an ell[2] or two long: The most wealthy among them lie on beds made with straps tied in knots at the four corners. Their minds are quick and subtle, therefore they are very capable of receiving the knowledge of sound doctrine, and easily inclined to embrace the principles of the catholic religion. They have good manners and a greater inclination toward civility than many other nations. This is because their lives are free from the care and distraction of the perplexity of business. Thus the very first ideas and instructions that are given them of our religion, kindle in their souls a great a desire for the sacraments and divine service of our church. As a result, the monks that instruct them need a great deal of patience to moderate their curiosity, the impulsiveness of their minds, and to answer all their questions. And it may truly be said that these Indians nations would be the happiest in the world, if they but had the knowledge of the true God. The Spaniards themselves, who have treated them so badly, cannot but confess the goodness of their natural temper, and the great disposition of their minds to every kind of virtue.

The almighty seems to have inspired these people with a meekness and softness of humor like that of lambs. But the Spaniards who have given them so much trouble, and fallen upon them so fiercely, resemble savage tigers, wolves, and lions, enraged with hunger. They massacred the poor wretches that inhabited this island for forty years. They have punished them with unheard of torments, such that this island which,

---

[2] **Ell**: a unit of measurement, generally the length of a man's arm from elbow to fingertip.

contained about three million people before the arrival of the Europeans, is now reduced to less than three hundred.

The island of Cuba, the length of which is equal to the distance between Valladolid and Rome, is entirely deserted and destitute of its inhabitants, and contains nothing but ruins. The Island of St. John and Jamaica, have met with similar treatment. They were very fertile and well populated but are now desolate and wasted. There are sixty some Islands near Cuba and Hispaniola on the north, which are commonly called the Isles of Giants. Even the least fruitful of these abounds more with plenty than the Royal Garden of Seville. But they are now destitute of inhabitants, though it contains as wholesome an air as men can breath in.

When the Spaniards fist landed in these isles, there were more than five hundred thousand souls. They cut the throats of a great number of these, and carried away the rest by force to make them work in the minds of Hispaniola. When some pious persons visited these isles after the ravages of the Spaniards, they found but eleven people left there. It was from the motive of charity and compassion that they undertook this difficult and perilous voyage, in hopes of instructing these poor creatures in the knowledge of Jesus Christ. More than 30 isles around St. John were entirely depopulated, so that there is scarce an inhabitant to be found in them.

As for the continent it is certain—and what I myself know to be true— that the Spaniards have ruined ten kingdoms there, bigger than all of Spain, by the commission of all sorts of barbarity an unheard of cruelties. They have driven away or killed all the inhabitants; so that all these kingdoms are desolate to this day, and reduced to the most deplorable condition, even though this continent was formerly the most inhabited county in the world. We say, without fear of criticism for exaggerating, that in the space of those forty years in which the Spaniards exercised their intolerable tyranny in this new world, they unjustly put to death above twelve million people, including men, women and children. It may be said without injury to truth, upon the just calculation, that during this space of time, more than fifty million people have died in these countries.

The Spaniards who invaded these isles, and boasted of their Christianity, mainly used two ways to exterminate the inhabitants. The first of which, was by an unjust and bloody war carried on with the utmost barbarity and cruelty. The other was that detestable policy that inspired them to massacre all that had any remains of liberty, or endeavored to shake off their tyrannical yoke, and to free themselves from so unjust and intolerable slavery. This was attempted by the bravest, strongest, and most warlike nation of the Indians. But when the Spaniard had killed all the men through war, they allowed the women and children to live, but imposed a yoke on them so cruel and insupportable, that their condition was as miserable as that of beasts. A multitude of other particular methods were taken for the destruction of these poor Americans, but they may be reduced in general to those two we have mentioned.

The gold and silver these people had in their possession was the motive that drove the Europeans to persecute and destroy them. The great desire they had of quickly enriching themselves, in order to gain an honor and dignity that far exceeded their condition, inspired them to all this inhumanity. In a word, their greed and ambition inspired them to an excess beyond imagination. The immense riches of the New World and the obedient, sweet, and good disposition of the Indians, which easily rendered access into their country to any that would attempt it, have made possible all these ravages and spoil, all the horrible massacres and cruelties, which the Spaniards have caused them to suffer. They thought so little of the miserable inhabitants of these islands that, I swear, without fear of being accused either of deception or of speaking inconsiderately—since I am an eyewitness—that they valued them less and treated them worse than beasts. They had so little regard to the salvation of their souls, that they would not even trouble themselves so much as to speak of the Christian faith and sacraments to these numberless multitudes of men and women whom they sacrificed to their ambition and tyranny. And the fact that these poor Indians offered them no injury, but on the contrary, gave them honor and respect as though they had been sent from heaven makes the enormity of their crimes even worse. They proceeded this way until the Spaniards wearied them out with repeated outrages and massacres, such that the Indians were forced to arm themselves contrary to their inclination and to repel the Spaniards by force to save themselves from the horrible violence and insults of their enemies, who invented various kinds of torments for them, with barbarity beyond all description.

At this island [of Hispaniola] the Spaniards arrived in their fist voyages, and there began to persecute and murder the Indians, taking way their wives and children and using them, or rather abusing them, at their pleasure. They devoured all that these poor creatures had amassed together for their subsistence with a great deal of care and labor. The Spaniards were not content with what the Indians freely offered them from their poverty and lowliness of their condition. For the Indians are satisfied with what is of pure necessity, not troubling themselves with luxuries, or laying up excessive provisions before hand. One Spaniard would consume in a day, that which would have sufficed three Indian families of ten persons each, for the space of the whole month. This ill treatment and waste soon made the inhabitants of this island lose the esteem they had for the Spaniards, whom they at first looked upon as messengers from heaven. As a result, they eventually began to hide from them their wives, children, and whatever goods they had. Some retired into caves, other fled up into the mountains to avoid meeting the Spaniards who now appeared so terrible and cruel to them. The Spaniards did not content themselves to merely beat them and to offer them many other indignities, but cut their throats in cold blood. And without any respect either to age or quality, put their princes and the governors of their cities to death. They came to that height of impudence and villainy, that a Spanish captain had the insolence to abuse the wife of the greatest kings of the island. This vile fact drove the Indians to such despair that from that time on they fought to drive the Spaniards out of their country. They armed themselves and did what they could to defend against these tyrants. But the weapons they used were neither capable of defending them, nor of injuring their enemies to any purpose. And to the Spaniards they were more like those that children use to play with than those fit for war.

The Spaniards, who were mounted on fine horses, and armed with lances and swords, looked upon their enemies so poorly equipped with the greatest contempt, and committed the most horrible slaughter with impunity. They passed through the several cities and towns, sparing neither age nor sex, they killed men, women and children. They ripped up women with child, that root and branch might be destroyed together. They made bets with each other, who could kill a man with one blow of his sword; or who could take a head clean off its shoulders; or who could run a man through with the most skill. They tore away children out of their mothers' arms and dashed out their brains against the rocks. Others they threw into rivers, entertaining themselves with this pitiless game, and gave great shouts [of laughter] while they saw them in their misery. They mocked them, advised them to struggle in the water, and try if they could to save themselves from drowning. They held the bodies of mothers and children together upon a single lance. They set up gallows, and hanged up thirteen of these poor creatures in honor of Jesus Christ and his twelve apostles (as they blasphemously expressed themselves). They kindled a great fire under these scaffolds, to burn those they had hanged upon them. They cut off the hands of those they left alive, and sent them away in that miserable condition, telling them to carry their news of their calamities to those that were hiding into the mountains.

They erected a small platform, supported with forks and poles, upon which to execute the chiefs, and those of the most esteemed rank among them. Then they laid them down upon this scaffold, they kinked a gentle fire, to make them feel themselves die gradually, till the poor wretches after the most exquisite pain and anguish, attended with horrible screeches and outcries, at length perished. One day I saw four or five persons of the highest rank in this island burned in this manner. However the dreadful cries this torment compelled from them, hindered the sleep of a Spanish captain. Thus he commanded them to be strangled immediately. But a certain officer whose name I know, and whose relations are well know at Seville, put gags in the Indians' mouths to stop them from making noise. He did not want to be deprived of the brutish pleasure of broiling them slowly until they breathed out their souls in this torment. I have been an eyewitness of all these cruelties, and an infinite number of other that I pass over in silence.

And because these poor people took all the care they could to hide themselves from these barbarous and wicked Spaniards, who had no sentiment of humanity, honor, or religion left, but acted as if they were made for nothing else but to destroy mankind. To add further to their brutish cruelty, they taught dogs to go hunting for these poor wretches, and to devour them as if they had been beasts. And because the Indians after they had been provoked with so many unheard of injuries, now and then killed one of the Spaniards when they found them alone, the Spaniards made a law among themselves to kill a hundred Indians for every Spaniard the Indians killed.

Description:_____

_____

_____

Inference:_____

_____

_____

Questions:

1. How does Las Casas emphasize the humanity of the Indians in this text?

2. Compare Las Casas's description of the nature of the Indians with his description of the nature of the Spaniards. How are these two different?

3. Reflect on the fact that the Spaniards "set up gallows, and hanged up thirteen of these poor creatures in honor of Jesus Christ and his twelve apostles." Why would they have killed the Indians in this manner? What role does religion play in the Spaniards' killing, and what role does it play in Las Casas's support of the Indians?

DOCUMENT 11-4

Juan Ginés De Sepúlveda

On the Just Causes for War Against the Indians

(or Democrates, pt. 2)

1545

"Is anyone born so unfortunately that they should be condemned to slavery by nature?"

—Leopold

Juan Ginés de Sepúlveda (c. 1490–1573) was the official royal chronicler of the Holy Roman Emperor, Charles V of Spain. Although an accomplished humanist scholar, today Sepulveda is most well known for his treatises defending the right of Christian sovereigns to use war for spreading the Catholic faith. In the text below, Sepúlveda presents these arguments in the form of a fictional dialogue between Democrates, a Catholic courtier supportive of forceful conversion, and Leopold, an impressionable German Protestant, who is slowly won over to this idea. This treatise follows up Sepulveda's earlier work, Democrates (pt. 1), *which justified Emperor Charles's many wars in Europe and criticized a school of Spanish pacifists, who claimed that war–even for defensive purposes–is inherently unchristian. In 1545, the president of the Council of the Indies, tasked with forging a policy on the proper use of violence in the New World, asked Sepulveda to expand Democrates to treat the recent conquests in the Americas. Although receiving some support at court, university theologians found Sepulveda's treatise "unsound" and blocked its Latin publication. In response, Charles suspended all further expeditions in the New World and called a special council to meet in Valladolid to clarify "how conquests*

My translation from *Boletín de la Real Academia de la Historia,* tomo 21 (October, 1892): 261-314.

may be conducted justly and with security of conscience." This set the stage for a showdown between the two premiere theorists on this issue, Bartolomé de Las Casas, who rejected the use of force in conversion as "iniquitous and contrary to our Christian religion," and Sepúlveda, who drew from the arguments presented below in its favor.

Themes: human nature, just war, slavery

Democrates: So, Leopold, what else could you want to hear from me concerning the respectability of a military action?

Leopold: Just a few more questions but they are hardly inconsequential for they deal with the justice of war. Recently, while I was walking with some friends in the palace of Prince Philip, Hernán Cortés, the Marquis del Valle, happened to pass by, and upon seeing him, we began a conversation. We discussed at length the deeds that he and others of the Emperor's captains had accomplished in the lands to the Southwest, which were completely unknown to the former inhabitants of our world. I confess that these stories astonished me greatly because of their excitement, originality, and unheard of nature. But considering them afterward, doubts arose in my mind. With dismay, I thought that it did not fit with Christian charity and justice that the Spaniards should have made war on such innocent people who didn't deserve any ill treatment. Now, Democrates, I want to hear what you think about this and similar kinds of wars, which are not waged because of necessity, but with a specific goal in mind, (indeed, I should say for lust and greed). And I also need you to lay out briefly—with your customary skill stemming from your singular genius and profound mind—all the reasons, as it seems to you, under which war can be waged justly....

[Sepulveda presents a number of justifications for war before coming to the following based on the supposed inferiority of the natives.]

Democrates: There are other causes of a just war that are less clear and happen less frequently. Nevertheless, they are most fair and depend upon divine and natural law. One of which is, if no another way is possible, for those whom servitude is their natural condition, ought to be forcibly driven under the authority of others, if, that is, they reject being ruled. In fact, the greatest philosophers attest that this is a just war according to the law of nature.

Leopold: Is anyone born so unfortunately that they should be condemned to slavery by nature? For what is the difference between being subjected by another's power than being a slave by nature? Do you think that judges, who for the most part follow the rule of nature, are joking when they claim that all men are born free, and that slavery was introduced contrary to nature by the laws of men?

Democrates: ...You could well understand, Leopold, if you only knew the customs and nature of another people, that the Spanish have a perfect right to rule the barbarians of the New World and the adjacent islands, who in all prudence, ability, virtue, and humanity are so far surpassed by the Spanish, as children by adults, women by men, the savage and cruel races by the most merciful, the careless and the intemperate by the most restrained and sober. In fact, I might almost say, as apes by men....[1] Compare, now, the prudence, talent, greatness, temperance, humanity, and religion of Spaniards with these half-men (*homunculos*), in whom you will hardly find a trace of humanity. They not only do not have any learning, but do not use or even know letters, nor retain any monuments of great accomplishments besides some unimportant and obscure histories recorded in paintings. Nor do they have written laws, only barbarian institutions and customs....

Some of the Indians seem to be clever at various works of artisanship, but that is no proof of human wisdom, since we observe various small animals, both birds and spiders, building structures which no human ability can completely imitate. [Consider, for example,] the civic way of life of those who live in New Spain and the province of Mexico, for these people, as I have said, are thought the most civilized of all, and they themselves take pride in their public institutions. They celebrate them as if unequaled either of industry or humanity; they possess cities built through reason and planning. They have kings, upon whom they confer power not by right of heredity, but by vote of

---

[1] The phrase "as apes by men" was removed from later manuscripts, which tried to moderate Sepulveda's view. See, Sepulveda, *Democrates Segundo*, trans and ed., Angel Losada, 33. However Indian comparisons to animals were common. See, Lewis Hanke, *All Mankind is One* (DeKalb: Northern Illinois University Press, 1995), 11, 12.

the people. And they exercise trade in the manner of civilized peoples. But see how greatly they are deceived and how strongly I disagree with their opinion of themselves, seeing as this serves more, through its being made known, to indicate the crudity, barbarity, and inborn slavery of those men than to indicate their ability to establish a civilized community. For what should one conclude from this argument–that is, that they have buildings, and commerce, and a particular plan in their manner of living (things which simple necessity dictates)–except that these people are not bears or apes, not [completely] without inward reason?

[Furthermore] these Indians have established the affairs of their state in such a way that nothing is their own property, neither a house nor a field, which one is either able to divide up and sell or leave to anyone in his will. Everything is in the power of their masters, who are improperly referred to as kings. These natives live not so much for the individual as for the will of kings, for the desire and pleasure of these rulers, not having any interest in their own freedom. They do all of this voluntarily and of their own free will, not compelled by force and arms. These are the surest signs of an uncivilized, downcast, and servile nature.... And if the servile and barbarous rule of their nation had not been to their nature and liking, it would be easy for them, following the death of a king–not one of which succeeds by hereditary law–to change their lives into a freer, better, and more honorable condition. And since they have neglected to do so, they reveal themselves to be born into slavery, not to civic and free life.

Description:_____

_____

_____

Inference:_____

_____

_____

Questions:

1. What hierarchical comparisons does Democrates make between Spaniards and Indians?

2. According to Sepulveda, why are Indian works of artisanship not evidence of human wisdom comparable to the Spaniards?

3. What is Democrates's evidence that American Indians "born into slavery, not to civic and free life"?

Document 11-5

Bernal Díaz del Castillo

The True History of the Conquest of New Spain

CA. 1570

"Gazing on such wondrous sights, we did not know what to say, or whether what appeared before us was real." -Bernal Díaz

The following excerpt comes from the memoires of Bernal Díaz del Castillo (ca. 1496—1584), a conquistador who participated in the conquest of the Mexica (Aztec) capital of Tenochtitlan under the leadership of Hernán Cortés. Díaz was a seventy-year-old encomendero and governor in Guatemala when he composed this account. He claims that he was driven to relate the "true" account of Cortés's mission in place of the apparent misinformation of Francisco López de Gomara's history of the conquest. This selection recounts Cortés's interaction with indigenous tribes along the way to Mexico and his party's first encounter with Montezuma and the Great city of Tenochtitlan.

Themes: tribal divisions, indigenous allies, encounter

We sent four different messages to Xicotenga the Elder and the great number of caciques at the capital of Tlaxcala requesting that they tell their captains not to attack or follow us unless they were coming to make peace.

Bernal Díaz Del Castillo, *The True History of the Conquest of New Spain*, ed. Genaro García, trans. Alfred Percival Maudslay (London: The Hakluyt Society, 1908), 1: 257-263; 2:39-44. Modernized by Andrew Fogleman.

As Xicotenga was bad tempered and obstinate and proud, he decided to send forty Indians with food, poultry, bread and fruit and four miserable looking old Indian women and much copal and many parrots' feathers. From their appearance we thought that the Indians who brought this present came with peaceful intentions, and when they reached our camp they fumigated Cortés with incense without doing him reverence, as was usually their custom. They said: "The Capitan Xicotenga sends you all this so that you can eat. If you are savage Teules (gods), as the Cempoalans say you are, and if you wish for a sacrifice, take these four women and sacrifice them and you can eat their flesh and hearts, but as we do not know your manner of doing it, we have not scarified them now before you; but if you are men, eat the poultry and the bread and fruit, and if you are tame Teules we have brought you copal (which I have already said is a sort of incense) and parrots' feathers; make your sacrifice with that."

Cortés answerer through our interpreters that he had already sent to them to say that he desired peace and had not come to make war, but had come to entreat them and make clear to them on behalf of our Lord Jesus Christ, whom we believe in and worship, and of the Emperor Don Carlos, whose vassals we are, that they should not kill or sacrifice anyone as was their custom to do. That we were all men of blood and flesh just as they were, and not Teules but Christians, and that it was not our custom to kill anyone; that had we wished to kill people, many opportunities of perpetrating cruelties had occurred during the frequent attacks they had made on us, both by day and night. That for the food they had brought he gave them thanks, and that they were not to be as foolish as they had been, but should now make peace.

It seems that these Indians whom Xicotenga had sent with the food were spies sent to examine our huts and ranchos, and horses and artillery and [to report] how many of us there were in each hut, our comings and goings, and everything else that could be seen in the camp. They remained there that day and the following night, and some of them went with messages to Xicotenga and others arrived. Our friends whom we had brought with us from Cempoala looked on and thought that is was not a customary thing for our enemies to stay in the camp day and night without any purpose, and it was clear to them that they were spies, and they were the more suspicious of them in that when we went on the expedition to a little town of Tzumpantzingo, two old men of that town had told the Cempoalans that Xicotenga was all ready with a large number of warriors to attack our camp by night, in such a way that their approach would not be detected, and the Cempoalans at that time took it for a joke or bravado, and not believing it they had said nothing to Cortés; but Doña Marina heard of it at once and she repeated it to Cortés.

So as to learn the truth, Cortés had two of the most honest looking of the Tlaxcalans taken apart from the others, and they confessed that they were spies; then two others were taken and they also confessed that they were spies from Xicotenga and the reason why they had come. Cortés ordered them to be released and we took two more of them and they confessed that they were neither more nor less than spies, but added that their Captain Xicotenga was awaiting their report to attack us that night with all his companies. When Cortés heard this he let it be known throughout the camp that we were to keep on the alert believing they would attack as had been arranged. Then he had seventeen of those spies captured and cut off the hands of some and the thumbs of others and sent them to the Captain Xicotenga to tell him that he had them punished for daring to come in such a way, and to tell him that he might come when he chose by day or night, for we should await him here two days, and that if he did not come within those two days that we would go and look for him in his camp, and that we would already have gone to attack them and kill them, were it not that we liked them, and that now they should quit their foolishness and make peace.

They say that it was at the very moment that those Indians set out with their hands and thumbs cut off, that Xicotenga wished to set out from his camp with all his forces to attack us by night as had been arranged; but when he saw his spies returning in this manner he wondered greatly and asked the reason of it, and they told him all the had happened and from this time forward he lost his courage and pride, and in addition to this one of his commanders with whom he had wrangles and disagreements during the battles which had been fought, had left the camp with all his men.

While we were in camp not knowing that they would come in peace, as we had so greatly desired, and were busy polishing our arms and making arrows, each one of us doing what was necessary to prepare for battle, at that moment one of our scouts came hurrying in to say that many Indians men and women with loads were coming along the high road from Tlaxcala, and were making for our camp, and that a second scout, his companion, who was on horseback, was watching to see which way they went; Just then this scout arrived and said the people were close by and coming straight in our direction, and every now and then were making short stops. Cortés and all of us were delighted at this news, for we believed that it mean peace, as in fact it did, and Cortés ordered us to make no display of alarm and not to show any concern, but to stay hidden in our huts. Then, from out of all those people who came bearing loads, the four chieftains advanced who were charged with seeking for peace, according to the instructions given by the old caciques. Making signs of peace by bowing the head, they came straight to the hut where Cortés was lodging and placed one hand on the ground and kissing the earth and three times made obeisance and burnt copal, and said that all the caciques of Tlaxcala and their allies and vassals, friends and confederates, were come to place themselves under the friendship and peace of Cortés and of his brethren the Teules who accompanied him. They asked his pardon for not having met us peacefully, and for the war which they had waged on us, for they had believed and held for certain that we were friends of

Montezuma and his Mexicans, who have been their mortal enemies for times long past, for they saw that many of his vassals who paid him tribute had come in our company, and they believed that they were endeavoring to gain an entry into their country by guile and treachery, as was their custom to do, so as to rob them of their women and children; and this was the reason why they did not believe the messengers whom we had sent to them. In addition to this they said that the Indians who had first gone forth to make war on us as we entered their country had done it without their orders or advice, but by that of the Chuntales Estomies, who were wild people and very stupid, and that when they saw that we were so few in number, they thought to capture us and carry us off as prisoners to their lords and gain thanks for so doing; that now they came to beg pardon for their audacity, and had brought us food and that every day they would bring more and trusted that we would receive it with the friendly feeling with which it was sent; that within two days the captain Xicotenga would come with other caciques and give a further account of the sincere wish of all Tlaxcala to enjoy our friendship.

As soon as they had finished their discourse they bowed their heads and placed their hands on the ground and kissed the earth. Then Cortés spoke to them through our interpreters very seriously, pretending he was angry, and said that there were [good] reasons why we should not listen to them and should reject their friendship, for as soon as we had entered their country we sent to them offering peace and had told them that we wished to assist them against their enemies, the Mexicans, and they would not believe it and wished to kill our ambassadors; and not content with that they had attacked us three times both by day and by night, and had spied on us and held us under observation; and in the attacks which they made on us we might have killed many of their vassals, but he [Cortés] would not, and he grieved for those who were killed; but it was their own fault and he had made up his mind to go to the place where the old chiefs were living and to attack them; but as they had now sought peace in the name of that province, he would receive them in the name of our lord and King and thank them for the food they had brought. He told them to go at once to their chieftains and tell them to come or send to ask for peace with fuller powers, and that if they did not come we would go to their town and attack them.

He ordered them to be given some blue beads to be handed to their caciques as a sign of peace, and he warned them that when they came to our camp it would be by day and not by night, lest we should kill them.

Then those four messengers departed, and left in some Indian houses a little apart from our camp, the Indian women whom they had brought to make bread, some poultry and all the necessaries for service, and twenty Indians to bring wood and water. From now on they brought us plenty to eat, and when we saw this and believed that peace was a reality, we gave great thanks to God for it. It had come just in time, for we were already lean and worn out and discontented with the war, not knowing or being able to forecast what would be the end of it....

Early the next day we left Iztapalapa with a large escort of those great caciques whom I have already mentioned. We proceeded along the causeway which is here eight paces in width and runs so straight to the City of Mexico that it does not seem to me to turn either much or little, but, broad as it is, it was so crowded with people that there was hardly room for them all, some of them going to and others returning from Mexico, besides those who had come out to see us, so that we were hardly able to pass by the crowds of them that came; and the towers and cues were full of people as well as the canoes from all parts of the lake. It was not to be wondered at, for they had never before seen horses or men such as we are.

Gazing on such wonderous sights, we did not know what to say, or whether what appeared before us was real, for on one side, on the land, there were great cities, and in the lake ever so many more, and the lake itself was crowded with canoes, and in the causeway were many bridges at intervals, and in front of us stood the great City of Mexico, and we did not even number four hundred soldiers! and we well remembered the words and warnings given us by the people of Huexotzingo and Tlaxcala and Tlamanalco, and the many other warnings that had been given that we should beware of entering Mexico, where they would kill us, as soon as they had us inside. Let the curious readers consider whether there is not much to ponder over in this that I am writing. What men have there been in the world who have shown such daring? But let us get on, and march along the causeway. When we arrived where another small causeway branches off (leading to Coyoacan, which is another city) where there were some buildings like towers, which are their oratories, many more chieftains and caciques approached clad in very rich mantles, the brilliant liveries of one chieftain differing from those of another, and the causeways were crowded with them. The Great Montezuma had sent these great caciques in advance to receive us, and when they came before Cortés they bade us welcome in their language, and as a sign of peace, they touched their hands against the ground, and kissed the ground with the hand. There we halted for a good while, and Cacamatzin, the Lord of Texcoco, and the Lord of Iztapalapa and the Lord of Tacuba and the Lord of Coyoacan went on in advance to meet the Great Montezuma, who was approaching in a rich litter accompanied by other great Lords and caciques, who owned vassals. When we arrived near to Mexico, where there were some other small towers, the Great Montezuma got down from his litter, and those great caciques supported him with their arms beneath a marvelously rich canopy of green colored feathers with much gold and silver embroidery and with pearls and chalchihuites suspended from a sort of bordering, which was wonderful to look at. The Great Montezuma was richly attired according to his usage, and he was shod with sandals (cotoras), for so they call what they wear on their feet, the soles were of gold and the upper part adorned with precious stones. The four Chieftains who supported his arms were also richly clothed according to their usage, in garments which were apparently held ready for them on the road to enable them to accompany their prince, for they did not appear in such attire when they came to receive us. Besides these four Chieftains, there were four other great caciques, who supported the canopy over their heads, and many other Lords who walked before the Great Montezuma, sweeping the ground where he would tread and spreading cloths on it, so that he should not tread on the earth. Not one of these chieftains dared even to think of looking him in the face, but kept their eyes lowered with great reverence, except those four relations, his nephews, who supported him with their arms.

When Cortés was told that the Great Montezuma was approaching, and he saw him coming, he dismounted from his horse, and when he was near Montezuma, they simultaneously paid great reverence to one another. Montezuma bade him welcome and our Cortés replied through Doña Marina wishing him very good health. And it seems to me that Cortés, through Doña Marina offered him his right hand, and Montezuma did not wish to take it, but he did give his hand to Cortés and then Cortés brought out a necklace which he had ready at hand, made of glass stones, which I have already said are called Margaritas, which have within them many patterns of diverse colors, these were strung on a cord of gold and with musk so that it should have a sweet scent, and he placed it round the neck of the Great Montezuma and when he had so placed it he was going to embrace him, and those great Princes who accompanied Montezuma held back Cortés by the arm so that he should not embrace him, for they considered it an indignity. Then Cortés through the mouth of Doña Marina told him that now his heart rejoiced at having seen such a great Prince, and that he took it as a great honor that he had come in person to meet him and had frequently shown him such favor. Then Montezuma spoke other words of politeness to him, and told two of his nephews who supported his arms, the Lord of Texcoco and the Lord of Coyoacan, to go with us and show us to our quarters, and Montezuma with his other two relations, the Lord of Cuitlahuac' and the Lord of Tacuba who accompanied him, returned to the city, and all those grand companies of caciques and chieftains who had come with him returned in his train. As they turned back after their Prince we stood watching them and observed how they all marched with their eyes fixed on the ground without looking at him, keeping close to the wall, following him with great reverence.

Thus space was made for us to enter the streets of Mexico, without being so much crowded. But who could now count the multitude of men and women and boys who were in the streets and on the azoteas, and in canoes on the canals, who had come out to see us. It was indeed wonderful, and, now that I am writing about it, it all comes before my eyes as though it had happened but yesterday. Coming to think it over it seems to be a great mercy that our Lord Jesus Christ was pleased to give us grace and courage to dare to enter into such a city; and for the many times He has saved me from danger of death, as will be seen later on, I give Him sincere thanks, and in that He has preserved me to write about it, although I cannot do it as fully as is fitting or the subject needs. Let us make no words about it, for deeds are the best witnesses to what I say here and elsewhere. Let us return to our entry to Mexico.

They took us to lodge in some large houses, where there were apartments for all of us, for they had belonged to the father of the Great Montezuma, who was named Axayaca, and at that time Montezuma kept there the great oratories for his idols, and a secret chamber where he kept bars and jewels of gold, which was the treasure that he had inherited from his father Axayaca, and he never disturbed it. They took us to lodge in that house, because they called us Teules, and took us for such, so that we should be with the Idols or Teules which were kept there. However, for one reason or another, it was there they took us, where there were great halls and chambers canopied with the cloth of the country for our Captain, and for every one of us beds of matting with canopies above, and no better bed is given, however great the chief may be, for they are not used. And all these palaces were [coated] with shining cement and swept and garlanded. As soon as we arrived and entered into the great court, the Great Montezuma took our Captain by the hand, for he was there awaiting him, and led him to the apartment and saloon where he was to lodge, which was very richly adorned according to their usage, and he had at hand a very rich necklace made of golden crabs, a marvelous piece of work, and Montezuma himself placed it round the neck of our Captain Cortés, and greatly astonished his [own] Captains by the great honor that he was bestowing on him. When the necklace had been fastened, Cortés thanked Montezuma through our interpreters, and Montezuma replied-" Malinche you and your brethren are in your own house, rest awhile," and then he went to his palaces which were not far away, and we divided our lodgings by companies, and placed the artillery pointing in a convenient direction, and the order which we had to keep was clearly explained to us, and that we were to be much on the alert, both the cavalry and all of us soldiers. A sumptuous dinner was provided for us according to their use and custom, and we ate it at once. So this was our lucky and daring entry into the great city of Tenochtitlan' Mexico on the 8th day of November the year of our Savior Jesus Christ 1519. Thanks to our Lord Jesus Christ for it all. And if I have not said anything that I ought to have said, may your honors pardon me, for I do not know now even at the present time how better to express it....

Description:_____

_____

_____

Inference:_____

_____

_____

Questions:

1. How did Cortés discover that Xicotenga's messengers were spies? Why is this important for understanding the eventual success of Cortés's mission?

2. Why did Xicotenga associate Cortés's party with Montezuma? What does this say about the tribal relations that existed before Cortés arrived?

3. What stood out to Bernal Díaz when first encountering Tenochtitlan?

Made in the USA
Las Vegas, NV
09 January 2021

15449870R00167